AIRLINES
REMEMBERED

Over 200 Airlines of the Past, Described and Illustrated in Colour

B I HENGI

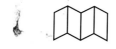

Midland Publishing

This book is dedicated to all
air transport pioneers who by their
courage and spirit of adventure have
made possible passenger flying
as we know it today

Airlines Remembered
© 2000 NARA-Verlag and Midland Publishing

ISBN 1 85780 091 5

First published in 1999 by
NARA-Verlag, Postfach 1241, D-85388 Allershausen,
Germany, as 'Vergangen, Vergessen, Vorbei'

This English language edition published 2000 by
Midland Publishing
24 The Hollow, Earl Shilton
Leicester, LE9 7NA, England.
Telephone: 01455 847 256   Fax: 01455 841 805
E-mail: midlandbooks@compuserve.com

Midland Publishing is an imprint of
Ian Allan Publishing Limited

Worldwide distribution (except North America):
Midland Counties Publications
Unit 3 Maizefield, Hinckley Fields,
Hinckley, Leics, LE10 1YF, England.
Telephone: 01455 233 747   Fax: 01455 233 737
E-mail: midlandbooks@compuserve.com

North American trade distribution:
Specialty Press Publishers and Wholesalers
11605 Kost Dam Road, North Branch, MN 55056, USA
Telephone: 651 583 3239   Fax: 651 583 2023
Toll free telephone: 800 895 4585

Design concept and layout
© 2000 NARA-Verlag and Midland Publishing

Printed in Hong Kong

Photograph on previous page:
National Airlines DC-10 N65NA. (Manfred Winter)

Contents

The Lockheed L-1011 TriStars ordered by BEA did not enter service with the airline before it became part of BRITISH AIRWAYS. This example, N305EA, was painted in BEA colours only for demonstration purposes. See page 60 (Manfred Winter)

4

Introduction

This book serves as a companion to *Airlines Worldwide* which is now becoming established as a perennial reference source to the current air transport scene, but here we take a look into the past, which is no less interesting in itself, and which provides insights into the background and development of the airline world as it is today.

Whatever became of well-known names such as Australian Airlines, Balair, Braniff, British European Airways, Court Line, CP Air, Eastern, Laker, National, Pan American, Spantax, UTA or Wardair? These airlines were all pioneers in their own way in the development of today's air transport business, be it charter or scheduled service.

Why do airlines disappear from the scene, sometimes as quickly as they have appeared? It is often financial difficulties which lead to closure or to merger or sale, or it can be overcapacity in a market, as has happened for instance in the European tourist market, or even political pressures.
Every single airline history reflects the story of the people who were involved. Mass redundancies, trade disputes and strikes go hand in hand with many bankruptcies or mergers.

Banks, insurance companies and other financial institutions and speculators can also be criticised.

These have had in the past, and still do have, a major influence on an airline and often can be more decisive as to success or failure than the management team.

However the object of this book is more to chart the histories and development of the various airlines portrayed, for the interest and information of those interested in civil aviation, for enthusiasts and historians, staff of now defunct airlines and to airline passengers, who recall their travels and experiences with these carriers.

Of course it is not possible to include every airline in this book - some lasted for a matter of only weeks - but a selection has been made to include all the major airlines and a selection of others which have interesting histories or which have played a significant part in the development of the air transport business. It is also more or less restricted to airlines from the 1970s and onwards, with the intention that a future volume will go back and cover the period from 1945 to 1970. The author and publishers hope that you will find the book enjoyable and informative.

This English edition has been translated from the original German version *Vergangen, Vergessen, Vorbei,* and edited by Neil Lewis.

Acknowledgements

The author wishes to thank all those who have contributed to this book. Special thanks go to Manfred Winter who made his extensive photo collection available for the first time. Thanks also go to Gottfried Auer, Martin Bach, Andrè Dietzel, Uwe Gleisberg, Wolfgang Grond, Stefan Höllering, Björn Kannengiesser, Albert Kuhbandner, Patrick Lutz, Gerhard Schütz, Lutz Schönfeld, Andreas Witek and Christofer Witt who have also provided photographs. Naturally the author also acknowledges the assistance of the owner and publisher of NARA-Verlag, Josef Krauthäuser, whose extensive knowledge of civil aviation and wide-ranging photo collection is also very evident in this book.

B I Hengi, Munich

This BAC 1-11-400 N5016 saw only brief service with AEROAMERICA and was returned to its leasing company after only five months. (Josef Krauthäuser collection)

AEROAMERICA   USA

This company will be well known to many watchers of the aviation scene in Berlin, as AEROAMERICA had several aircraft based here and carried out many military charter flights.

This charter and non-scheduled operator had its origins in AIR CLUB INTERNATIONAL and began flying in January 1974. The fleet was brought together in a higgledy-piggledy fashion and included examples of the Boeing 707, Boeing 720, and BAC 1-11. In 1978 AEROAMERICA was granted a licence for American domestic services; a Boeing 707 was used to inaugurate a service from Seattle to Hawaii and this route proved to be successful.

Close examination of the airline's operations by the US Civil Aviation Board followed, with the result that AEROAMERICA lost its licence to operate charter flights to Europe and Hawaii. On the 15th November 1979 the Company went under the bankruptcy protection of Chapter 11 and finally lost its operating authority in June 1980. In spite of that, several charter flights were operated, using the licence of Jet Set Flying Club. As it became clear that AEROAMERICA was under too great a financial burden to escape from Chapter 11, the owners eventually gave up the struggle in 1982. Those aircraft which had not been leased in were put up for sale, and the company dissolved.

AEROCANCUN appeared in Europe in the guise of of this leased Airbus A310-300 VR-BMU, seen here at Munich. (Uwe Gleisberg)

AEROCANCUN   Mexico

A new charter company called AEROCANCUN was founded in 1989 in Mexico. The shareholders were Mexican hoteliers and the Spanish airline OASIS, via whom three Airbus A310-300 were ordered.

The airline first operated in November 1989 with the McDonnell Douglas MD-83. The principal target was the financially strong United States and flights were operated to Miami, New Orleans, New York and Boston.

At the end of 1991 AEROCANCUN received the first of the Airbus A310-300s which it had ordered, and from May in that year services to Europe were also begun. However, delivery of further Airbus aircraft was put into abeyance, since following economic recession in several countries, the European market had not developed as had been anticipated. Indeed, in August 1994 AEROCANCUN suspended European services on financial grounds. In the end, only the single Airbus A310-300 was in use, the MD-80s having been passed on to PRIVATE JET and OASIS. These concerns belonged to the same group of owners, and so were also suffering from financial difficulties. During the main Winter season 1994/95 services were principally concentrated on the South American market, and led to the use of a further Airbus A300-600 and an MD-83. In conjunction with AIR AMBER a subsidiary company was established in the Dominican Republic, and this flew the Airbus A310 especially to the growing European market. Following the collapse of OASIS at the end of 1996, AEROCANCUN also had to file for bankruptcy.

The Boeing 720 came into service with AEROCONDOR from 1972 for longer range routes. (Gerhard Schütz)

AEROCONDOR   Colombia

This company was established in Barranquilla in February 1955 by former AVIANCA pilots as AEROVIAS CONDOR DE COLOMBIA Ltda. (AEROCONDOR) At first, freight services were flown between Barranquilla and Bogota, using Curtiss C-46 Commando and later Douglas DC-4s. It was some years until AEROCONDOR was to carry passengers. On the 12th January 1960 several destinations in Colombia were selected for these passenger services. The first international service was undertaken in 1963 with a Douglas DC-6 from Bogota via Medellin, Barranquilla and San Andres to Miami. Again it was freight which would be carried first, and then a year later passenger service was added on this important route. Further destinations in the Caribbean were Aruba and Curacao. As a replacement for the ageing DC-4s several Lockheed L-188 Electras were taken on in 1968/69, this

also marking the first acquisition by the company of a turboprop aircraft. AEROCONDOR grew quickly to become the second largest airline in Colombia and with the purchase of the Boeing 720 in 1972, it entered the jet age. Further international routes to Guatemala City, Port au Prince and Santo Domingo were opened up and the Miami service was turned over to jet-only operation.

At a time when Airbus Industrie was only finding customers rather slowly for its products worldwide, AEROCONDOR ordered an Airbus A300B4, which was delivered at the end of 1977. On the showcase route to Miami this was soon successful and gained great passenger approval. However, AEROCONDOR suffered badly from worldwide business crisis and the collapse of the Colombian currency. In 1979 the Airbus, which had been leased with payments due in US dollars, was returned to the lessor, and as a result several

routes had to be suspended. The negative financial situation could no longer be borne, and the search for new investors, or government help, could not stave off the bankruptcy which came in 1981.

Boeing 737-300 F-GFUA was used for charter services within Europe, to North Africa and the Middle East. It was leased from BRITISH MIDLAND and in 1990 further leased on to AUSTRALIAN AIRLINES. (Gerhard Schütz)

AEROMARITIME   France

Founded in 1966 as a subsidiary of UTA, COMPAGNIE AEROMARITIME D'AFFRETEMENT S.A. was dedicated to special and charter flights. In 1967 the Douglas DC-6 entered service. However, AEROMARITIME was principally tasked with operating the Airbus Skylink, to transport aircraft assemblies on behalf of Airbus Industrie. Using Super Guppys, of which some were converted at the UTA workshops in Paris, aircraft parts were flown from the various European factory sites to the final assembly location at Toulouse. Four of these rebuilt Boeing 377 Super Guppys were eventually brought into service.

From the mid 1980s AEROMARITIME also took on passenger charters from UTA and concentrated mainly on intra-European flights. Boeing 737-300s and 737-400s were used from a variety of French airports in what was a district colour scheme, though quite similar to

that of the parent company. As the cost structure at AEROMARITIME was appreciably more favourable than at UTA , the traditional charter services to the French overseas provinces were also taken over. A further business activity was the leasing of its own aircraft to other companies, be it for a brief time on an ad hoc basis, or for a longer duration. In1990 AIR FRANCE took a 70% shareholding in UTA and thereby the majority of the subsidiary company AEROMARITIME. Under the umbrella of the AIR FRANCE group there followed a new division of activities within the whole assemblage, to which also belonged AIR INTER and AIR CHARTER. AEROMARITIME received the Boeing 767-200ER for operation on overseas routes and these were flown on behalf of the whole Air France group. A change of name to AERO-MARITIME INTERNATIONAL was to be only short-lived, as at the

end of 1991 AEROMARITIME and UTA were integrated into AIR FRANCE and thereby lost their independent identities.

Tupolev Tu-154 YN-CBT of AERONICA, also known as the 'rainbow airline' is seen here already taken out of service and stored.
(Manfred Winter collection)

AERONICA   Nicaragua

Political changes in one country can lead to appreciable changes in the infrastructure of neighbouring states. Thus it was in Nicaragua, where the national airline LANICA was grounded in 1979 as a result of the war, and following the onset of the Somoza dictatorship in 1980, a new airline was established. AERONICA was henceforth the only and therefore the national airline, which also took over several of the aircraft of LANICA, such as the Curtiss C-46, Douglas DC-3 and Boeing 727. A Boeing 720, leased from OLYMPIC AIRWAYS, was used for service to Miami, while Boeing 727s served destinations in Central and South America. One of these 727s was destroyed by a bomb attack in Mexico. Two CASA C.212 Aviocars augmented the small fleet used for domestic and regional services. Additionally DC-3s and C-46s, confiscated from the LANICA fleet were brought back into service for freight flights.

Nicaragua remained politically unstable, and a civil war developed. As the ruling political parties were not to the liking of the United States, a trade embargo was imposed against Nicaragua. Consequently this had an effect on the fleet policies of AERONICA, who acquired Soviet-built equipment in the form of a Tupolev Tu-154, two Antonov An-26s and two Antonov An-32s, with the Boeing 727 being taken out of service due to a shortage of spares. The country's economic difficulties also had its effects on AERONICA and led to the cessation of flying at the end of 1991.

Fresh political changes (see above) had further repercussions for the company, which was dissolved in 1992 following a further change of government.

Nord 262 F-BVPP, seen here at Colmar waiting for its next service, was for some years on the inventory of AIR ALSACE for the regional routes flown from Colmar, Belfort and Strasbourg. (Manfred Winter)

AIR ALSACE   France

The air taxi company AIR ALSACE was founded in Colmar on 15th August 1962. The concern was active with small Cessnas and Piper Navajo aircraft, but also had ambitions for a regional scheduled network. These were fulfilled in June 1974 with service from Colmar via Belfort to Lyon, and at this time Aerospatiale Corvette light jets were introduced to the fleet. In a close co-operation with AIR FRANCE the airline also offered flights with these from Strasbourg to several destinations such as Amsterdam, Brussels, Cologne/Bonn or Rome, whilst for London-Gatwick and Milan the larger Fokker F.28 Fellowship was used. The company grew quickly and in 1974 took over AIR VOSGES, which had as its main route Epinal to Paris. In 1975 larger Nord 262s and Fokker F.27s displaced smaller aircraft, which were still in service on the less frequented routes. The first of a total of three leased VFW 614

jets came into service with the company on 3rd June 1976 and was mostly used on the route from Colmar to Paris. AIR ALSACE was one of the very few airlines to choose to use this modern but unusual aircraft, with its engines mounted on pylons

above the wings. To replace these jets AIR ALSACE leased in 1979 another Fokker F.28. In 1981 the airline was merged with TAT-TOURAINE AIR TRANSPORT and AIR ALPES to become TAT-TRANSPORT AERIEN TRANSREGIONAL.

Fokker F.27 F-GCMR in the last colour scheme before the amalgamation with TAT. (Manfred Winter)

11

Douglas DC-3 G-AGJV was for many years the workhorse of AIR ANGLIA and was used for both passenger and freight work. (Josef Krauthäuser collection)

AIR ANGLIA   Great Britain

Formed by the amalgamation of ANGLIAN AIR CHARTER, NORFOLK AIRWAYS and RIG-AIR on 22nd July 1970, AIR ANGLIA was intended to become a regional airline based in Norwich. Business was commenced in August, using aircraft which ranged from the small Auster to the Douglas DC-3, the latter already in use on international routes including to Amsterdam, Esbjerg and Stavanger. The first scheduled service was flown with the Britten Norman BN-2 Islander from Norwich via Edinburgh to Aberdeen. The company was particularly active with charter work for various oil companies in Scotland and in the Shetland Islands and had need of more aircraft. 1972 was a year of rapid expansion for AIR ANGLIA and more routes licences were gained. The delivery of a Fokker F.27 Friendship in May 1972 marked the advent of its first turboprop and this was employed on the Norwich-Amsterdam route.

The booming North Sea oil business meant that there was a need for more flights to Aberdeen and to meet this a second Fokker F.27 Friendship was brought into service, whilst two Douglas DC-3s were sold. Airports such as Humberside, which up to then had been served only by smaller aircraft, were linked into the steadily growing network of AIR ANGLIA. During the summer season there were many weekend charters undertaken from airports in the Midlands and North of England to the Channel Islands. The company acquired a further F.27 in 1975, and this was likewise employed on the popular Norwich to Aberdeen service. The last two DC-3s, which had by now become freighters, left the company at the end of 1975 and were replaced with an Armstrong-Whitworth Argosy. This specialised freighter was the first four-engined turboprop in the fleet, though it was later joined by a leased Vickers Viscount. During

the second part of the 1970s AIR ANGLIA was one of the fastest growing regional airlines. With the addition of a Fokker F.28 on 21st May 1979 AIR ANGLIA took on its first jet, with a second F.28 following during the course of the year. The new type was well suited for new routes which were inaugurated to Bergen and Paris.

The need to strengthen the company in order to meet competition from the newly formed BRITISH AIRWAYS and other companies led, on 1st January 1980, to an amalgamation with BRITISH ISLAND AIRWAYS, AIR WALES and AIR WESTWARD to form the new AIR UK.

Boeing 727-100 N7083U was built for UNITED AIR LINES and first flew in 1967. From 1983 to 1987 it was leased from General Electric Credit Corp. to AIR ATLANTA and after the bankruptcy sold to FEDEX for freighter conversion. (Josef Krauthäuser collection)

AIR ATLANTA   USA

AIR ATLANTA was formed in 1981 by lawyer Michael Hollis, with financial support from investment companies. It set out to provide service to points within a range of up to 500 miles from Atlanta, with especially competitive fares and conditions. Under attack would be the two 'majors' DELTA AIR LINES and EASTERN AIRLINES who until then had control of over 90% of the traffic from Atlanta The necessary authority from the US aviation authorities was forthcoming in June 1982, yet it was to be more than a year before the first service was flown. This gave the competition enough time to formulate their own initiatives, and they were correspondingly well prepared when service was begun on 1st February 1984 with a Boeing 727 on the route Memphis-Atlanta-New York.

From the outset there was a code-share arrangement with PAN AM in order that their passengers could be fed into international flights from New York. While the expected results and the resultant profits were there initially, further finance had to be sought via the issue of new shares.

More aircraft – the Boeing 727 again, in order to maintain a homogeneous fleet – were obtained to undertake further services, including to Fort Myers, Miami, New York, Orlando, Philadelphia.This should have helped to make a breakthrough, but a flawed pricing policy led to further losses. Discussions were held with KLM with a view to them taking a 25% share in the company and there was a plan to sell the Boeing 727s which were relatively expensive to maintain, or to swap them for Boeing 737s. However none of this came in time to avoid the impending failure of the enterprise. On 3rd April 1987 services were ceased and bankruptcy proceedings commenced.

The BAe 146-200 of AIR ATLANTIC was used for the longer-range and busier routes. The aircraft had detectors on the wings, which could differentiate between icing, snow or sleet, and indicate this via an instrument in the cabin. (Josef Krauthäuser)

AIR ATLANTIC   Canada

In 1985, at a time when the Canadian air transport market was in a state of radical change, AIR ATLANTIC was founded in St Johns, Newfoundland. Following the collapse of EPA-EASTERN PROVINCIAL AIRWAYS there was something of a vacuum in the provision of air services in this part of Canada. Services were begun towards the end of its year of incorporation with two de Havilland Canada DHC-7s. These were however quickly replaced in 1986 with the modern DHC-8. From the outset the company worked closely with CP AIR and following their merger with PWA, with the resulting CANADIAN INTERNATIONAL AIRLINES. The airline was a CANADIAN PARTNER, an association of regional airlines whose flights appeared in the timetables and reservations system of CANADIAN.

In 1990 the first BAe 146 jets were introduced and with these aircraft AIR ATLANTIC started its first routes to the east coast of the United States. In Autumn 1990 the collapse of AIR ATLANTIC was signalled; analysis showed too many aircraft flying with too great a frequency on routes with too little traffic. In order to stave off the crash, CANADIAN AIRLINES bought a 45% share of AIR ATLANTIC in 1991. British Aerospace also helped in the solution of the problems by taking a shareholding in lieu of the unpaid BAe 146 leasing fees. The relatively expensive DHC-8s were reduced in number and replaced by leased BAe Jetstream 41s, in order to progress to a positive outcome through cost reductions. The investment company IMP International acquired AIR ATLANTIC in 1995 and developed a long-term plan for consolidation. At this time a strike lasting several months at AIR CANADA Partner AIR NOVA was helpful, in that they were the principal competition. The company headquarters was

moved to Halifax, the fleet reduced to twelve aircraft and the routes optimised. After CANADIAN AIRLINES decided that they no longer wished to maintain the links with their partner airlines, and imposed restrictions on fleet and routes, the service to Toronto was barred and so AIR ATLANTIC ceased flying on 24th October 1998. The remaining aircraft were put up for sale.

Boeing 727-200 CS-TCH on approach to Frankfurt. DELTA AIR LINES took delivery of this aircraft in 1974, and it progressed via a dealer to TAP in 1986. After several months with AIR ATLANTIS and GULF AIR it went to FEDEX where it was converted as a freighter. (Josef Krauthäuser)

AIR ATLANTIS   Portugal

At a time when the tourist industry in Portugal was a 'secret tip' for future investment, the national airline TAP-AIR PORTUGAL decided to participate in the anticipated boom by starting its own charter company.

AIR ATLANTIS was therefore set up as a charter operator at the beginning of 1985 , with TAP as the sole shareholder. Boeing 707s, which were to prove too inflexible for the charter market, and Boeing 727s were leased from the parent company. These were painted in the airline's own colours and had different seating arrangements, and began internal European service from June 1985. During the summer season the aircraft of AIR ATLANTIS were seen at the airports of, amongst others, Stockholm, Copenhagen, Amsterdam, Frankfurt, Brussels, London and Zurich, from where they carried holidaymakers to the sunny Algarve via the airport at Faro. To meet changing requirements aircraft could be returned to or loaned from TAP-AIR PORTUGAL. In 1987 the old Boeing 727s were exchanged for Boeing 737-200s and the first brand new aircraft bought specifically for AIR ATLANTIS were Boeing 737-300s which appeared for the 1988 summer season. One by one the 737-200s were supplanted by the newer series 300s in the fleet. As a result of delivery delays from Boeing, 737-300s from other airlines were leased in until their own aircraft could enter service. With about a half a million passengers in a season, an independent operation was not really viable. Increasing costs meant that the airline was not in a position to meet the competition. As part of a restructuring of TAP-AIR PORTUGAL and its operations and fleet AIR ATLANTIS was dissolved at the beginning of 1993.

Saab 340 D-CHBA named 'Paula Modersohn Becker' was one of a total of three leased by AIR BREMEN, and delivered in February 1989. (Josef Krauthäuser collection)

AIR BREMEN Germany

At the beginning of 1988 a new regional airline was founded in Bremen, with the aim of providing direct flights from its home base at Bremen airport to important cities in Europe. Shareholders were the Bremen industrial company HIBEG, an insurance company and two shipping concerns. Flights began in March 1989 with two Saab 340s. Destinations were Amsterdam, Brussels, Copenhagen and London. In March 1990 AIR BREMEN received a third Saab 340.

In the middle of 1990 the signs of financial crisis brought about by undercapitalisation of the airline were becoming more apparent. The state of Bremen introduced several million DM of tax revenues, and thus ensured the continuation of services.

Negotiations with KLM and LUFTHANSA with a view to connecting into their networks failed, since in 1990 there was no pressing need for European companies to link with smaller partners as there is now. Several years later AIR BREMEN would have had better prospects and more success.

Since the search for a financially strong partner was fruitless, AIR BREMEN ceased operations on 22nd August 1990 and the owners decided on liquidation.

Boeing 737-200 N461GB was leased in 1968 by AIR CALIFORNIA and later bought. It was taken over by AIR CAL and then AMERICAN AIRLINES. It was taken out of service in 1992 and stored initially in New Mexico, before becoming a fire brigade training aid in Phoenix, Arizona. (Manfred Winter)

AIR CALIFORNIA/AIR CAL USA

AIR CALIFORNIA was formed in 1966 with the objective of providing regional service between Santa Ana (Orange County) to the south of Los Angeles and San Francisco. Services began with two Lockheed Electras on 16th January 1967 and were expanded in the Autumn of that year with the addition of routes to San Jose and Oakland. Two more Electras were bought for these services and two Douglas DC-9s were also leased, introducing jet operation to the growing company. In October 1968 came the first of six Boeing 737-200s which had been ordered. By and by these replaced the leased aircraft. The quickly growing and profit oriented airline attracted interest from investment companies, which led to the acquisition of an 81% stake by the Westgate-California Corporation in AIR CALIFORNIA in June 1970. In 1977 the subsidiary company Westgate-Waeco Inc purchased

the rest of the share capital. Further Boeing 737s were bought and options were already held on the new McDonnell Douglas MD-80. In addition to the scheduled services, charter work was also undertaken to Reno, Las Vegas and Mexico. In 1981 Westgate-California engaged in a takeover battle for AIR FLORIDA, which led to the bankruptcy of Westgate. AirCal Investments, a newly formed firm from Orange County took over the whole of AIR CALIFORNIA for $61.5 million. With this takeover came a change of name to AIR CAL and the company's aircraft were given a new colour scheme.

From 1st June 1981 Seattle was served by scheduled service for the first time, and more than 3.5 million passengers carried in the year. In 1985 the first of the new generation Boeing 737-300s arrived, and especially for flights to the noise-sensitive Orange County airport six BAe 146 were leased in 1986. In spite of all

efforts the airline was still making losses. As a result of this a stronger partner was sought, who could help them to expand from the restricted West Coast services into the entire USA.

Negotiations were held with US AIR who opted, however to take over rival PSA. ACI-Holdings and AMR Corporation, the two holding companies of AIR CAL and AMERICAN AIRLINES then agreed a purchase of AIR CAL by AMERICAN AIRLINES with the merger taking place on 1st July 1987.

Airbus A320 F-GLGM entered service with AIR CHARTER to replace the older Boeing 727s. (Albert Kuhbandner)

AIR CHARTER   France

Founded as a subsidiary company of AIR FRANCE (80% holding) and AIR INTER (20%) on 3rd February 1966 under the name SAFA – SOCIETE AERIENNE FRANCAISE D' AFFRETEMENT, this airline was known from 1970 as AIR CHARTER INTERNATIONAL (ACI). Services were begun in July 1966 with SE 210 Caravelles, provided by AIR FRANCE and AIR INTER. The main destinations were the holiday resorts in the Mediterranean area. In May 1979 came the Boeing 727 and then in 1988 the first Airbus A300B4 in the fleet. The arrival of the Airbus also marked the introduction of a new colour scheme for the aircraft, and the shortened name of AIR CHARTER was introduced. For the first time the company operated outside of its traditional routes, with service to the USA using a leased Boeing 747. During 1994 and 1995 the older Boeing 727s were replaced by modern Airbus A320s.

With the amalgamation of AIR FRANCE and AIR INTER and the consequent rationalisation and cost reduction exercises, there was no obvious need for a subsidiary charter company to continue to exist.

Thus it was already clear at the beginning of 1998 that the dissolution of AIR CHARTER would take place at the end of the 1998 summer season. The business was discontinued in November 1998.

AIR FRANCE brought this SE 210 Caravelle F-BJTJ into its sister company. It remained in service with AIR CHARTER INTERNATIONAL until April 1984. (Manfred Winter)

Caravelle Series 10B3 HB-IKD, c/n 249 was built for STERLING and came via service in the Central African Republic and France to Switzerland. Here it is taxying into take-off position at Zurich. (Stefan Höllering)

AIR CITY   Switzerland

AIR CITY GENEVE, set up in 1987, was at the outset a company which operated a business jet for its owner. With the acquisition of the Sion-based JONATHAN AIRWAYS, also in 1987, the company then took on the name AIR CITY S.A. In 1988 it acquired its first SE 210 Caravelle for planned charter flights, and during the summer of 1988 this was put to work on behalf of smaller tour operators. AIR CITY received a second SE 210 Caravelle in May 1989 and moved its operational base to Basle-Mulhouse.

It was planned to operate freight flights with a Douglas DC-8, but these plans were abandoned during 1989/90 over the financing of such an aircraft.

On 2nd May 1991 AIR CITY went into bankruptcy, because the capital necessary for expansion and fleet renewal was not available, and negotiations over co-operation with other partners broke down.

HB-ICJ was the second Caravelle 10B3 c/n 69 and came via FINNAIR, ALTAIR and EAS into Air City service. (Josef Krauthäuser collection)

19

Airbus A310-324 C-GCIT was in service for only a short time with AIR CLUB, having flown previously with PAN AM and DELTA AIR LINES as N818PA. (Josef Krauthäuser collection)

AIR CLUB   Canada

AIR CLUB INTERNATIONAL started up in June 1994 with a leased Boeing 747-200 from Vancouver, Montreal and Toronto to Paris, London and Frankfurt. The formation of the airline, which was really not a club at all despite its name, was initiated at the beginning of 1993 by employees of the former NATIONAIR CANADA. Airbus A310-300s were also leased from 1994 for less well patronised routes and to give operational flexibility. At the beginning of 1995 the fleet had been turned over solely to the Airbus A310-300, the Boeing 747 having been returned to the lessor. The 1995 summer season saw especially many trips to Europe where Amsterdam, Belfast, Cardiff, Frankfurt, Gatwick, Glasgow, Manchester and Newcastle were all served.

Alongside charter flights for various tour operators, aircraft were also leased out as required to other companies for short periods. During the winter season operations were concentrated on the Caribbean and especially Cuba, a traditional destination for sun-seeking Canadians. At the end of November 1995 two more A310s were brought into service. 1996 was not a very successful year for AIR CLUB, since other operators with aggressive pricing policies lured away the business of first one, then another tour operator. The small capital base was such that the company filed for bankruptcy in 1997.

A striking appearance marks out this Boeing 737-300 CS-TKD named 'Caravela Nino', which had already flown into bankruptcy with AIR EUROPE. (Andrè Dietzel)

AIR COLUMBUS   Portugal

Set up in 1989, TRANSPORTE AEREO NAO REGULAR was a joint venture between Portuguese companies and the Danish airline STERLING AIRWAYS, with the latter holding 34% of the capital. Using leased Boeing 727s, the intention was to take a slice of the Portuguese tourist market. The bulk of the flying was carried out on behalf of German tour companies and at first the business was successful.

In 1991 AIR COLUMBUS, a name which had been chosen for the company's operations for marketing reasons, took on three more aircraft – Boeing 737-300s, with options for more, as well as for the larger Boeing 757.

With the break up of the most important of the German tour companies MP Travel and facing competition from STERLING AIRWAYS, during 1993 the company had major financial problems, which were however cushioned by new shareholders. At the end of 1993, a consolidation of business was envisaged for 1994, but this did not come about and there were more financial setbacks, as Portugal was no longer as popular with tourists.

Several aircraft were leased out, but even so operations had to cease at the end of 1994 when the last aircraft remaining in service was grounded by Eurocontrol on account of unpaid fees. From that point there was no chance of recovery, and the company entered bankruptcy at the beginning of 1995.

Boeing 707 D-ADAQ was delivered to QANTAS in 1959 as VH-EBF 'City of Adelaide' and saw nine years service. AIR COMMERZ took over the aircraft, which had been mothballed for two years, at the end of January 1971. (Dieter Sandner)

AIR COMMERZ   Germany

This German company was set up in 1970, apparently only for the benefit of an investor who wanted to take advantage of tax write-off possibilities. With the benefit of hindsight, it looks as if this is the way the history of this short-lived company turned out anyway. With two leased Vickers Viscounts alongside two owned Boeing 707s services were started from the Summer of 1971 from several German airports, though the airline's base was at Hamburg. The airline was predominantly occupied with 'guest-worker' flights, with occasional ad hoc charters, which included such exotic destinations as Bali.

In business terms, the company was from the outset lacking the relevant security or capital for expansion, with the result that the Vickers Viscounts were returned to the leasing company after a time.

Apparently the Boeing 707s were also compulsorily removed from service on account of outstanding payments for state taxes. Following unsuccessful searches for an increase in capital or for a stronger financial partner, the path to the receiver's door was taken in August 1972 .

AIR EUROPE leased numerous Fokker 100s directly from the manufacturer for use on European scheduled services. PH-ZCK was delivered in November 1989 and is seen here arriving at Düsseldorf on the daily service from London-Gatwick. (Josef Krauthäuser)

AIR EUROPE   Great Britain

Established in mid-July 1978 as INTER EUROPEAN AIRWAYS, the company began operations on 4th May 1979 and changed its name to AIR EUROPE. Boeing 737-200s entered service on behalf of tour operator Intasun Holidays. The Intasun Leisure Group Limited (ILG) was the owner of both companies. In April 1983 AIR EUROPE received two Boeing 757s and the fleet continued to grow, with aircraft from foreign companies having to be rented in at times of peak demand.

In 1985 AIR EUROPE also achieved the status of scheduled airline, and from this time expanded strongly. The main base for schedules was London-Gatwick, with charters being flown from many British airports including Birmingham, Cardiff, East Midlands, Leeds/Bradford, Luton and Manchester, which became a second base alongside Gatwick.

AIR EUROPE was one of the first airlines to put into operation the european trans-border plans for an international airline, and set up fully-owned subsidiaries in several countries or took up shares in already existing airlines. Thus came about AIR EUROPA in Spain, AIR EUROPE ITALY in Italy and there were shareholdings in NFD – NÜRNBERGER FLUGDIENST and NORWAY AIRWAYS. With AIR EUROPE EXPRESS in the UK came also the airline's own internal airline. Fokker 100s were used on the scheduled services, whilst for charter operations Boeing 737s and 757s predominated.

On 8th March 1991 AIR EUROPE ceased flying operations, and a few days later filed for bankruptcy. After that, ILG, saddled with a debt mountain of some £480 million, also had to seek bankruptcy as there was no hope of financial rescue. The reason for this was the impenetrable Chinese-puzzle type company relationships and the arcane behaviour of OMNI Holding and its break-up; this was the owner of 49% of ILG, in turn the owner of AIR EUROPE.

An AIR FLORIDA Boeing 737-200 N37AF on the approach to Miami. AIR FLORIDA received this aircraft in 1979, returning it to the leasing company in 1982. (Josef Krauthäuser collection)

AIR FLORIDA   USA

AIR FLORIDA began operations on the 28th September 1972 with a Lockheed L-188 Electra, the company having been founded in September 1971 and receiving its necessary licences to operate as a regional carrier. From its Miami base, St Petersburg, Tampa, Jacksonville, Orlando and smaller cities were served. In 1973 a Boeing 707 was leased, flying also to these destinations as required, but this was particularly used for flights to the Caribbean. By the end of the decade AIR FLORIDA had developed to become a booming company. With the introduction of fresh capital, and the opportunities offered by deregulation, AIR FLORIDA grew so rapidly that new destinations appeared almost weekly in the timetable. The Electras were at last replaced by Boeing 727s, 737s and Douglas DC-9s and the expansion targets widened to include Central America and Europe.

In 1981 the regional airline AIR FLORIDA COMMUTER was founded. This served over 30 points and functioned as a feeder. After PAN AMERICAN NATIONAL AIRLINES had been acquired, a route from Miami to London was announced. Before AIR FLORIDA gained acceptance for this in 1981, charter flights to Amsterdam were undertaken with a leased Douglas DC-10-30, which was switched over to the scheduled services once route licences had been granted. Brussels and London-Gatwick were other destinations in Europe.

Three more DC-10s were leased for these routes, but because of financial difficulties these had to be returned to the lessor during 1982. However, the combination of falling passenger numbers and the crash of a Boeing 737 in the Potomac River in Washington had adverse effects. A reorganisation was set in train in 1983 with the loss of

over 1,000 jobs, a fleet reduction, and the abandonment of several routes, with a view to making the carrier profitable again. As this showed no positive developments during 1984 AIR FLORIDA sought the bankruptcy protection of Chapter 11 on 3rd July. Only a few flights were maintained in co-operation with MIDWAY AIRLINES, who specifically set up a subsidiary company MIDWAY EXPRESS and at the end of 1984 took over the remaining routes and aircraft. With that AIR FLORIDA was liquidated.

Airbus A300B2 F-BUAO on approach to Paris-Orly. It was originally delivered in 1977 to LUFTHANSA as D-AIAD. Later on, this Airbus was in service with NORTHEASTERN and OLYMPIC before AIR INTER bought it in 1986. (Patrick Lutz)

AIR INTER EUROPE   France

In 1954 LIGNES AERIENNES INTERIEURES was brought into existence by AIR FRANCE, UAT, French Railways and some banks. However, the first flight did not take place until four years later. Until a temporary cessation of services, only a few seasonal routes, for example from Strasbourg to Paris, were served on behalf of AIR FRANCE. After an extensive reorganisation as AIR INTER, services were resumed in November 1958 using leased aircraft. Douglas DC-3s, DC-6s and Lockheed L-1049 Constellations entered service, until in 1962 the first Vickers Viscounts were bought. These aircraft were taken over from AIR FRANCE, as were the first jets, SE.210 Caravelles which arrived in 1965. For less well supported routes Nord 262s were added in 1964, and later Fokker F.27 Friendships.

On 16th May 1974 AIR INTER received the first of a total of eleven Dassault Mercures, a French short and medium range jet which was developed in direct competition to the Boeing 737, but which was a commercial failure. With this type, later AIR INTER 'shuttles' were opened from Paris to Lyon. In October 1976 AIR INTER took on its first widebody in the form of the Airbus A300. With the takeover of UTA in 1992 AIR FRANCE also acquired the majority of AIR INTER's shares. AIR INTER became the launch customer for further Airbus products: the A320, A330 and A319, the latter being introduced in 1996. Over a period of several years, the French government's airline operations were loss-making, and this led to a major reorganisaton in the mid 1990s. Thus in 1996 AIR INTER became AIR INTER EUROPE and was tasked with flying intra-European routes in competition with privately-owned airlines.

However, this reorganisaton did not last for very long, because with the advent of a new board at AIR FRANCE the whole group was again reshaped and during 1998 AIR INTER EUROPE was completely integrated into AIR FRANCE.

25

Douglas DC-8-63CF N6162A was received directly from Douglas in 1969 and remained in service with AIRLIFT INTERNATIONAL until 1981. (Manfred Winter)

AIRLIFT INTERNATIONAL USA

In May 1945 J P Riddle set up his own airline called RIDDLE AIRLINES, with its base in Miami. In 1946 RIDDLE AIRLINES began charter flights from Miami to Puerto Rico, but from 1947 specialised in freight transport. Curtiss C-46s and Douglas DC-4s were brought into service.

In 1951 a CAB licence for scheduled freight services between New York, Miami and Puerto Rico was granted. UNITED STATES AIRLINES, another air freight company was taken over in 1951, and thereby the route network was expanded to include Chicago and Detroit. Two Douglas DC-7s were added in Spring 1960 and were used for group charter and military transport flights to Europe. During 1960/61 seven Armstrong-Whitworth Argosy turboprop freight aircraft were acquired from Great Britain in order to undertake a special freight contract on behalf of the US military, but these were sold in

1962 on cost grounds and replaced in 1963 by the first Douglas DC-8s. Also in 1963 RIDDLE AIRLINES changed its name to AIRLIFT INTERNATIONAL. A further expansion of the fleet and route network came in 1966 with the takeover of SLICK AIRWAYS. This company was also active in the scheduled airfreight business in the USA and operated Lockheed L-1049 Super Constellations and Canadair CL-44s, which were integrated with the AIRLIFT fleet. 1967 was marked by the arrival of three new types for different tasks: the Lockheed L-382 Hercules, Boeing 707 and Boeing 727. The two Boeing 727 series 100s were in the Quick Change version and were flown during the daytime as passenger aircraft for NATIONAL AIRLINES and at night for AIRLIFT INTERNATIONAL as freighters. Three more Boeing 707s were leased from other companies.

As well as the freight

schedules, many passenger and freight charters were operated especially to South America, until the company, following mounting financial difficulties, was forced to seek Chapter 11 bankruptcy protection. Following a reorganisation, flights were recommenced in mid 1982 with four Douglas DC-8s. At the end of 1985 came a further cessation of operations and the provisions of Chapter 11 were again used to enable reorgansiation. A DC-8-54 and a Fairchild F-27 were initially the only aircraft in the fleet at the new start in 1986. Two stored DC-8s were sold, and this allowed the purchase of further Fairchild F.27s in 1988. These were more flexible in service than the DC-8s and were given a new colour scheme. During 1990 and 1991 however the financial losses were so great that in June 1991 the company stopped all flights and gave way to a final bankruptcy. AIRLIFT was liquidated in June 1991.

Fokker F.27 VH-FNM in the old colour scheme with the well-known 'Q' on the tailfin. (Josef Krauthäuser collection)

AIR QUEENSLAND Australia

BUSH PILOTS AIRWAYS had been set up in Cairns in June 1951 and it was occupied during its early years with the needs of several small settlements and outlying farms in northern Queensland, before its first scheduled routes from Cairns were initiated in 1957.

In 1972 QUEENSLAND PACIFIC AIRWAYS was acquired, thus augmenting the network with routes in the south of the state. The Douglas DC-3, well-suited for rough service and for the small, undeveloped strips, was brought into use. These were later replaced by de Havilland DHC-6 Twin Otters and Fokker F.27 Friendships. ANSETT AIRLINES transferred over several local routes and in 1982 the name AIR QUEENSLAND was chosen, as this was much better suited for marketing purposes than the old name.

TRANS AUSTRALIA AIRLINES (TAA), which later was to become AUSTRALIAN AIRLINES, acquired

the majority of the shares in1985 and began with a reconstruction of the routes and of the fleet; however the independent existence of the company was maintained. Modern ATR 42 Aircraft were introduced from the 1st May 1986, and at this time the airline's colours were changed to

a new scheme which resembled that of the parent company.

By the mid 1980s AUSTRALIAN AIRLINES was having financial problems and the state ordered rigorous economy measures to be taken, as a result of which AIR QUEENSLAND ceased operations at the end of 1987.

With the introduction of the first ATR 42 the colours were changed to those illustrated here. VH-AQC is in colours similar to those of TAA. (Josef Krauthäuser collection)

Boeing 707-131 HS-VGC came via TWA, with whom it was originally N736TW, and Israel Aircraft Industries to AIR SIAM, who used it predominantly on the route to Tokyo for a year and a half. (Josef Krauthäuser collection)

AIR SIAM   Thailand

For patriotic and political reasons, in that in his opinion foreign investment was having a negative influence on Thailand's airline industry, particularly with SAS's partnership with Thai Airways, Prince Varanand established his own airline in 1965, and called it VARAN AIR-SIAM. Being a member of the Thai royal family and a former pilot with the British Royal Air Force, he quickly gained traffic rights to Hong Kong, Japan and the USA, but the airline was lacking the most important thing for its flights – aircraft. Efforts to acquire these and to find an airline which would give start-up assistance faltered at first, and the airline searched until 1969 for a powerful and financially strong partner. Eventually a Douglas DC-4 was received from TAA-TRANS AUSTRALIA and in 1970 a freight route to Hong Kong was started, with the airline also becoming an IATA member. On 31st March 1971 the first service from

Bangkok to Los Angeles was undertaken, using a Douglas DC-8-63 leased from ONA – OVERSEAS NATIONAL AIRLINES; at first this was flown in a mixed passenger/freight configuration, so that the route could be slowly built up and become successful, yet because of the high leasing costs, results were modest. Eventually after ten months the service to the USA was abandoned and the airline split away from ONA.

A disappointed Prinz Varanand pulled out of the business, as with hindsight he saw that he had been cheated by his partners. AIR SIAM resumed service to Hong Kong with a single BAC 1-11, and then extended this to Tokyo with a leased Boeing 707. Inscrutable political wranglings over the status of a carrier and financial contributions to 'contact persons' seemed to be the way of life at AIR SIAM but with a change of political direction in Thailand the influence of the company waned

and financial problems set in. Likewise the choice of fleet, with one DC-10, one Airbus A300, one Boeing 707 and one Boeing 747, was hopelessly labour intensive and expensive in maintenance. As the financial burdens mounted in 1975 and tickets were sold in a 'wild-west' manner at giveaway prices in order to to fill the aircraft, it was not surprising that AIR SIAM declared bankruptcy in September 1976 as a result of its excessive debts.

A Boeing 737-200 of AIR SOUTH on approach to Miami, which was served by several flights a day from Atlanta. (Josef Krauthäuser)

AIR SOUTH

USA

New airlines in the United States have often been set up following the example of the very successful SOUTHWEST AIRLINES, and thus it was with AIR SOUTH from South Carolina, established at the beginning of 1984.

Conceived as a 'low cost-low fare' company, on-board service was restricted to the essentials, and assumed that passengers would forego snacks on flights of only one or two hours, if the prices were correspondingly cheap.

On 23rd August 1994 services were inaugurated between Atlanta-Miami and Atlanta-St Petersburg with two leased Boeing 737-200s. The turnaround times at the destination airports were very short, and in this way it was possible to provide several round trips on these routes each day. Within a short time the route network was extended to further destinations in Florida and on the US east coast, with service to

Jacksonville, Myrtle Beach, Tampa and Raleigh-Durham. In parallel with the network expansion there were additions of further Boeing 737-200s and -300s to the homogeneous fleet. At the main base at Atlanta, maintenance was restricted to smaller inspections, with major overhaul and checks being contracted out to other companies. By the end of 1995 seven Boeing 737s were in service. Further expansion would have to be slow, and solidly financed. As well as the daily schedules AIR SOUTH offered charter services and was active on behalf of a tour operator. In 1996 AIR SOUTH found a new investor who introduced fresh capital; even so services on some routes were reduced, as they had not been profitable.

Also in 1996 a marketing alliance and codeshare was set up with KIWI INTERNATIONAL AIR-LINES. However in the Autumn of 1996 both companies

were having great difficulties, in that the Federal Aviation Administration was looking especially closely at new companies and had found many shortcomings. This led to flight cancellations and a loss of confidence amongst customers, who after the VALUJET accident, and in Europe the BIRGENAIR accident, were being put off 'cheap' airlines by media attention. Lacking sufficient capital to ride out this rough time, AIR SOUTH had to seek Chapter 11 bankruptcy protection in August 1997. Flight operations could not be pursued for the lack of working capital, and the company went bankrupt in September 1997.

This Fokker F.27 Friendship G-BNAL saw service for several years in Australia before AIR UK took it on in August 1986. The aircraft is seen here in the first AIR UK colour scheme at Amsterdam. (Josef Krauthäuser collection)

AIR UK   Great Britain

On 1st January 1980 AIR ANGLIA, AIR WALES, AIR WESTWARD and BRITISH ISLAND AIRWAYS came together to form a united company called AIR UK. The route networks and aircraft fleets were harmonised and the airline soon grew to become one of the most important regional operators, carrying over a million passengers a year.

The financial arrangements were that British Air Transport Holdings held the majority of the shares in AIR UK, but in 1987 KLM took on a minority shareholding of 14%, with the result that Amsterdam became even more a hub of operations in Western Europe. In 1980 AIR UK operated its first charter flights, but these operations were sold off to the newly founded BRITISH ISLAND AIRWAYS, which carried forward a name with a rich tradition. Modern Fokker 50 and Fokker 100 aircraft usurped older types such as the Fokker F.27 and Shorts 360. Numerous BAe

146s were acquired for the steadily growing scheduled network.

In 1987, in association with the tour operator Unijet, AIR UK LEISURE was set up as a charter operator. However, this remained an independent company and in 1996 was sold off fully to Unijet. KLM increased its shareholding at the beginning of 1992 to 45% and this led to even closer co-operation between the two airlines, especially in building up Amsterdam as a hub. It therefore came as no surprise that in the Autumn of 1997 KLM took over the airline completely. With the advent of a new identity as KLM uk and a new colour scheme closely matching that of the parent, AIR UK lost its separate identity from the beginning of 1998, and became from this point another subsidiary of the growing KLM group.

A Boeing 707-321 of AIR VIETNAM in the last version of the colour scheme which was employed in the 1970s. (Josef Krauthäuser collection)

AIR VIETNAM   South Vietnam

AIR VIETNAM was founded in 1951 in what was then still French-occupied Indochina, in order to take over regional flights from AIR FRANCE. Air France held 25% of the capital of the new company, with the majority of the shares resting with the new Vietnam government. Douglas DC-3s, DC-4s and several Bristol 170 Freighters, all taken over from AIR FRANCE, formed the initial fleet and on 1st October 1951 services were begun from Saigon to Bangkok, Hong Kong, Phnom Penh and Vientiane. These flights were carried out either in co-operation with, or on behalf of AIR FRANCE. Internal services to Da Nang, Hanoi, Haiphong, Hue and other smaller towns and cities were also in the timetable and were expanded to provide connections with AIR FRANCE flights to and from Europe. Following the French withdrawal from Vietnam and the partition of the country into North and South in the mid 1950s,

services in the northern part were dropped on political grounds. From 1961, using leased Vickers Viscounts, several international services were commenced on the airline's own account. In 1962 Douglas DC-6s were bought to replace the DC-4s and by 1964 AIR VIETNAM had begun various international services with the SE.210 Caravelle. New destinations included Kuala Lumpur, Manila, Singapore and Taipei. The latter was particularly important, in that this country had been especially supportive to Vietnam during the war, and also gave technical support to AIR VIETNAM. With the entry of the United States into the Vietnam conflict, there came also an American influence into AIR VIETNAM. Boeing 727s were leased from PAN AMERICAN and this company also gave technical and logistical support; services were often disrupted during Vietcong attacks. Aircraft were also shot down or damaged by

warfare. As the war intensified there was in increasing demand for refuge to 'safer' areas and the passenger total passed 1½ million in 1969. CHINA AIRLINES put aircraft at the airline's disposal alongside PAN AMERICAN, with the pattern of service moving more and more from domestic towards external routes. The end for AIR VIETNAM came with the end of the Vietnam war. From the prevailing chaos, and with the reunification of the country in 1976, CAAV-Civil Aviation Administration of Vietnam took on the rebuilding of civil aviation, taking over the previously grounded aircraft, and founded HANG KHONG VIETNAM for this purpose.

AIRWORLD Airbus A320 G-BVJW was one of the first aircraft leased from ORIX and here returns holidaymakers to London-Gatwick. (B I Hengi collection)

AIRWORLD Great Britain

AIRWORLD was set up in October 1993 by tour operator Iberotravel with the initial intention only of participating in summer season charters to Spain, Portugal and Greece. Two Airbus A320s were leased from Orix and operated for the airline by AIR FOYLE in the absence of the airline's own Air Operators Certificate.

The first flight took place on 28th April 1994 from Manchester to Faro in Portugal. One aircraft was based in Cardiff and the other in Manchester. At the end of the season AIRWORLD ceased operating and leased out the two A320s. In Spring 1995, by now with its own licence, the airline restarted operations to more destinations, with a third Airbus A320 added. AIRWORLD received on 8th April 1997 an Airbus A321, the first of the type to enter service with a British carrier, and this entered service three says later with a trip from Manchester to Tenerife. The three Airbus A320 were exchanged for four newer aircraft of the same type, and at the end of 1997 a second A321 also joined the growing fleet.

Following the purchase of the tour operator Iberotravel by Sunworld, this was in turn taken over by the Thomas Cook travel concern, already the owner of the FLYING COLOURS charter airline, into which AIRWORLD was merged at the end of October 1998.

DC-10-30 9Q-CLI was the first and only widebody with AIR ZAIRE, in service since 1973. (Josef Krauthäuser collection)

AIR ZAIRE   Zaire/Congo

AIR ZAIRE was the country's flag carrier, having been set up in June 1961 as AIR CONGO by the government and SABENA. The state held 65% of the shares, and SABENA 30% with the balance held by smaller companies. SABENA gave assistance with the setting up of the organisation, and technical help in order to establish services. The intensive route network of this one-time Belgian colony was taken over from SABENA, who had already been serving the country since the 1930s with Douglas DC-3s, DC-4s and DC-6s. These older propeller-driven types were used for regional service including to neighbouring countries, and these were supplemented by Beech 18s and Curtiss C-46s for freight services. For scheduled services to Brussels, Rome and Paris SABENA and AIR CONGO used a Boeing 707 until 1963.

This was replaced by a larger Douglas DC-8. Following the build-up period, a split from

SABENA came in 1965, and the airline operated independently. Two Sud Aviation SE 210 Caravelles acquired in 1967 represented a fleet renewal for medium length routes. There were organisational difficulties with the operation of the airline, and further DC-8s were acquired from PAN AM, with whom a partnership for technical support was formed. In 1971 the country was renamed as Zaire, and logically the airline from that time on was known as AIR ZAIRE. In 1973 the first widebody, a Douglas DC-10-30 entered service. To replace the DC-3s on regional services, eight Fokker F.27 Friendships and Boeing 737-200s were acquired. Following the takeover of the company from Belgian hands, profits disappeared, and the losses mounted from year to year and with hindsight it can be seen that even a full reorganisation in the 1980s made only minor improvements to the business

position. Services ceased at the end of 1994 and the company went into bankruptcy.

Boeing 737-300 G-BNCT belonged to leasing company ILFC and was in service with CYMRU during the 1987 summer season. (B I Hengi collection)

AIRWAYS INTERNATIONAL CYMRU Great Britain

With its headquarters in Cardiff, Wales, the company was founded in 1984 as a charter operator and took to the skies with a BAC 1-11. Alongside Cardiff, Manchester was the principal departure point, though operations were also conducted from Bristol and other smaller British airports. In1986 came the delivery of the first Boeing 737-300, with a second following at the end of 1986. Destinations were the Mediterranean countries, North Africa and the Canary Islands. Charters in the winter operated to, amongst others, Salzburg and Geneva. By 1987 CYMRU found itself in financial difficulties, as a result of the loss of charter contracts from Manchester to other companies, and because the airline was not aligned with its own tour operator. Plans to merge with another operator foundered, and efforts to recapitalise also came to nought.

AIRWAYS INTERNATIONAL CYMRU was therefore obliged to cease operations suddenly on 19th January 1988, following which the two BAC 1-11s and a Boeing 737-300 were taken back by the leasing companies. The operating certificate was withdrawn by the Civil Aviation Authority.

Taking off from Zurich on one of the few flights conducted from here, Airbus A300B4 TC-TKC was only in service for a short time with AKDENIZ AIRLINES. (Andrè Dietzel)

AKDENIZ AIRLINES   Turkey

At the beginning of 1995 AKDENIZ HAVA YOLLARI, or AKDENIZ AIRLINES was founded. Things went badly from the outset and there were difficulties in obtaining aircraft. The envisaged Boeing 757s could not be financed, and so flight operations were begun in June 1995 with Airbus A300B4s. Three leased aircraft were flown in the high season for several tour operators, but the aircraft were often to be seen standing idle at Antalya or Istanbul.

By the end of December 1995 it was all over for the company. One Airbus A300B4 was returned to the US leasing company in November, with the other two sitting at London-Stansted, impounded against unpaid leasing bills. Thus the dream of success in the charter market for this Turkish enterprise ended in short order. Several attempts at a revival of the airline were made in the following year 1996 but were however unsuccessful, because the Turkish authorities had in the light of its previous experience imposed stronger financial regulation of airlines.

The strange mixture of types in the ALBATROS AIRLINES fleet was a surprise to tour operators. Here is Yakovlev YAK 42 TC-ALY in use. (B I Hengi collection)

ALBATROS AIRLINES   Turkey

ALBATROS AIRLINES was set up in Turkey at the beginning of 1992. In May of that year it took on two Boeing 727-200s and started operations, carrying tourists from German and other european airports to the well known Turkish holiday resorts. The airline was also active in providing service for the numerous Turkish 'guest-workers'.

Following the introduction of new regulations for airlines in Turkey, ALBATROS had to suspend services with its Boeing 727s at the beginning of 1993 for a while, but was able to use them for the summer season.

In the winter 1994/95 traffic slowed down, and having no other work, a Boeing 727 was available for charter to MACEDONIAN AIRLINES. However, for the 1995 summer season the airline was back in the market. Using Boeing 737-200, Yak 42 and various other aircraft from time to time, the airline was not at the top of the passenger popularity scale, but then cheap prices must inevitably lead to shortcomings in service and in the aircraft.

In March 1996 ALBATROS AIRLINES ceased services completely, as following the BIRGENAIR crash, no charter work was forthcoming, particularly from German tour operators. Thus its principal market sector had been taken away.

This MD-82 HB-IKK was leased long-term from SWISSAIR. It was used for scheduled and charter flights and likewise flew for MERIDIANA.
(Josef Krauthäuser collection)

ALISARDA   Italy

The Sardinian business group Consorzio della Costa Smeralda established an air taxi business in Olbia on 24th March 1963 in Olbia, initially operating charter work. In 1965 ALISARDA SpA gained a licence for scheduled flights from Olbia to Rome and Milan. Leased Nord 262s were introduced into service, and these were replaced in 1969 by Fokker F.27 Friendships, following which the route network was extended to include Pisa, Bologna and Cagliari. It also became possible to run charter flights into Switzerland or to Germany, and with this in mind two Douglas DC-9-14s were initially leased. These were however quickly replaced by owned DC-9s, so that by 1975 the airline had a pure jet fleet at its disposal. In 1986 AVIANOVA was set up as a 100% owned subsidiary. This was tasked with meeting increasing passenger demand to serve regional airports, and to act as feeders for the DC-9s and the

new MD-80s, which had been bought as part of further expansion. Paris, Frankfurt and London were now regularly served. As the island of Sardinia is popular with holidaymakers, an increasing number of operators offered vacation travel here. Thus in the summer season many charter flights are offered from European airports to Cagliari and Olbia. In 1991 ALISARDA and the Spanish airline UNIVERSAIR concluded an operational alliance, and from 1st September 1991 flew as a new business under the new, combined name of MERIDIANA.

Airbus A310 F-ODSV leased from the manufacturer, served for a short time before the merger with YEMENIA on routes to Western Europe, Africa and Bombay. (B I Hengi collection)

ALYEMDA   Yemen

ALYEMDA DEMOCRATIC YEMEN AIRLINES was founded in 1971 as the national airline of the separated southern part of Yemen. The fleet consisted partly of Soviet-built aircraft, but also western types such as the de Havilland DHC-7 or Boeing 707. From Aden the route network radiated principally to Africa and the Middle East. A weekly service to Bombay carried mainly Indian expatriate workers. In contrast to what has happened in other divided countries, ALYEMDA did fly to Sana'a, the capital of northern Yemen.

Following political reunification there were already plans since 1990 to combine ALYEMDA with YEMENIA, but continuing political disputes and power struggles thwarted this.

As a result of the conclusion of the civil war at the end of 1993/beginning of 1994, which led to the eventual reunification of the two Yemeni states, ALYEMDA was able to recommence operations in October 1994. A new Airbus A310-300, complete with new colour scheme, altered name ALYEMEN and new logo was used. The economic sense of unifying the two carriers became more pressing, as it was not really possible to support both companies. The merger of YEMENIA and ALYEMEN had been long awaited and planned, but it finally came about at the beginning of 1997 when ALYEMEN was incorporated into YEMENIA, the airline of the 'victorious' North.

AMBASSADOR AIRWAYS Boeing 737-200 G-BAZH ready to depart on its return flight from Graz to London-Gatwick. (Andreas Witek)

AMBASSADOR AIRWAYS Great Britain

AMBASSADOR AIRWAYS was brought into existence in 1992. Following the collapse of AIR EUROPE there were capacity shortages amongst British tour operators and the airline's founders hope that there would be realistic chances of success for a new charter company. Delivery positions were quickly secured for two Boeing 757s, even though the necessary licensing procedures had not been completed.

As the airline did not have its own operating licence, two Boeing 757s from CALEDONIAN AIRWAYS were used. Operating approval followed in the Spring of 1993. From Newcastle, London-Gatwick and Glasgow flights were operated principally to Cyprus and Greece; other airports such as Birmingham and Manchester were also served.

In Summer 1994 the fleet consisted of three Boeing 757s and two Boeing 737-200s, and two Airbus A320s were operated exclusively for the tour operator Goldcrest. However, on 28th November 1994 AMBASSADOR had to cease flying. The tour company Best Travel, which was associated with the airline, had been forced into bankruptcy. The business of another important customer, the Inspirations travel company, was lost through its purchase of CALEDONIAN AIRWAYS and another charter operator thus disappeared.

This Boeing 737-200 OB-1511 was leased from AERO CONTINENTE to cover for the loss of capacity caused by the grounding of its Boeing 727. (Christofer Witt)

AMERICANA   Peru

Following a liberalisation of air transport regulation in South America, and especially in Peru, there were numerous airline start-ups. Thus in 1990 AMERICANA DE AVIACION was set up and started operations in May 1991 with the Boeing 727-100. Initially services were provided on regional routes to Aerequipa, Ayacucho, Chiclayo, Cuzco, Juliaca, Piura, Pucallpa, Porto Maldonado, Tacna, Trujillo and Tumbes. In 1994 the Peruvian government imposed a prohibition on flights by Boeing 727-100s over twenty years old, or which had more than 60,000 flying hours. Along with other airlines, AMERICANA was affected by this ruling, and the two aircraft had to stand idle. As a replacement Boeing 737-200s were brought into use, taking over completely the work of the 727s. Increasing concentration on the regional markets and price-pressure from competing airlines made life difficult for AMERICANA as a newcomer. Then came business recession in South America, which led to the collapse of some other companies. Following efforts to put the airline back in shape, or to merge the debt-ridden company with another operator, which failed to succeed, flights were ceased in 1997, and bankruptcy followed.

Fokker F.27 VH-FNR was used on routes out of Adelaide. Following takeover the aircraft was integrated into the ANSETT fleet. (Josef Krauthäuser collection)

ASA-AIRLINES OF SOUTH AUSTRALIA Australia

AIRLINES OF SOUTH AUSTRALIA had its origins in New Guinea, where it had been established in November 1927 as GUINEA AIRWAYS. Using Junkers W 34s and Junkers G 31s they flew principally freight and equipment for the newly established gold mines near Wau in the interior, operating from the port town of Lae. Often under the severest conditions – there were no made-up airfields – pioneering feats were achieved in air freight service, which today are inconceivable. In 1937 GUINEA AIRWAYS also opened up two routes in Australia. Using Lockheed L-10A aircraft, services were flown from Darwin to Adelaide and from Adelaide to Sydney. Numerous intermediate stops were made on these routes. In 1939 the airline took over from MAC ROBERTSON MILLER the rights to several routes from Adelaide, which would form the basis of the post-war route network. As a result of the Second World War and the landing of Japanese forces in parts of New Guinea the company withdrew from New Guinea. The routes from Darwin to Adelaide were also suspended. In July 1959 ANSETT AIRLINES took over the company and renamed it as ANSETT AIRLINES OF SOUTH AUSTRALIA. Adelaide was the main base. Flights to five destinations in South Australia and to Broken Hill in New South Wales were operated on a daily basis, and the well-proved Fokker F.27 was brought into service.

In 1981 out of ANSETT AIRLINES OF SOUTH AUSTRALIA came AIRLINES OF SOUTH AUSTRALIA, after ANSETT decided to organise its numerous subsidiaries as individual profit centres. Over the years, passenger totals dwindled and ASA produced only losses. In July 1986 ASA – AIRLINES OF SOUTH AUSTRALIA was dissolved as an independent company and integrated into ANSETT.

Convair 580 N5808 was in service for more than ten years with ASPEN AIRWAYS until on 2nd February 1988 at Durango it left the runway and was irreparably damaged. (Josef Krauthäuser collection)

ASPEN AIRWAYS   USA

ASPEN AIRWAYS started in 1953 as an air taxi company flying between Denver and the well-known recreation area at Aspen in the Rocky Mountains of Colorado.

In 1966 it was tasked by the state authorities with the provision of scheduled services, though only within the state of Colorado. A Fairchild F.27 was used for this at first, but this was quickly replaced by Convair 440s and 580s. Over the course of several years the route network was carefully expanded. Following deregulation at the end of the 1970s, flights were added into the neighbouring states of New Mexico, Arizona, Kansas and Utah, as well as charter services to California.

With the purchase of a BAe 146 in 1985 ASPEN joined the jet era and from September 1986 became a Partner of UNITED AIRLINES, providing feeder services for flights from Denver. Several Convairs were painted in UNITED EXPRESS colours. With the sale of the privately-owned ASPEN AIRWAYS in October 1989 came the 'beginning of the end' for the airline. The new owners sold a part of the airline's operation in 1990 to MESA AIRLINES. The jet operations and the facilities at Aspen Airport were disposed of to AIR WISCONSIN, another UNITED EXPRESS carrier. ASPEN AIRWAYS remained independent for only a year after that, when for reasons of cost, the support services and flight operations were rationalised and from 1st. June 1991 the two undertakings were merged.

This Douglas DC-9-32 I-ATIW was one of ATI's first jets, delivered on 2nd December 1971. (Josef Krauthäuser collection)

ATI   Italy

AERO TRASPORTI ITALIANI was established by ALITALIA on 13th December 1963; the base of the new airline was Naples. SOCIETA AEREA MEDITERRANEA which had previously been responsible for the provision of internal flights, passed these over to ATI. Fokker F.27s came into service, and from 1969 the first jets in the form of the Douglas DC-9 which were taken over from ALITALIA. In 1985 ATI took over AERMEDITERRANEA, a domestic carrier which had financial links with ATI, and integrated their services into the ATI network. McDonnell Douglas MD-82s supplemented the DC-9 fleet from 1988 and ATR 42s were brought into use for shorter routes The network incorporated over 30 destinations, and ATI was also active with charter work to european and North African destinations.

In 1993 AVIANOVA came into full ownership of ATI and thereby the ALITALIA Group. This airline took over the whole of the short-haul network, including the ATR 42s which had been unpopular with ATI.

Following the production of immense losses by the whole ALITALIA Group, in 1994 ATI was integrated into ALITALIA with the takeover of all routes and aircraft.

The first aircraft of ATLANTIS was this Douglas DC-7C D-ABYF, leased from SAS. It flew for one year with ATLANTIS and was then returned and scrapped. (Manfred Winter)

ATLANTIS AG   Germany

With the purchase of the existing operating licence of the former NORDSEEFLUG at the beginning of 1968, ATLANTIS GmbH was in a position to develop from August 1968 into one of the leading non-scheduled operators in Western Germany. The first aircraft with which ATLANTIS inaugurated services was a Douglas DC-7C, which was leased from SAS for one year. At first ad hoc charters were operated: included in these were numerous flights for immigrant workers, which formed a good basis for the airline. On 1st November 1968 ATLANTIS received its first Douglas DC-8-32, which was leased from Greyhound Leasing. The aircraft had already operated in Germany for SÜDFLUG; a second DC-8-32 followed in December 1968. The granting of traffic rights in connection with some inclusive tour charters to the United States brought the one-sided organisation of air transport in the Federal Republic into such a

muddle, that the company of necessity had to resort to legal means to protect its traffic rights. This success frustrated several German competitors on transatlantic routes. Following this defeat, the obviously biased Federal Transport Ministry made an about-turn on its position and awarded regular IT-flights to ATLANTIS. In order to facilitate the further development of the company and to achieve a greater capital base, the 'GmbH' (limited company) was changed in 1969 into an 'Aktiengesellschaft' (joint stock company).

Likewise an independent finance company was established with Flugkapital GmbH. This was to raise limited partnership capital of DM 40-50 million, to be used for the acquisition of new aircraft. This form of capitalisation was at the time strongly promoted and widely used by independent operators and the self-employed to provide necessary capital. A larger DC-8-63 was delivered

directly from Douglas in April 1970. Alongside this ATLANTIS also put into service the DC-9 for flights to the Mediterranean area. In 1970 over 300,000 passengers were carried. These totals would have been increased with the further delivery of DC-8s in April and May 1971. One of the older DC-8s was leased out. Dubious complications of the capital structure led to unrest amongst the shareholders and although the passenger total exceeded 500,000 the yield was falling. The company entered turbulent financial waters, as the aircraft were not leased out during the winter months. Personal differences among the management also failed to produce a positive atmosphere in the company. ATLANTIS AG needed to increase its capital for 1972, but this could not be accomplished and the company filed for bankruptcy on 20th October 1972.

The strikingly painted BAe/HS.748 C-GFFU was used particularly in the north of Ontario and is seen here at Timmins. (Josef Krauthäuser collection)

AUSTIN AIRWAYS   Canada

One of the privately-owned pioneer airlines in northern Ontario, Canada AUSTIN AIRWAYS was set up on 1st March 1934 with its base in Timmins. Over the course of the years AUSTIN undertook varied work with a mixture of aircraft types. Also, several smaller operators such as ECLIPSE AIRWAYS, HOOKER AIR, ONTARIO CENTRAL AIRLINES were taken over. Forestry patrol and firefighting, supply flights to outlying settlements, passenger and freight services were carried out using DC-3, HS.748, and de Havilland Canada Beaver, Otter and Twin Otter aircraft. Even Consolidated Canso flying boats were used, both as water bombers and freighters. Scheduled services were developed to over 40 destinations, including some in the USA such as Minneapolis.

In 1974 AUSTIN AIRWAYS was disposed of to the owners of WHITE RIVER AIR SERVICES and the two companies continued under the well-known AUSTIN name.

However, scheduled services were transferred to AIR CREEBEC and to AIR INUIT, marking a withdrawal of services to northern Ontario. In 1988 GREAT LAKES AIRLINES of London, Ontario and AUSTIN AIRWAYS joined forces to form the new AIR ONTARIO.

This Douglas DC-3 C-GWYX was built in 1942, with constructors number 13343. Following retirement from the RCAF in1975 it passed into a civilian career.

45

Airbus A300B4 with the meaningful registration VH-TAA carried QANTAS colours from 1993 and was sold in 1998.
(Uwe Gleisberg)

AUSTRALIAN AIRLINES   Australia

The name AUSTRALIAN AIRLINES appeared in timetables for the first time in 1986, though this 'new' company had been active since 1946. On 12th February 1946 the Australian National Airline Commission founded a national airline known as TRANS-AUSTRALIA AIRLINES, or TAA for short, and on 9th September 1946 service began between Melbourne and Sydney with Douglas DC-3s. By the end of the year TAA was flying to the most important points in the whole of Australia with eleven DC-3s and four DC-4s and in the following years the airline concentrated on building up a complex route network. More modern Convair 240s flew from 1948 and the first Vickers Viscount 700 from December 1954. By the use of the modern turboprop Viscount TAA gained a significant advantage over its main competitor ANA-ANSETT. Further turboprops in the form of the Fokker F.27 replaced DC-3s

on shorter routes from 1959. A further type was also introduced in the same year: the Lockheed L-188 Electra which supplemented the Viscounts on the longer routes. In 1960 TAA took over from QANTAS several DC-3s and de Havilland Canada DHC-3 Otters, along with the whole of the route network in Papua-New Guinea, which at this point was still under Australian government care. This network alone embraced more than 40 destinations. Port Moresby and Lae were served by scheduled flights from Brisbane.

With the introduction of the first Boeing 727 on 2nd November 1964 came the jet era. DC-9s followed in 1967 and little by little the propeller-driven types were withdrawn from the main routes. In 1973 AIR NIUGINI was founded with participation from TAA. This airline took over flights from and to, and within New Guinea, following the country's independence.

The first widebody on the Australian continent, an Airbus A300 for TAA, entered service from July 1981. Starting with these new aircraft TAA changed its colours, and aircraft were painted in a new scheme with a bold 'T' logo on the fin. Only five years later, when the Boeing 737-300 was being introduced to the fleet as a new type, TAA changed not only its colours, but also its name. The worldwide recession of the late 1980s did not leave Australia unscathed and AUSTRALIAN suffered heavy losses, bringing it near to collapse. The Australian government, in the course of a complete rationalistion, decided first to merge the two state-owned companies AUSTRALIAN AIRLINES and QANTAS and then to privatise them.

On 1st November 1993 the two airlines were combined, with the AUSTRALIAN AIRLINES aircraft being integrated into the QANTAS fleet.

Boeing 727-200 VH-TBH named 'Freeman Cobb' in the colours of TAA with the prominent 'T' on the fin. (Gerhard Schütz collection)

Fokker F.27 VH-TQS seen in the final colour scheme, before the company was taken over. (Josef Krauthäuser collection)

AVIANOVA received its first ATR 42-300 I-NOWA on 26th July 1987; it is seen here in its first colour scheme. (Josef Krauthäuser collection)

AVIANOVA

Italy

After MERIDIANA sold its shares in AVIANOVA to ATI in 1993, this company also came into the ownership of the ALITALIA group. AVIANOVA was founded in 1986 as a regional airline on the island of Sardinia

Service was begun in 1987 with three ATR 42s. As early as 1989 ALITALIA had taken a financial stake in AVIANOVA. Using the extra capital thus available, more ATR 42s were ordered in order to be able to build up the route network. In 1990 AVIANOVA took over another regional carrier, ALIBLU. After the bringing together of ALISARDA and UNIVERSAIR into MERIDIANA, the latter sold its remaining shares to ATI and thereby to the ALITALIA group, which was at the time undergoing radical changes. The earlier brown and orange colours were swapped for ALITALIA livery, with only the titling on the aircraft acknowledging the company name. When as part of a re-

organisation, the whole of the regional services were recast, in 1995, larger ATR 72s were added to the AVANOVA fleet, and the first jets came in the form of the Fokker 70. In 1997 the whole

ALITALIA group was again reorganised and ATI along with AVIANOVA was fully integrated into ALITALIA, and the AVIANOVA titling passed into history.

Fokker 70 PH-EZW was repainted into ALITALIA colours in Autumn 1995 but still with AVIANOVA titling for use on shorter European scheduled services. (Albert Kuhbandner)

BALAIR received this DC-9-34 directly from manufacturer McDonnell Douglas on 4th November 1976. HB-IDT is seen here at Zurich. (B I Hengi collection)

BALAIR   Switzerland

The name BALAIR occurs twice in Swiss air transport history. The first BALAIR was founded on 2nd September 1925, and merged in 1931 with AD ASTRA AERO to form SWISSAIR.

After the Second World War, a co-operative was formed as a flying school in Basle, using the same name. In 1953 this became a company. Until 1957 the enterprise limited itself to pilot training, aircraft preparation, aerial photography and general transport work. With the delivery of their first Vickers Viking however, real commercial services were begun in the form of passenger charters. In1959 the capital was increased to 40 million Swiss Francs, with SWISSAIR taking a 40% interest. The fresh capital injected allowed the acquisition of larger aircraft. Two Douglas DC-4s were taken over from SWISSAIR in 1959 and used for longer range charter work. During 1960 BALAIR flew for the first time on behalf of the

United Nations; relief flights were undertaken to the Belgian Congo. Later on, BALAIR was to be often involved with relief work on behalf of UNO or the International Red Cross, for instance during the Biafra crisis. The aircraft wearing the Swiss cross flew relief supplies to Bangladesh, Cambodia and Vietnam. From 1960 Douglas DC-6s supplemented the three DC-4s with long-distance trips to Asia and Africa particularly in demand from charterers. BALAIR aircraft were also made available to other companies for ad hoc or supplementary flights

In 1965 BALAIR also carried out scheduled services on the routes Basle-Geneva-Berne-Zurich, Basle-Frankfurt and Basle-London for SWISSAIR. Fokker F.27 Friendships took over passenger duties from the DC-4s, which were then used for freight work. BALAIR's first jet was a Convair 990 Coronado, taken on lease in 1968 from SWISSAIR, until the airline acquired the first

jet of its own, a Douglas DC-9, in 1970. In1972 BALAIR acquired a Douglas DC-8-63 for long-range routes, including flights to Colombo, Bangkok and Rio de Janeiro. With the introduction of flights to the USA in 1974 passenger figures increased markedly and despite the oil crisis, the airline was in confident mood. A further advance was made by BALAIR with the intro-duction of the DC-10 widebody in 1979. With the disposal of the last of the DC-6s, which had been used only as freighters for some years, BALAIR became an all-jet airline in 1982, and with the introduction in 1986 of the Airbus A310 and MD-80 the fleet was brought up to the latest standards. Two Airbus A310-300s replaced DC-10s in 1992. SWISSAIR had become the majority shareholder, and there was close co-operation between the two airlines; in 1993 BALAIR was merged with the other SWISSAIR subsidiary CTA to form the new BALAIRCTA.

BAC One-Eleven D-AMAS of the new BAVARIA GERMANAIR exhibits a combined colour scheme with the red and blue of GERMANAIR and the Bavarian lion with chequered mane adopted by BAVARIA. (Manfred Winter)

BAVARIA GERMANAIR Germany

Formed on 1st January 1977 by the merger of the existing BAVARIA and GERMANAIR airlines, BAVARIA GERMANAIR only lasted for a few months before being sold in Spring 1977 to HAPAG LLOYD. An Airbus A300 which had been on order was however delivered in the new colours in February 1978 and flew for the whole season. There was a lapse of time until the merger with HAPAG LLOYD was approved by the German federal monopoly authority; this took place in January 1979 and marked the official end of BAVARIA GERMANAIR.

The longstanding independence of these two companies was extinguished by this episode. Max Schwabe & Co KG was founded in Munich in 1957, but from January 1958 became known as BAVARIA FLUGGESELLSCHAFT. The first aircraft was a Piper Apache which was used for air-taxi work. In 1959 the fleet was increased with a Beech 18 and

not only newspapers and freight were flown, but prominent personalities from the worlds of politics, film and broadcasting. At the end of 1960 BAVARIA took on a Douglas DC-3 and in practice a freight contract which this undertook. In 1961 and 1963 came two more DC-3s and BAVARIA became Germany's second largest freight operator. The capital base was increased in 1964 and Handley Page Dart Herald turboprops brought into service; this also allowed BAVARIA to enter the holiday flight business. By 1966 three Heralds were in service, with passenger boardings at about 80,000 a year. In March 1967 the DC-3s were sold and as a first jet came a BAC 1-11, temporarily leased from BAC. However this was immediately leased out to LUFTHANSA for several months for use on schedules. In 1970 the last Herald left the fleet, to be replaced again by the BAC 1-11 and a new Handley Page

Jetstream 31, which was used on regional schedules; it crashed during the course of a service to St Moritz on 6th March 1970. Amongst those killed was the company founder Schwabe, who was flying as pilot. On 19th July of the same year there was a further accident with the BAC 1-11 at Gerona but this time without injury. More 1-11s were delivered to BAVARIA at the end of 1970, so that from 1971 activities could be dedicated to the tourist business. BAVARIA flew not only from Germany, but was quite active from England; in 1972 flights were made into the German Democratic Republic for the first time, for the Leipzig Trade Fair.

The capital structure of BAVARIA was changed in 1974, when Josef Schörghuber took over 76% of the shares from the insolvent Bankhaus Mertz. At this point, Schörghuber had two similarly structured airlines at his disposal in Germany, BAVARIA and GERMAN AIR.

Douglas DC-3 D-CADO of BAVARIA FLUGGESELLSCHAFT seen in Basle in 1972. (Manfred Winter)

GERMAN AIR Bedarfsflug GmbH succeeded SÜD-WESTFLUG in 1968, this originally having been founded in 1966. GERMAN AIR had flown three Douglas DC-6s until 1970 when they were sold to TF-FLUG. The name GERMAN AIR was retained and three BAC 1-11s were acquired in 1970 for passenger work. Also a Douglas DC-9 was used for a short time. The principal destinations were the Mediterranean countries, Spain and Tunisia. In January 1971 the company was once again sold, to the Munich businessman Schörghuber, who already had a considerable shareholding in ATLANTIS AG and a minority shareholding in BAVARIA. Alongside the BAC 1-11s, four Fokker F.28s were brought into service. During 1971 the Frankfurt base was built and the airlines' own maintenance hangars constructed. Route licences were available for the USA, but were not used because

of a shortage of suitable aircraft. The larger aircraft came in the shape of an Airbus A300, the first Airbus aircraft in Germany, delivered in GERMANAIR colours on 23rd May 1975. The two Schörghuber airlines were the second largest charter operators in Germany and during 1976 flew two Airbus A300B4s, nine BAC

1-11s and four Fokker F.28s. Flight planning, purchasing and outstation operations were combined and and in practical terms there was little division between the two companies. The merger into BAVARIA GERMANAIR from 1st January 1977 was thus a logical consequence.

Airbus A300B4 D-AMAX was the first Airbus aircraft to be registered in Germany. (Manfred Winter)

Ilyushin IL-18 D-AOAO leaving the hangar at Berlin-Schönefeld. It is in a colour scheme that only lasted for a few days, as it was then decided to adopt a more conservative livery. (Lutz Schönfeld)

BERLINE   Germany

The first new enterprise to start up following the break up of the former East German state airline INTERFLUG was IL-18 AIR CARGO in the Spring of 1991. On 1st November 1991, two years after the fall of the Berlin Wall, and shortly after reunification of the two Germanys, this airline was renamed as DIE BERLINE, BERLIN-BRANDENBURGISCHES LUFTFAHRTUNTERNEHMEN GmbH. Five former INTERFLUG Ilyushin IL-18s were brought into service, three for passengers and two as freighters. From the outset, the company had to struggle with an excess of bureaucracy, be it over the installation of freight doors in the IL-18s, or in the acquisition of the necessary operating permits. Despite all these hindrances, the company was eventually able to take to the air and within a short time became successful. Alongside numerous freight contracts, many passengers were able to discover the joy of flight in the legendary

IL-18, one of the largest turboprops, which had of course been built for passenger work. In order to appeal to a different clientele, several Fokker 100s were leased in the summer to undertake passenger charters to the Mediterranean, with a particular emphasis on Greece.

The airline's first Fokker 100 was ordered, to take advantage of the good prospects for 1994. However in the Spring of that year the participating banks, for not entirely fathomable reasons, refused further credit, which led to a cessation of operations on 30th April 1994, and bankruptcy.

The same IL-18 after the failure of BERLINE in GERMAN EUROPEAN AIRLINES colours. This putative successor airline failed to take to the skies. (Patrick Lutz)

This Boeing 767-200ER TC-ASK flew previously with KUWAIT AIRWAYS and was not a victim of the Gulf War, since KUWAIT AIRWAYS managed to fly part of the fleet to safety. After service with BIRGENAIR it went on to LAN CHILE and AIR GABON. (Uwe Gleisberg)

BIRGENAIR   Turkey

The proprietor of BIRGENAIR, which was set up in 1988, was the Birgen Celtin company, an influential Turkish enterprise, which was active in may areas. For service on the routes from many West European airports to sunny holiday destinations in Turkey a DC-8-61 and Boeing 737-300 were first used. During the tourist high season aircraft were rented in from other companies in order to meet demand. Öger Tours, a well-known German tour operator had BIRGENAIR under exclusive contract and thus filled its aircraft.

With Boeing 757-200s from 1992 and later with Boeing 767-200ERs in 1994, winter destinations in the Caribbean were also served. Additionally aircraft went out on wet-lease or subcharter ALAS NACIONALES or CARIBBEAN AIRWAYS INTERNATIONAL. During one of these Caribbean flights on 7th February 1996 a Boeing 757-200 crashed. On board were German holidaymakers, who regrettably lost their lives along with the crew. This was the trigger, particularly for the German media, to engage in an orgy of supposition, speculation, and half-truths, fuelled, even though they should have known better, by a pilots union and government authorities, to jump on this tragic accident and bring into question the whole matter of non-German holiday flights. The consequence of these attacks was not only that BIRGENAIR aircraft were boycotted and the company ceased flying in April 1966, but also a softening of the market for undesirable competitors to German charter operators.

BIRMINGHAM EUROPEAN took over several BAC 1-11 Series 400s from BRITISH AIRWAYS. G-AWBL is seen here departing on another flight to Birmingham. (Josef Krauthäuser collection)

BIRMINGHAM EUROPEAN – BEA Great Britain

Established in January 1983 as BIRMINGHAM EXECUTIVE AIRWAYS, service began with BAe Jetstream 31s on 8th June 1983.

Beginning with routes from Birmingham to Copenhagen and Zurich, the company expanded quickly following the purchase of a Saab SF340 and ordered further aircraft of this type, but in 1986 following continuial technical problems with the Saab, it was abandoned and four Grumman Gulfstream 1s acquired. BEA was under sharp attack from BRITISH AIRWAYS on several routes, leading to a price war. Via its subsidiary company Plimsoll Line Ltd MAERSK AIR invested in BEA and put Fokker F.27s including crews into service. Five BAC 1-11-400s acquired in Spring 1990 paved the way towards a jet fleet, which could be used on services throughout Europe. These BAC 1-11s came from the BRITISH AIRWAYS fleet and took on the new colours and the newly-revised name of BIRMINGHAM EUROPEAN. They were used on routes to Amsterdam, Belfast, Cork, Düsseldorf, Copenhagen, Milan, Stockholm and Stuttgart from the base at Birmingham International Airport. These routes were all built up by BEA, which came to be the airline with the most movements at Birmingham.

The name BIRMINGHAM EUROPEAN was chosen to reflect the change in business targets of the company. Newcastle was served in the UK from Birmingham, still using the Jetstream 31s. In a time of radical changes in Britain's airline industry, many companies were taken over or merged in partnerships in order to gain strength to succeed in business, and BEA likewise sought such a partner.

In Autumn 1992 BIRMINGHAM EUROPEAN was taken over by BRYMON AIRWAYS, part of the BRITISH AIRWAYS group. After a short period of merger, the Birmingham operation later re-emerged as a separate entity known as MAERSK AIR (UK) and to this day this continues to operate as a BRITISH AIRWAYS franchise from Birmingham.

This Douglas DC-10-10 TC-JAY was, like its sister machine, taken over from TURKISH AIRLINES. (Josef Krauthäuser)

BOGAZICI HAVA TASIMAZILIGI – BHT Turkey

Also known as BOGAZICI AIR TRANSPORT, the company was founded on 1st December 1986. TURKISH AIRLINES held 85% of the capital, with the rest split between banks and other companies.

In December 1987 the new carrier commenced services from Turkey with two Douglas DC-10-10s. Both aircraft were taken over from TURKISH AIRLINES , along with two Boeing 707s, which were put into service as freighters. These were used for freight charters to America and within Europe, and to Asia and Africa. The range of passenger services offered by BHT was focused on Turkish emigrant workers, who were to be found throughout Europe.

BHT shared traffic rights between Istanbul and Ankara with THY, ISTANBUL AIRLINES and NESU AIR. The price structure and correspondingly the quality of the service meant that most travel operators shied away from sending large numbers of holidaymakers with BHT. A leased Boeing 727, came into service from the Turkish-occupied part of Cyprus. In 1988 the company was handed over to the state development bank, with a view to it being privatised. As the passenger services over several years had not been particularly successful, no investors could be found.

Service was therefore ceased in 1989 and the company liquidated during that year.

Boeing 737-300 TC-CYO was leased from JAT and was impounded, when BOSPHORUS AIRWAYS allegedly continued with the lease against UN sanctions. (B I Hengi collection)

BOSPHORUS AIRWAYS   Turkey

This Turkish company was active for only a short time. At the end of April 1992 it began services with two Boeing 737-300s. The operation of Douglas DC-10s for the summer season was quickly shattered by the outbreak and consequences of the Gulf War.

At the end of May 1993 a Boeing 737-300 leased from JAT, was temporarily impounded in Dublin as the lease broke the conditions of the United Nations embargo against Serbia. In order to maintain services, other aircraft had to be rented from other airlines on a day to day basis, as the other Boeing 737 was also leased from JAT – YUGOSLAV AIRLINES. This stressful circumstance brought BOSPHORUS AIRWAYS into financial difficulties and led to a cessation of flights at the end of the 1993 season. As the 1994 season would not ameliorate the financial position BOSPHORUS AIRWAYS gave up the struggle completely in March 1994.

BRANIFF was a company which always stood out because its colourful aircraft markings Here is Boeing 727-200 N470BN in the last colour scheme used before the first bankruptcy. (Josef Krauthäuser collection)

BRANIFF INTERNATIONAL AIRWAYS USA

In 1928 brothers Paul and Tom Braniff began a service between Tulsa and Oklahoma City with a Stinson Detroiter. With Paul as pilot and Tom as the financial brains, they did not achieve great success and thus sold the service on. In 1930 however they set up BRANIFF AIRWAYS afresh and expanded strongly, as the postal service granted some routes to the airline in 1931. In 1937 Douglas DC-2s were introduced and these were supplemented from 1939 by the modern DC-3. In 1941 the headquarters and operating base of BRANIFF moved to Dallas. Directly after the ending of the Second World War, the first flights to Mexico were undertaken. On 4th June 1948 the first Douglas DC-6 took off from Houston via Havana to Lima, Peru. The name was now changed to BRANIFF INTERNATIONAL AIRWAYS. Further destinations in South America were added so that nearly every capital city had a

service. Domestically BRANIFF also expanded further through the purchase of MID-CONTINENT AIRLINES. Lockheed L-188 Electra turboprops were used to provide a Dallas to New York connection in 1959. BRANIFF received its first Boeing jet – a 707 – for use on its South American routes in December 1959, and in 1965 was the first US company to bring the BAC One-Eleven into service. In the same year the company also hit the headlines with the introduction of its 'Flying Colors' campaign. The aircraft were painted in up to nine different variations of the colour scheme, the two most famous being a Boeing 727 and a Douglas DC-8 decorated by artist Alexander Calder. With the takeover of PAN AMERICAN GRACE AIRWAYS from 1st February 1967, BRANIFF became market leader in South American services. PANAGRA had ruled the market for a long time and had a monopoly of

traffic between Panama and Chile, and to Buenos Aires and the USA. Along with the traffic rights BRANIFF also inherited DC-8s from PANAGRA. Following air traffic deregulation in the USA, BRANIFF embarked on further expansion in 1978, this time to Europe, where London, Paris, Brussels, Amsterdam and Frankfurt were served. The aircraft received another new colour scheme, still colourful, but not so garish. Further expansion to Hawaii and Guam followed. All this necessitated a larger fleet and Boeing 747s, 747SPs and more Douglas DC-8s were bought or leased. There was also the spectacular use of Concordes from Washington to Dallas with direct onward services to Paris and London; however, this made enormous losses and the route was soon given over to the 747s. Recession at the beginning of the 1980s and the fall in airline bookings hit BRANIFF hard in its expansion phase. As mounting

This Boeing 727-200 was in service with BRANIFF for only a few months The aircraft was leased from AIR HOLLAND in November 1986. (Josef Krauthäuser collection)

losses, even in the face of countermeasures including staff and route reductions and the sale of aircraft, could not be reduced in 1981, BRANIFF ceased operations on 12th May 1982 and entered bankruptcy.

The Hyatt Company bought the company out of this bankruptcy, recapitalised it, and within a couple of years there emerged a new BRANIFF airline. It was constrained to US domestic services, used the Boeing 727 as its sole aircraft type and employed about 2,200 people.

After six months the service was converted into a 'low-fare' operation. Yet again however, services had to be cut back and personnel numbers reduced to minimise further losses. Early in 1989 FLORIDA EXPRESS was taken over; this operated from Orlando as BRANIFF EXPRESS. By taking over PAN AM's orders for up to 50 Airbus A320 BRANIFF became the first operator of this type in the USA.

Sixteen had been delivered by the time of the second failure of BRANIFF on 6th November 1989.

However, BRANIFF made more comebacks than Frank Sinatra and so another 'new' BRANIFF was established. This harked back to the 'Flying Colors' era and the aircraft were once again brightly painted. On 1st July 1991

service was re-established between New York and Orlando, though Chapter 11 protection had to be sought, until fresh capital and the recovery of the Reagan era made survival possible until 1992. However with the cessation of flying again on 2nd July 1992, BRANIFF INTERNATIONAL was finally doomed.

The final colour scheme of BRANIFF INTERNATIONAL, shown on a Boeing 727. (Gerhard Schütz)

Using BAC 1-11s, such as this Series 500 G-AWUY, B.CAL flew to Amsterdam and Frankfurt, in Europe but also to several domestic destinations. Delivered to BUA in 1969, this aircraft went through two mergers, first to B.CAL and then in 1988 to BRITISH AIRWAYS. (Josef Krauthäuser collection)

BRITISH CALEDONIAN AIRWAYS Great Britain

The merger of BRITISH UNITED AIRWAYS – BUA and CALEDONIAN AIRWAYS in 1970 led to the creation of CALEDONIAN/BUA. However the new company changed its name in September to BRITISH CALEDONIAN AIRWAYS or B.CAL for short. B.CAL took over from BOAC routes to Africa and flew to Abidjan, Accra, Banjul, Dakar, Freetown, Lagos and Monrovia. Boeing 707s were brought into use for these routes, while BAC 1-11s were flown in Europe. In 1973 B.CAL opened up its own routes to New York and Los Angeles, but these had to be abandoned after a year because of business recession and the oil crisis.

In 1976 the UK authorities passed over route licences to Bogotá, Caracas and Lima from BOAC to B.CAL, thereby nominating B.CAL as the second British flag carrier to Africa and South America. At the end of March 1977 the first widebody arrived, a Douglas DC-10-30, as a

Boeing 707 replacement. B.CAL also few services for numerous small or developing airlines such as AIR SEYCHELLES or CARIBBEAN AIRWAYS. In 1983 flights to the USA were re-introduced and the network grew to eight destinations. Boeing 747s were used to Los Angeles and Dallas. During 1982 B.CAL set up BRITISH CALEDONIAN COMMUTER as a feeder service for its international flights. The participating companies were BRYMON AIRWAYS, CON-NECTAIR, GUERNSEY AIRLINES, JERSEY EUROPEAN AIRLINES and METROPOLITAN AIRWAYS. A further subsidiary, alongside B.CAL HELICOPTER, was BRITISH CALEDONIAN AIRWAYS CHARTERS, set up in 1983. This flew predominantly for single charterers and for the Rank Group with a DC-10. When the British government in 1984 – yet again – re-organised its air transport policies and rejected the idea of two flag carriers, B.CAL

transferred all of its South American and Caribbean routes to BRITISH AIRWAYS. In exchange its routes to Africa and the Middle East were expanded, and Hong Kong was served on a daily basis from London. B.CAL received two Airbus A310s in March 1984, and Airbus A320s were taken on as replacements for the BAC 1-11s. McDonnell Douglas MD-11s were ordered as successors to the DC-10s. From1984 B.CAL had financial problems, which led to large losses during the course of the year. At the end of 1987 BRITISH AIRWAYS announced the takeover of BRITISH CALEDONIAN. As a result of that the delivery positions for the MD-11s were sold, but the A320s were delivered from March 1988 and taken into the BA fleet. The merger took place officially on 14th April, but practically was consummated during the course of 1988, so that Britain's second largest airline disappeared.

Vickers Vanguard G-APEN at Hanover in 1970 operating a German internal flight. While with BEA it was named 'Valiant' and was delivered in 1961. BEA used it until the end of 1973, when it went on to serve with MERPATI NUSANTARA AIRLINES in Indonesia. (Manfred Winter)

BRITISH EUROPEAN AIRWAYS – BEA Great Britain

After the end of the Second World War, the state airline BOAC set up BRITISH EUROPEAN AIRWAYS CORPORATION-BEA, on 1st August 1946 in order to take over the services of the BOAC-European Division. BOAC had recommenced flights to Amsterdam, Brussels and Paris from 1st January 1946. BEA also took over all the airlines which had been active during wartime, such as ALLIED AIRWAYS, RAILWAY AIR SERVICES, SCOTTISH AIRWAYS and CHANNEL ISLANDS AIRWAYS. The departure point for BEA flights was the military airfield of Northolt, some 15 miles west of London. Douglas DC-3s, de Havilland Dragon Rapides, Junkers Ju 52/3ms and Avro 19s formed the backbone of the fleet.

The route network grew quickly and alongside the Vickers Viking, the Airspeed Ambassador (known as the Elizabethan with BEA) formed BEA's second generation of aircraft. The latter was first

used on the London-Paris run from 13 March 1952. For the longer European routes the first turboprop, the Vickers Viscount, came into service in 1953. As had already been demonstrated by a series of test flights in 1950 using prototype aircraft, the aircraft soon won the trust of passengers and led to further expansion. The 700 series Viscounts were followed by the re-worked and larger 800 series and from December 1960 the even larger Vickers Vanguard. This was specially designed and built to BEA's specifications. The first route operated by jets was London-Moscow in 1960 with de Havilland Comet 4Bs. Further British-built aircraft, again to the wishes of BEA, were the de Havilland developed DH.121, which following the merger of de Havilland and Hawker Siddeley came to be known as the HS.121 Trident 1; this type first flew for BEA on 11th March 1964. The BAC 1-11-500 entered BEA

service on 18th November 1968. Some lesser known types such as the Hawker Siddeley A.W. 650 Argosy, a pure freighter and de Havilland DH.114 Heron also served in the fleet. A special operation was the BEA German Internal Service, which connected West Berlin with other German cities and other European points. Following the end of the war it had been decreed that only the victorious nations would fly from and to Berlin. Whilst developing as a leading European company, BEA was also building up internal services in the UK, and in order to do this, help was sought from partner airlines. In 1967 BRITISH AIR SERVICES was founded, a company which principally took financial stakes in other concerns such as CAMBRIAN and BKS AIR TRANSPORT, who conducted regional flights on behalf of BAS. BEA also had shareholdings in CYPRUS AIRWAYS and GIBRALTAR AIRWAYS. Another subsidiary set up was BEA-

This HS-121 Trident 3B was delivered to BEA on 23rd March 1972 and carries the up-to-the-minute livery, which was in fact to be the last livery of the airline, with the Union Flag on the tailfin. (Manfred Winter)

AIRTOURS in 1969. From 5th March 1970 this offered services from London-Gatwick using Comet 4Bs. BEA-AIRTOURS used a total of seven Comet 4Bs and established London-Gatwick as the charter airport of the future. After the merger of BEA, BEA-AIRTOURS would become BRITISH AIRTOURS. At the beginning of 1972 BEA was one of the first airlines to order widebodies, with nine Lockheed L-1011 TriStars. Following Parliament's decision in the Civil Aviation Act of 1971, on 1st September 1972 BEA and BOAC merged into the new BRITISH AIRWAYS BOARD. In this were seven divisions, out of which on 1st April 1974 BRITISH AIRWAYS emerged to take on all the flying operations of the former individual divisions.

de Havilland Comet 4B G-ARJK of BEA-AIRTOURS at Paris-Le Bourget (Manfred Winter)

BIA bought this BAC 1-11-500 G-AWWZ from MONARCH AIRLINES in October 1985. It was sold to leasing company AIV-Holdings in 1989 and leased back. After BIA's failure, it was leased by both DAN AIR and RYAN AIR. (Josef Krauthäuser collection)

BRITISH ISLAND AIRWAYS Great Britain

BRITISH ISLAND AIRWAYS – BIA was founded in 1981, in order to undertake the charter flights of AIR UK. The first operation using the historic name was on 1st April 1982 with a BAC 1-11. The company was independent and self-sufficient, and had simply taken over from AIR UK the rights to the name, but had nothing at all to do with the previously existing company.

The fleet grew quickly to a total of seven BAC One--Elevens, which were used for flights to the holiday regions of the Mediterranean. In order to finance this and planned further expansion, shares were issued and the company quoted on the stock exchange. In order to modernise the fleet in the long term, two McDonnell Douglas MD-83s were ordered and entered service in 1987. BIA was active on behalf of independent tour operators, and was not linked to its own operator who could fill the aircraft in the off-

seasons. There was a trend in the travel market towards larger groupings by mergers and takeovers in Great Britain at the end of the 1980s and the resulting big operators either already owned, or newly established, their own airlines, so that times became hard for independent airline companies.

At the end of 1989 the company found itself in financial difficulties and trading in the BIA's shares was suspended. As a form of rescue for the company, the six BAC One-Elevens were sold to leasing company Atlantic International Aviation Holdings and then leased back in order to operate services. The MD-83s were also removed from service in order to cut costs. Despite all these endeavours, the rescue effort failed and BRITISH ISLAND AIRWAYS was obliged to file for bankruptcy on 1st February 1990.

The Boeing 747-100 was first used by BOAC in 1971 on the London-New York run. The whole fleet was transferred over to BRITISH AIRWAYS. (Christofer Witt collection)

BRITISH OVERSEAS AIRWAYS CORP - BOAC Great Britain

On 24th November 1939 the British government decided to merge IMPERIAL AIRWAYS and BRITISH AIRWAYS to form the new BRITISH OVERSEAS AIRWAYS CORPORATION, or BOAC for short. During the Second World War BOAC managed to keep open several of the former IMPERIAL routes, forming the most important connection of the Commonwealth with Britain. After the end of the war BOAC had no less than 170 aircraft of 18 types in its fleet., and a rationalisation and reduction of types and tasks was called for. BOAC became responsible for all routes outside Europe, with the newly formed BEA taking over the European services. Lockheed Constellations, Boeing 377 Stratocruisers and Canadair North Stars, known as Argonauts with BOAC, entered service. Until 1950 Short Solent flying boats were also used on routes to Southern Africa. With the takeover of BSAA – BRITISH

SOUTH AMERICAN AIRWAYS on 30th July 1949 services to South America and the Caribbean were improved. In 1952 on the London-New York route a cheaper 'second class' service was introduced for the first time. In doing this BOAC was a pioneer for developments which would later lead to mass tourism. More seats were simply installed in the Constellations or Argonauts and the comfort and service reduced. BOAC was the first airline in the world to introduce jet aircraft, when the de Havilland Comet 1 flew its first route to Johannesburg on 2nd May 1952. A year later Tokyo followed and the first commercial transatlantic jet flight was made by BOAC on 4th October 1958. The further developed Comet 4 was used for this London-New York service. Bristol Britannias were however also used for longer range routes. The first 'Round the world' flight on 22nd August 1959 began in the easterly direction with a

Comet to Tokyo and westbound via New York and San Francisco with the Britannia across the Pacific to Tokyo. The Boeing 707 introduced on 2nd July 1960 took over the roles of the Comet. During 1962 BOAC and the Cunard shipping line set up a joint company BOAC-CUNARD with BOAC owning 70% of the shares. It took over the network of CUNARD-EAGLE to Nassau and the Caribbean. From 1964 Vickers VC-10s, and from 1971 Boeing 747s increased the fleet. They flew on routes to Africa, Australia and North America. In 1971 BRITISH OVERSEAS AIR CHARTER was founded, using BOAC Boeing 707s as required for its flights to the USA, the Far East and Australia. The end for the 'Speedbirds' was signalled in a parliamentary act in 1971 which envisaged the merger of BEA and BOAC On 1st September 1972 BOAC became one of the seven divisions of the BRITISH AIRWAYS BOARD.

BUA used the Vickers VC-10 on routes to South America and Africa. G-ASIX is seen here being towed into the hangar for preparation for its next flight. (Josef Krauthäuser collection)

BRITISH UNITED AIRWAYS – BUA Great Britain

BRITISH UNITED AIRWAYS came into being in July 1960 by the merger of AIRWORK Ltd and HUNTING-CLAN with their associated companies AIR CHARTER, AIRWORK HELICOPTER, BRISTOW HELICOPTER, MORTON AIR SERVICE, OLLEY AIR SERVICE and TRANSAIR. The new company was split into three divisions – air transport, helicopters and overseas charter. The fleet at takeover consisted principally of Douglas DC-3s, DC-4s, DC-6s, Vickers Viscounts and Bristol Britannias.

BRITISH UNITED AIRWAYS flew scheduled services to east, west and central Africa. On behalf of SUDAN AIRWAYS, BUA also flew scheduled services via Cairo to Europe and in the Middle East. The company was also active for the British armed services with many services to overseas bases. In particular several trooping flights were operated each month to Germany and military bases such as Gütersloh and

Wildenrath, but also to Aden, Gibraltar or Hong Kong. BUA was a large and independent company, the first in the world to order the BAC 1-11 which entered service in May 1965; ten One-Elevens were ordered to replace Vickers Viscounts. The new aircraft allowed new routes to be opened up. In January 1962 BUA bought the British Aviation Service Group with their airline SILVER CITY AIRWAYS, which flew a mixed fleet including DC-3s, Bristol 170 Freighters and Vickers Viscounts. A new holding company, Air Holdings brought the interests of the group under one umbrella and co-ordinated the numerous separate divisions. The shareholders in Air Holdings were well-known British shipping companies P & O, Blue Star Line and several insurers.

During 1962 there followed a re-organisation, and in May JERSEY AIRLINES became a member of the group. Newly created were BRITISH UNITED

(CHANNEL ISLANDS) AIRWAYS on 1st November 1962 and BRITISH UNITED AIR FERRIES on 1st January 1963. BUA (CHANNEL) was responsible for schedules and freight services to the Channel Islands and the Isle of Man. Vickers VC-10s ousted the Bristol Britannias in 1964 and were used on routes to Africa and to Chile. By 1968 BUA was running an international network which was profitable for the owners. The airline was also busy with charter operations for various well-known holiday tour operators and also introduced the Africargo-Service with VC-10s. One sells a successful company when one's investment can be doubled by a sale. In any event, Air Holdings thought so, and put it up for sale in 1970. CALEDONIAN AIRWAYS bought the company for £6.9 million on 30th November 1970; the companies were merged as the new CALEDONIAN/BUA , later to become BRITISH CALEDONIAN AIRWAYS.

Fokker F.27 Friendship LN-NPC operating a charter flight at Düsseldorf. (Josef Krauthäuser collection via USP)

BUSY BEE   Norway

The company was founded in 1966 as BUSY BEE AIRSERVICE, and operated from 1972 to 1980 under the name AIR EXECUTIVE NORWAY – BUSY BEE. The staple aircraft was the Fokker F.27 and with this type the airline was active both with scheduled and charter flights. As a subsidiary of the Braathens Shipping Group, which also owned the airline BRAATHENS SAFE, it was in a position to take over work from this sister airline. It also undertook regional flights for other companies, such as SAS, to airports which could not be used by their own aircraft. Additionally, charter flights on behalf of the Norwegian Army, both internal and overseas, were frequently carried out. At weekends, leased Boeing 737-200s were used for tourist flights to the Mediterranean, or to other holiday destinations. At the beginning of 1990 six Fokker F.27s were taken over from the Australian airline EAST WEST AIRLINES and used to build up regional services. BUSY BEE was one of the launch customers for the new Fokker 50 and ordered five examples.

However, business difficulties, and a recession in the Norwegian economy, and a dramatic fall in the number of passengers on the regional services brought losses to BUSY BEE. No quick fix was possible, and takeover by or merger with the parent company BRAATHENS was not possible on technical grounds.

Thus the company succumbed to bankruptcy quickly on 17th December 1992 and ceased flying.

This HS 121 Trident 2E B-280 (later B-2204) was delivered to CAAC in 1976, and remained in service until the end of 1988 when it was eventually retired and stored. (Josef Krauthäuser collection)

CAAC

CIVIL AVIATION ADMINISTRATION OF CHINA – CAAC or otherwise MINHAIDUY was the state airline of the Peoples Republic of China and was created by the merger of the former Soviet-influenced company SKOGA and the CHINA CIVIL AVIATION CORPORATION in 1954. Douglas DC-3s, Lisunov Li-2s, Ilyushin IL-12s and IL-14s formed the basis of the CAAC-fleet. In 1960 with the Ilyushin IL-18 came the first turboprop type for use on longer routes. The route network was overwhelmingly focussed on internal needs, with the only destination in neighbouring countries being Alma Ata. Spares supply and maintenance problems with the Soviet-built aircraft led to the acquisition of Western types. Vickers Viscounts were used first on the Peking (now Beijing) to Shanghai route in 1964. A further British-sourced type was the HS.121 Trident 1E/2E, which entered service in 1970. As the

country began to open itself up a little more to the outside world, a service to Karachi was begun. CAAC was closely influenced by political considerations, and as a result, routes to Laos, North Korea and North Vietnam were operated. However other decisions were made which were far from influenced by political ideology – thus Boeing 707s were acquired for longer overseas routes; Tirana, Paris, Moscow, Tokyo, Teheran, were all served from 1974. After the Mao era and the end of the Vietnam War, political relationships with the USA were broadened. Just as with AEROFLOT in the USSR, CAAC was also responsible for other aerial tasks. The organisation of airports, agricultural flying and many other special tasks were carried out on a daily basis by CAAC aircraft and helicopters.

The political changes in China helped Boeing and McDonnell Douglas particularly to achieve

large aircraft orders; however BAe and later Airbus Industrie were also able to secure a share of the new aircraft sales.

The structure of the Chinese aviation industry did not follow the flat pattern of the socialist economy and from 1985 a fundamental reform took place, allowing a plethora of new and privately financed airlines to come into being. CAAC withdrew more and more from the actual business of flying operations and became more the umbrella company and overseeing body for civil aviation in the Peoples Republic, a role in some ways similar to that of the FAA in the USA or the CAA in the UK.

CAMBRIAN Vickers Viscount G-AOYG leaves Hannover for Berlin. CAMBRIAN served some internal German routes on behalf of BEA. (Manfred Winter)

CAMBRIAN

Great Britain

On 25th April 1935 S Kenneth Davies set up CAMBRIAN AIR SERVICES LTD at Lisvane near Cardiff, bringing his own de Havilland Gipsy Moth into the company. The main activities until the outbreak of war were sightseeing flights for tourists and training flights for the air force. During the war CAMBRIAN AIR SERVICE looked after spares for aircraft and parachutes. On 1st January 1946 CAMBRIAN started flying again with a freight charter from Cardiff to Bristol, marking the rebirth of civil aviation in Great Britain after the war. De Havilland Dragon Rapides, Auster Autocrats and Percival Proctors formed the basis of the fleet when in co-operation with BEA in 1948 the airline first operated the route from Cardiff to Weston-Super-Mare. During the summer season of 1949 flights were inaugurated to Birmingham and Jersey. During 1953 CAMBRIAN took over several aircraft from OLLEY AIR SERVICE, who gave up their

own services and flew in association with MORTON AIR SERVICES from Bristol to Jersey and Guernsey. Furthermore, MURRAY CHOWN AVIATION complete with its own airport at Staverton near Gloucester, was taken over during the year. Also this year services commenced via Southampton to Dinard and Paris.
In 1954 this route would be served by the de Havilland Dove, but two Douglas DC-3s (a type later to become a staple of the fleet) were added as the airline moved to the new airport at Cardiff-Rhoose. On 7th February 1958 BEA acquired by agreement one third of the share capital of CAMBRIAN AIRWAYS, as the company had been known from 1956, in order to further develop the previous co-operation. In February 1964 CAMBRIAN received its first Vickers Viscount. Numerous group charters to Rimini, Palma, Nice, Valencia and Barcelona were undertaken. In November 1967 BEA took over

the remaining two thirds of the capital. With the last DC-3 flight on 31st October 1968 an era ended, as numerous short routes were also abandoned at that time. At the end of December 1969 the delivery of the first BAC 1-11 marked the company's entry into the jet set; three more One-Elevens were added in the following year. One BAC 1-11 was based in Berlin and flew German domestic services on behalf of BEA; the others were used predominantly on charter work to the Mediterranean. Vickers Viscount 700s were supplanted by the more modern Viscount 800s, flying overwhelmingly for BEA. In 1972 CAMBRIAN was incorporated into the newly formed BRITISH AIRWAYS initially in the Regional Division, but lost its home base in Cardiff, and more and more its independence. From 1975 it operated only in the colours of BRITISH AIRWAYS and CAMBRIAN AIRWAYS formally came to an end on 1st April 1976.

Short SD 360-300 'City of Leeds' G-BNDM was delivered on 9th October 1987 and was used on the Leeds-Gatwick route. (Christofer Witt)

CAPITAL AIRLINES   **Great Britain**

This company founded in 1983 was originally known as BROWN AIR INTERNATIONAL and was based at the airport at Leeds/Bradford in the north of England. Using Cessnas and a Grumman Gulfstream 1, regional services between Leeds/Bradford and London-Gatwick, Cardiff-Leeds-Glasgow and air taxi operations were flown, until at the beginning of 1987 the company was re-named as CAPITAL AIRLINES. Using a leased Vickers Viscount scheduled services were operated, until with the delivery of a Shorts SD-360 in October 1987 the company had its own larger aircraft with which to operate from Leeds/Bradford to London-Gatwick. The sole international route to Norway, which had been flown with a Cessna 401 and later with the Shorts SD-360 was closed down in 1988 and the airline concentrated on building up routes from Leeds.

Following the failure of the parent company, the Brown

Group International at the beginning of 1990, CAPITAL AIRLINES suspended services in June 1990. After attempts at re-organisation failed, the company was eventually wound up.

This Vickers Viscount 806 G-AOYN was leased from BRITISH AIR FERRIES for several months during 1987 and carried CAPITAL titling. (Christofer Witt)

Douglas DC-8-63s were the workhorses of CAPITOL INTERNATIONAL AIRWAYS for many years on routes to Europe. (Josef Krauthäuser collection)

CAPITOL AIR   USA

CAPITOL INTERNATIONAL AIRWAYS was set up in 1946 in Smyrna, Tennessee and concentrated initially on group charters within the United States. The fleet of Curtiss C-46s and Douglas DC-4s was augmented by Lockheed L-749A Constellations from 1957. These were used occasionally for military charters including to Europe, a destination area which would become significant for the company. The airline grew quickly to become the largest charter concern in the USA, with 17 Constellations in use by 1960. In 1962 a freight contract on behalf of the USAF was taken over from RIDDLE AIRLINES, and this included the corresponding aircraft in the form of the Armstrong Whitworth Argosy. These were replaced for this work by the old Curtiss C-46s, when in 1963 the first DC-8 entered service with CAPITOL. A further expansion followed, especially on transatlantic routes,

where almost 50% of the capacity was allocated to MAC-Military Airlift Command use. However over the years the amount of military charter declined and by 1973 formed only about 20% of capacity. Using around a dozen DC-8s freight was flown as well as passengers and concentrated more and more on Europe. In 1978 CAPITOL INTERNATIONAL AIRWAYS obtained permission for a scheduled service between Newark and Brussels, which was first operated on 5th May 1979. In September of the same year a scheduled service between New York and Los Angeles was also introduced. Neither route was a commercial success and this led to a sale in 1980 to Batchelor Enterprises, the owner of ARROW AIR in Miami and of International Air Lease. The name was changed to CAPITOL AIR and the aircraft repainted in the new colour scheme.

More scheduled services and more aircraft was the thrust of an

expansion policy, with services to more destinations in the USA, to Puerto Rico and Europe. Two Douglas DC-10s were acquired for the famous 'SKY SAVER' service to Europe. Despite all this activity the company still finished up in the red and in 1983 was taken over by Capitol Holding, a newly-formed company owned by Farhad Azima. Farhad Azima was also at this time the owner of GLOBAL INTERNATIONAL AIRWAYS and attempted to breathe life into the company by further expansion. More flights to the Caribbean, to Tel Aviv in Israel and within the USA were undertaken. The company however failed to make profits, and had debts everywhere, so by mid 1984 it had to drastically cut routes, lose 1,000 workers and park up numerous aircraft.

On 25th November 1984 a creditor began bankruptcy proceedings and CAPITOL AIR ceased flying.

Fort Lauderdale was the base and headquarters for CARNIVAL AIR LINES. Here it was busy with the Boeing 727, and 737 as seen here, and the Airbus A300B4. (Josef Krauthäuser)

CARNIVAL AIR LINES   USA

PACIFIC INTERSTATE AIRLINES was founded in 1984 in Las Vegas, with the Riviera Hotel as a shareholder. At first, group charters from Los Angeles to Las Vegas were undertaken; these could be booked in conjunction with a hotel package. In 1985, in anticipation of the award of a scheduled service licence, the name was changed to PACIFIC INTER AIR. Only two years later came another change, to BAHAMAS EXPRESS; the company was now flying from airports on the US east coast to Freeport in the Bahamas. In 1988 Carnival Cruise Line bought the company. Again the name was to be changed, and the marketing people at the shipping line put forward the name FUN AIR. However this was not adopted and the cruise passengers were flown to and from their ports of embarkation and disembarkation by MAJESTIC AIR. In order to give a single identity to the whole product, in 1989 there was a final

change of name to CARNIVAL AIR LINES. Scheduled services from Miami to Chicago, Houston, Los Angeles, New Orleans and New York were started. In 1992 a code-share agreement was concluded with IBERIA, with CARNIVAL providing connecting services for IBERIA passengers in Miami. In 1996 CARNIVAL AIR LINES opened a new route from

Miami to Lima in co-operation with FAUCETT,whose licence had been withdrawn. A further agreement was made with LADECO, whereby their passengers from Chile arriving at Miami could fly on to New York.

In March 1997 came the merger with the new PAN AM. The Fort Lauderdale base, all aircraft and staff were taken over.

Boeing 727 N5609 when the company was known as MAJESTIC AIR. (Josef Krauthäuser collection)

CHANNEL AIRWAYS Vickers Viscounts formed the basis of a successful fleet for several years for charter work from the British Isles to the Mediterranean holiday resorts. Here is G-AVIW at Ostend, ready for its return flight across the English Channel to Southend. (Manfred Winter)

CHANNEL AIRWAYS   Great Britain

One of the best known of the British post-war airlines was CHANNEL AIRWAYS Ltd, set up in 1946 as EAST ANGLIAN FLYING SERVICE, with a base at Southend from 1st January 1947. Using Puss Moths or Miles Aerovans it was a busy charter undertaking, with occasional flights to Cyprus from as early as 1947. Four de Havilland Dragon Rapides were bought from the RAF in 1948 and used from Southend for flights to Le Touquet and Ostend. A schedule from Southend to Rochester was flown on behalf of BEA, and from 1950 services were added from Birmingham via Southend to Ostend with de Havilland DH 104 Doves entering service. By 1957, the company now known as CHANNEL AIRWAYS opened its first year-round route to Rotterdam, bought two Bristol 170 Freighters and began combined car/passenger services across the Channel. Other larger aircraft came in 1958 with Vickers Vikings, supplemented

in 1960 with Douglas DC-3s and CHANNEL AIRWAYS expanded its network. Scheduled services to the Channel Islands were initiated with the DC-3s, with the London-Jersey 'Coach Service' becoming a great success; passengers travelled by coach from London to Southend and flew on to Jersey. In1962 TRADAIR was taken over and its Vikings and a single Viscount integrated into the fleet, giving CHANNEL AIRWAYS its first turboprop. This laid the basis for later success as a leading charter company, particularly using Viscount 800s acquired from CONTINENTAL AIRLINES in the USA. Further Viscounts came from BEA, but were leased out to other airlines. HS.748s supplanted the DC-3s from 1966 and a year later the first BAC 1-11-400 was introduced. CHANNEL AIRWAYS expanded its operations to other UK airports during the 1960s, particularly for charters. East Midlands became a hub for services to northern

England and Scotland. HS-121 Trident 1Es entered the fleet in 1968 as a Viscount replacement. The base for jet services was moved to Stansted, as Southend's runway was deemed too short. In 1970 five DH.106 Comet 4Bs were brought into service to fulfil a contract with a tour operator. CHANNEL AIRWAYS received a licence for inclusive tour work to the USA and Canada, but never operated these services. In 1970 the last of the DC-3s were finally retired, and for the first time flights were undertaken to southern Europe from Berlin for a German tour operator. 1971 was a poor year for CHANNEL and as the situation was not improving in the early part of 1972, the company came under bankruptcy protection. All jet services were suspended from 15th February 1972 so that these could be sold off. On 29th February 1972 the last flight was operated by a DH 114 Heron and CHANNEL AIRWAYS was liquidated.

Using leased MD-80 VH-LNH COMPASS AIRLINES attempted to make a new start in Australian scheduled services. (Josef Krauthäuser collection)

COMPASS AIRLINES   Australia

Following the deregulation of Australian domestic services from 1st November 1990, the new company COMPASS took advantage of the situation and began scheduled services on 1st December 1990 between Sydney, Perth, Melbourne and Brisbane.

Two Airbus A300-600s leased from Britain's MONARCH AIRLINES formed the equipment. From the outset COMPASS was seen as a low-fare operator, undercutting the prices of the previously monopolistic competition by up to 20%. In 1991 the first of the airline's own Airbus A300-600s arrived, allowing frequencies to be increased and the network to be expanded. Even so, two further Airbus A310-300s were leased in during the year. On 20th December 1991 COMPASS ceased flying and the Airbus aircraft were stored in Brisbane. The reason for this was mounting business problems, because the two large and established Australian carriers ANSETT and AUSTRALIAN had made life difficult for the unwelcome new competition, apparently doing so by means which led to or would lead to numerous court hearings, ultimately to the detriment of the consumers. A hoped-for reorganisation of the company faltered initially at the beginning of 1992. However, in the summer of that year SOUTHERN CROSS AIRWAYS was set up, taking over the assets from the COMPASS bankruptcy, including the old name which it continued to use. MD-80s were brought into service, again leased in. Even so, this second start was short-lived and the airline failed after only a few months. On 11th March 1993 COMPASS AIRLINES finally gave up flying , as even the new owners could not stave off bankruptcy.

With a fleet of brightly coloured BAC 1-11s, such as G-AZEB seen here at Palma de Mallorca, COURT LINE was the leading British charter company at the beginning of the 1970s. (Manfred Winter)

COURT LINE   Great Britain

COURT LINE stands out as a pioneer of English mass charter traffic, but also as an example of an airline company being too dependent on tour operators and their sales policies.

AUTAIR began life in 1953 as a helicopter operator in London and grew quickly as a specialist company. There were contracts in Europe, Africa, India and Canada for various tasks, such as pesticide application and earth survey work. During 1960 AUTAIR took on a single DC-3, which was however leased out for much of the time. Following the erection of the necessary maintenance base at Luton, more DC-3s were taken on for charter flights. These were also used for ad hoc services on behalf of other companies. Two Vickers Vikings were also added to the fleet, and were used for inclusive tour work to the Mediterranean. Berlin was an important market for AUTAIR. The first scheduled service between Luton and Blackpool was initiated

on 1st October 1963. The Court Line Shipping Company acquired a controlling interest in AUTAIR in 1965 , but without changing its type of operations. The signs pointed towards expansion and further aircraft including Airspeed Ambassadors, HS 748s and Handley Page Heralds replaced the older DC-3s and Vikings. New UK domestic services were also introduced. In 1967 AUTAIR took over the routes of TREFFIELD INTERNATIONAL which had gone into bankruptcy, with flights from Bristol and Cardiff to destinations in the Mediterranean. During 1967 the first of the BAC 1-11s were introduced, being used overwhelmingly on behalf of Clarkson Holidays. On 1st April 1969 AUTAIR moved all its scheduled services from Luton to London-Heathrow, only to drop these routes completely in October of the same year. All the Handley Page Heralds were sold and the BAC 1-11 fleet increased to five aircraft. At this time the

Court Line Group was putting up several holiday complexes in the Caribbean and further changes were in the offing. From 1st. January 1970 AUTAIR changed its name to COURT LINE and and the rise to becoming a leading charter airline was begun. The company's livery was particularly outstanding. Brightly coloured aircraft reflected the holiday atmosphere. In 1971 75% of the shares in LIAT were acquired and during the winter months BAC 1-11s were introduced into service on their Caribbean routes. COURT LINE received its first Lockheed L-1011 TriStar in 1973 and this was the first widebody for a charter company; they were used mostly for services to the Mediterranean, and in winter to the Caribbean. In 1973 COURT LINE took over the ailing Clarkson Holidays tour company, which had until then been responsible for filling 80% of their aircraft seats. Another smaller tour company, Horizon Holidays, was also bought.

In 1973 the first widebody operations from Berlin were carried out by the Lockheed L-1011 TriStar. Here G-BAAA receives attention from technical and ground personnel. (Manfred Winter)

COURT LINE thus found itself in the difficult position that it had to fill its aircraft in the face of the first oil crisis, business recession and falling numbers of bookings with the situation worsening daily. The company was able to lease out two One-Elevens at the beginning of 1974, but even so the financial crisis was obviously coming to a head. The British government took over the shipping line for £16 million and thus ensured the immediate survival of the group. On the evening 15th August 1974 at 7pm, COURT LINE ceased flight operations and entered bankruptcy. More than 50,000 holidaymakers were at this moment stranded abroad, since the six tour companies were also bankrupt. A further 150,000 holidaymakers lost their anticipated holidays and deposits, and about 1,200 employees of COURT LINE lost their jobs. It was at that time the largest collapse in the history of the British tour industry.

The second Lockheed L-1011 TriStar G-BAAB at London-Gatwick awaiting its next passengers. 80% of the passengers had booked their holidays though Clarkson, a company which became bankrupt and whose takeover led COURT LINE into financial ruin. (Manfred Winter)

The leased Airbus A320 has a mixed colour scheme and carries the name 'Zorbas'. (Josef Krauthäuser collection)

CRETAN AIRLINES   Greece

CRETAN AIRLINES was founded in 1992 by local tour operators and business people in Crete and began flying in April 1993. Using leased Airbus A320 equipment services were principally flown from German airports to Crete and to other destinations in Greece. A scheduled service was also instituted between Thessaloniki-Athens and Crete, but in spite of this the two Airbus A320s could not be fully employed throughout the year. During the summer season extra capacity, also in the form of A320s had to be leased in, in order to fulfil the existing commitments. CRETAN AIRLINES was one of the first to order the new Dornier Do 328 and intended to use these from 1995 on domestic routes, particularly inter-island services. However, before this could happen, CRETAN AIRLINES had to face bankruptcy in June 1995. Services ceased and the Airbuses were returned to their lessors.

Boeing 737-200ADV PP-CJT of CRUZEIRO. The aircraft was delivered directly from Boeing in 1975 and continued to fly after the merger with VARIG. (Josef Krauthäuser collection)

CRUZEIRO DO SUL   Brazil

This company could trace its origins to 1926, when it was founded in Porto Alegre by the German Condor-Syndikat and Brazilian business interests. On 3rd February 1927 the single route from Porto Alegre via Pelotas to Rio Grande was started; a year later this route was extended as far as Rio de Janeiro. During 1934 the first flights to neighbouring countries began, to Argentina and to Chile. Junkers Ju52/3ms and two Focke Wulf Fw200s joined the carefully managed company. With the beginning of the Second World War, the German influence with the company was reduced, and from 1941 the name was changed to SERVICIOS AEREOS CONDOR. During 1943 the Brazilian government took over the whole of the shares and thus there was a further name change to become SERVICIOS AEREOS CRUZEIRO DO SUL on 16th January 1943. Douglas DC-3s were brought into service, and

the twelve Junkers Ju 52s were slowly withdrawn. By 1953, with a fleet of 38 DC-3s, there were no longer any German-built aircraft in the fleet; Convair 340s and 440s followed on from the DC-3s. More and more CRUZEIRO concentrated on services throughout Brazil, but international services to Montevideo, La Paz and Caracas were added. At the beginning of the 1950s smaller companies had been supported in their growth such as TRANSPORTES AEREOS CATARINENSE and VIACAO AEREA GAUCHA, both of which were integrated into CRUZEIRO in 1967. Following the collapse of PANAIR DO BRASIL in 1965, their network and aircraft were taken over. Using the SE.210 Caravelle CRUZEIRO began its first longer range routes as early as 1962, particularly international services. Boeing 727s and 737s replaced all the propeller-driven types by and by. In 1975 the Ruben Berta Foundation acquired the majority of the CRUZEIRO shares. Behind

this foundation hid the holding company of VARIG, the Brazilian national carrier. In future the flight timetables would be harmonised and the infrastructure of the two airlines rationalised. In 1980 CRUZEIRO received its first Airbus A300, for use on the most important domestic services. Further rationalisation and the drive towards cost-savings led the two airlines to ever-close co-operation, which quickly led in January 1993 to the merger of CRUZEIRO into VARIG.

A DC-10-30 C-GCPC of CP AIR/CANADIAN after the merger with PWA, in a mixed scheme with the colours of CP AIR and the new CANADIAN titling on the forward fuselage. (Josef Krauthäuser)

CP AIR   Canada

This company, rich in tradition, had its origins in several bush-flying and smaller undertakings which came together on 16th May 1942 to form CANADIAN PACIFIC AIR LINES – CPAL. The driving force behind this amalgamation was majority shareholder Canadian Pacific Railway, also the owner of CANADIAN AIRWAYS, which played a leading role in the mergers. The new airline thus had about 120 aircraft from over twenty manufacturers on hand; significant amongst these were numerous Junkers W33s and W34s. During the Second World War, a lot of flying was carried out for the RAF and USAF ; CPAL pilots ferried many C-47s, C-54s and even B-17s. The biggest problem was rationalisation of the fleet and after the war Douglas DC-3s were ordered. In 1949 CPAL opened a route from Vancouver to Sydney and Auckland. Canadair North Stars (a Canadian-built version of the Douglas DC-4) were used.for this service. Following the

outbreak of the Korean War CPAL DC-4s were chartered to fly contingents of troops to Tokyo. More comfortable Douglas DC-6s were brought into service on the Pacific routes from 1953. The airline was always in competition for licences with with TCA-TRANS CANADA AIR LINES, decisions often going in favour of the state airline. In spite of much discrimination, CPA became a successful company, which by the mid-1950s offered service to South America and after SAS, was only the second airline to fly over the North Pole to Europe. Here, Amsterdam was the destination of a DC-6 service in 1955, upgraded to the new Bristol Britannia from 1956. Further European destinations were Rome, Lisbon, Madrid and Athens. On 25th March 1961 the first Douglas DC-8 flight was undertaken from Vancouver to Honolulu,and a month later, Amsterdam was being served by the new jet. During1968 the remaining propeller types were

usurped by the Boeing 737. In this year also a new corporate identity was introduced and the name changed to CP AIR. With the arrival of the Boeing 747 in 1973 the airline had its first widebody in service. DC-10-30s supplemented 747s from March 1979; in 1985 four Boeing 747s were exchanged for DC-10s with PIA – PAKISTAN AIRLINES. With additional fuel tanks, the range of the DC-10s was increased and CP AIR was one of the largest users of the DC-10-30. Business conditions dictated that in the mid 1980s there would have to be a concentration of airline activities in Canada. In 1984 CP AIR took over a majority shareholding in EASTERN PROVINCIAL AIRWAYS and their subsidiary company AIR MARITIME. In December 1986 PACIFIC WESTERN AIRLINES bought CP AIR for Canadian $300 million and shortly afterwards merged the airlines to become the basis of the new CANADIAN AIRLINES.

More than half of the Comets built served at some time with DAN-AIR. Here Comet 4C G-BDIU is seen landing at London-Gatwick. This aircraft saw five years' service with DAN-AIR. (Josef Krauthäuser collection)

DAN-AIR LONDON   Great Britain

Davies and Newman Ltd, a British shipping agency, founded DAN-AIR SERVICES in March 1953 with a capital of £5,000. The name stems from the initials of the founding company. Using a Douglas DC-3, ad hoc flights were started from Southend. In 1955 with the introduction of Avro Yorks, the base was moved to Blackbushe, with their own maintenance company, DAN-AIR Engineering, set up at Lasham. Many freight flights were operated to Africa, and on behalf of the government, to Singapore, resulting in the aircraft being well utilised. However in 1956 the first scheduled service to Jersey was flown. In the same year the DC-3 was used for many aid and evacuation flights in connection with the Russian invasion of Hungary. Bristol 170 Freighters carried numerous rockets and equipment to the test centre in Australia. By the end of the 1950s the summer season would account for many IT-charters

carried out to Italy, Spain, Belgium and Germany. Domestically, new scheduled services were added from the new airport at Bristol and from Cardiff. De Havilland Doves were acquired for these services, and three Airspeed Ambassadors were also added to the fleet. During the 1967 summer season DAN-AIR used three Comet 4Bs on charter work for the first time, and during subsequent years DAN AIR managed to fly at one time or another more than half of all the Comets which were built. Scheduled services were also added to Belgium, Norway and to the Netherlands. In 1969 DAN-AIR received further jets – more Comets, and BAC One-Elevens. In the same year the German tourist market was entered from Berlin and the airline remained active here until closure. Following the grant of transatlantic ABC-licences, two Boeing 707s were bought in 1971 from PAN AM. DAN-AIR bought

SKYWAYS INTERNATIONAL for £650,000 in 1972; this then operated scheduled services for a while as DAN-AIR SKYWAYS with HS 748s on the 'City Network'. Almost 20 HS 748s flew with DAN-AIR and in 1972 the airline became the first, and for a long time the only, UK operator of the Boeing 727. These were to replace the fuel-thirsty Comets. It is surprising how with the variety of types in the fleet, it was possible for DAN AIR to fly profitably. One of the 727s was based in Berlin and flew to the Canary Isles; in order to do this it was modified with an additional fuel tank. DAN-AIR also participated in the oil business. A single HS 748 based in Aberdeen flew oil company crews and personnel to Sumburgh in the Shetland Islands, to meet this growing demand. The activities of DAN-AIR were not however limited to flying services. Through shareholdings or as fully-owned companies in the group, they had

Boeing 727 G-BAFZ was often used from Berlin-Tegel on behalf of German tour operators. The aircraft was taken over by DAN-AIR in 1972. In 1985 it was sold but then leased back for serveral months (Josef Krauthäuser collection)

aircraft handling, catering, leasing, tour operation and sales organisations. More than 3,000 people were employed as the yearly passenger figures grew. DAN AIR rode out the recession and oil crisis of the 1970s and by the mid 1980s was carrying over three million passengers a year. Newer aircraft, which DAN-AIR almost always acquired second-hand, were bought or leased. During the European winter season, DAN-AIR aircraft could be seen in the USA or in South America, where they had been leased out to other airlines. Boeing 737-200s, Boeing 737-300s, Airbus A300B4s and BAe 146s all found employment on the expanding route network. At the end of the 1980s DAN-AIR felt the pressure of numerous newer airlines and lost various contracts, particularly as more and more tour operators were lining up with their own airlines. The ageing fleet did not help in this respect. As a radical cure, older aircraft

were replaced with newly-built Boeing 737-400s. These were leased, since DAN-AIR was no longer flying profitably. Unprofitable routes were axed, personnel numbers reduced and shareholdings sold off. In 1991 4.7 million passengers were carried with a turnover of £325

million, but this produced a bottom line of a £35 million loss. For the symbolic price of £1 BRITISH AIRWAYS took over the company at the end of 1992 in a rescue move which ensured the continuity of services. Another illustrious British airline with strong traditions had passed into history.

This 1968 photo shows G-AMAH, one of ten Airspeed Ambassadors which flew for DAN-AIR. (Manfred Winter)

Originally built for ANA-ALL NIPPON AIRWAYS, DOMINICANA received this Boeing 727-200 in April 1992 as HI-616CA, but it was reregistered only a month later as HI-617CA. (Josef Krauthäuser collection)

DOMINICANA DE AVIACION Dominican Republic

The COMPANIA DOMINICANA DE AVIACION was established on 4th May 1944 and began services with a Ford Trimotor from Santo Domingo to Santiago de Cuba. Following the introduction of further Trimotors and a Stinson Reliant, the network was expanded. In 1947 DOMINICANA received two Douglas DC-3s from United States Air Force stocks, and a Fairchild F-24. Using the Curtiss C-46 Commando, a freight service was also started between Santo Domingo and San Juan, transporting only deeply refrigerated meat to San Juan. The return services were flown empty, since the United States authorities had granted no licence. In 1955 DOMINICANA gained permission to undertake passenger services between Miami and Santo Domingo. Modified Curtiss C-46s were brought into use. A special feature of these aircraft was the installation on board of 'one-armed bandits', which allowed

the passengers to pass away the time and if they were lucky to take away some cash. Following the introduction of Douglas DC-4s from March 1958 , the C-46s were again relegated to freight work. After the ousting of the dictator Trujillo and the dissolution of his clan, who had been very influential in the business world and had owned DOMINICANA, the company was nationalised. In 1962 came the first Douglas DC-6B, with more following until 1964. A co-operative jet service with VIASA was flown from Caracas to Santo Domingo, but this operated only from May 1967 until February 1970. As a result of the crash of the sole DC-9-32 which the airline had, this service was suspended. Using a Boeing 707, service was provided from April 1972 to New York, which quickly became one of the most important destination cities, alongside Miami. In support of the 707, two Boeing 727s were added, and as a result the last of

the DC-6s could be converted for freight work; one of these then remained in service until 1992. During 1991 IBERIA took a shareholding in DOMINICANA; however mounting business difficulties and operating restrictions imposed by the US authorities led to a cessation of the New York and Miami routes at the beginning of 1995. All flights were stopped in April 1995 and the company was dissolved.

Bristol Britannia 312 G-AOVF was one of three former BOAC aircraft of the type to see service with DONALDSON. (Josef Krauthäuser collection)

DONALDSON   Great Britain

DONALDSON INTERNATIONAL AIRWAYS was set up as a subsidiary of the Waverley Shipping Company in 1964. Another business in the group was Mercury Air Holidays, whose holidaymakers were being flown on aircraft operated by other charter companies. It took three years before DONALDSON received its first aircraft, a Bristol Britannia 312, but this was leased out, and services did not begin until 1969 from London Gatwick, where a base was established, two further former BOAC Britannias having been acquired. Prestwick in Scotland was also an operating base for charter flights, which predominantly served the traditional Mediterranean resorts. Some flights were however also carried out to the United States and to Canada. In December 1970 DONALDSON received two Boeing 707s, which were brought into service from May 1971 and replaced the Britannias on routes over the North Atlantic. One

Britannia was converted as a freighter, while the other two were configured as combis, for mixed passenger and freight work. Two more Boeing 707s were added in 1972 and these were used on services to the Far East, finally displacing the Britannias. Disputes with the United States authorities, over the form of group charters, led to losses in America – the part of the business which had become the most important to the company. Increasing financial security bonds to the US authorities (CAB) led to the sale of two of the Boeing 707s. In 1973 the airline went over to ABC charters with multiple flights each week to Toronto and New York. From 1st May 1974, the airline took over IRAQI AIRWAYS' daily flights to the Middle East and Europe using three leased Boeing 707s. However, the charter business continued to decline and it was decided to convert the last remaining 707 to a freighter, though this did not enter service.

On 8th August 1974 DONALDSON ceased operations. The operating licences were withdrawn, and services did not recommence.

Boeing 737-200 TF-ISA after landing in Amsterdam. This particular 737 joined EAGLE AIR in April 1988 and remained with the airline until the merger with ISLANDSFLUG after which it was sold to CASINO EXPRESS. (Josef Krauthäuser)

EAGLE AIR/ARNARFLUG Iceland

EAGLE AIR was set up on 10th April 1976 by former employees of the bankrupt AIR VIKING, which had operated two Boeing 720s for a short time. The official first flight of the new Icelandic charter company followed on 5th June 1976 from Keflavik to Malaga in Spain. Leased Boeing 707-300s were used to continue this service and to fly to further destinations in the Mediterranean holiday region, and the company was active with charter work and sub-leasing until 1979. After the collapse of another smaller company, EAGLE AIR was granted the status of a scheduled service airline by the Icelandic government. Thus the routes of VAENGIR HF AIRTRANSPORT were taken over. This airline had operated a network of services to the west and north-west of Iceland using smaller aircraft – DHC-6 Twin Otters and Britten-Norman Islanders. Additionally there were ambulance and rescue flights on behalf of the

government. In order to make full use of these aircraft, seasonal sightseeing flights showing tourists the wonders of Iceland were flown. On 14th September 1979 EAGLE AIR/ARNARFLUG (the title in Icelandic), began its first scheduled services. These were quickly built up, serving 14 points in Iceland. In the same year two Boeing 707s which had been leased out to other airlines, were taken out of service and broken up. EAGLE AIR however remained loyal to the 707, as more examples were acquired in 1980 and 1981, though these were not used on the airline's own services, but again leased out. In 1981 EAGLE AIR was licensed for scheduled services outside Iceland. Amsterdam, Hamburg and Zurich appeared in the timetable at first, but Hamburg was dropped in favour of Düsseldorf. For these new services EAGLE AIR leased a Boeing 737-200, though later on this was exchanged for other 737s.

In 1984 the last Boeing 707 was sold, since because of rising fuel prices it was no longer profitable to operate. Harder times in Iceland, which led in the mid 1980s to a business recession, necessitated a reconstruction of the company. A reduction in passengers and tourists staying away led to drastic economies and a reduction in services. In 1990 the scheduled service rights were given up and negotiations with ISLANDSFLUG led to a merger with this small regional carrier from 1st January 1991.

Handley Page Dart Herald F-BLOY was for many years the mainstay of EAS and was used for both passenger and freight work. (Manfred Winter)

EAS-EUROPE AIRLINES France

EUROPE AERO SERVICE SA was set up as a subsidiary company of SOCIETE AERO SAHARA in 1965. The parent company was especially involved in the oil exploration business in Algeria and managed several chartered aircraft for oil companies. It also gained permission for regular flights between Perpignan and Palma de Mallorca. These services were however operated for only 2½ years, and it was a condition that no aircraft larger than 5.7t could be used. EUROPA AERO SERVICE, EAS for short, took over these flights from the beginning of 1966. As demand increased, the weight restriction was lifted and from 1968 the Handley Page Dart Herald came into service. Further domestic routes were instituted using this new type: Valence-Paris, or Metz-Paris and Paris-Rennes. These routes were flown for AIR INTER, and in addition there were numerous seasonal charter flights from Perpignan or Nimes to

destinations in various holiday regions. In 1971 EAS took over extensive freight work from AIR FRANCE. At night newspapers were flown from Paris to Marseilles and Toulouse, and further freight contracts led frequently to Algiers, Casablanca, Frankfurt, Milan, Tunis and Zurich. At first the Heralds were used for this, and later, from the end of 1972, Vickers Vanguards were introduced. For passenger services SE.210 Caravelles replaced the ageing Heralds and were brought into use on the Valence to Paris service; for courier and small package flights the airline also had Dornier Do 28s, Do 27s and Cessna 180s. At the beginning of the 1990s the Caravelles were supplanted by Boeing 727s and 737s, but the company was running into financial difficulties and had to seek bankruptcy protection. A new owner was found in the shape of Francis Lagarde, who built the company up again,

established a second base at Paris-Orly, bought after the collapse of TEA-FRANCE and was also the owner of AIR TOULOUSE. In 1993 he also took over the remaining activities of STELLAIR and JET FRET, and a merger of EAS and TEA-FRANCE was negotiated. The name was changed to EAS EUROPE AIRLINES in order to better reflect its Europe-wide activities. There also had to be negotiations with the creditors, but EAS's financial conduct was inscrutable, and at the end of 1993 it was again placed under bankruptcy protection. On 6th March 1995 EAS ceased operations and the bankruptcy was carried through.

Vickers VC-10 5Y-ADA was the only VC-10 of EAST AFRICAN AIRWAYS registered in Kenya and was delivered to the company on 1st April 1964. EAST AFRICAN AIRWAYS flew weekly to Frankfurt, where this photo was taken. (Manfred Winter)

EAST AFRICAN AIRWAYS Kenya, Uganda & Tanzania

EAST AFRICAN AIRWAYS CORPORATION (EAAC) was founded in Kenya as early as 1st January 1946. Until the independence from Britain of the three countries, Kenya (1963), Uganda (1962) and Tanzania (1964), all aircraft were initially based in Nairobi. The fleet consisted mainly of the indestructible Douglas DC-3, though there were smaller aircraft in addition. Using leased Canadair Argonauts, EAAC began a route to London in April 1957. Karachi in Pakistan and Bombay in India followed. Johannesburg in South Africa was also served in the same year. In 1960 de Havilland Comet 4 jets took over these routes. 1966 saw the introduction of the first Vickers Super VC-10. While the main base remained in Nairobi, various aircraft used on regional services were based and registered in Tanzania and Uganda. Fokker F.27 Friendships formed the backbone of the fleet for these duties, while the VC-10s appeared on services to an increasing number of destinations in Europe and Asia.

EAAC received its first Douglas DC-9 on 22nd December 1970 signalling the conversion to jet service on internal African routes. Stemming from the differing political systems and regimes in the three partner countries, there were inevitable conflicts, and especially when it came to financial settlements between them. The airline's costs were to be calculated and apportioned, but from 1975 there were differences of opinion which had consequences for these costs. Tanzania and Uganda did not agree their calculated obligations of about $13 million and did not pay Kenya. This led in January 1977 to the bankruptcy of the airline, since Kenya was not willing to support all the costs alone.

Lockheed L-1011 TriStar 1 N329EA on approach to Miami. EASTERN AIR LINES was the largest user of the L-1011 in the USA. After Eastern's collapse, LTU took on this aircraft as D-AERC. (Josef Krauthäuser collection)

EASTERN AIR LINES

In 1927 PITCAIRN AVIATION was founded, flying the postal run from New York to Atlanta. From 1st May 1928 a route licence was also granted for postal service between Atlanta and Miami. North American Aviation Corporation took over PITCAIRN in 1929 as their Eastern Division; this was to become known from 1930 as EASTERN AIR LINES. Several smaller airline companies were taken over in the 1930s and '40s. North American Aviation sold out in 1938 to Eddie Rickenbacker, who was the President of EAL for many years. Douglas DC-3s were used throughout the route network and from 1946 DC-4s followed for a Miami-San Juan route. Non-stop flights using the Lockheed Constellation were begun in 1951 on the most profitable route between Miami and New York. COLONIAL AIRLINES was bought up in 1956, with their routes to Canada and to Bermuda. EASTERN's first turboprops were to be another

Lockheed product, the L-188 Electra, which from 12th January 1959 took on the route from Miami to New York. Convair 440s and Martin 4-0-4s were also used. The airline's first jet came in 1960 in the form of the Douglas DC-8, which again was first introduced on the Miami-New York run. Boeing 720Bs followed, and with EASTERN being a launch customer for the new Boeing 727, with what at that time was a hefty order for 40 aircraft, jets came to dominate the fleet. EASTERN AIR LINES set innovative standards in 1961 with the introduction of the 'Air Shuttle' between New York-Washington and New York-Boston. The system was as easy as a New York subway journey; turn up, buy a ticket, and get on the next hourly flight. There were no reservations and no on-board service, and thus the fares were correspondingly cheaper. During 1967 MACKEY AIRLINES with routes between Miami and the Bahamas was taken over. In

October 1970 Boeing 747s became the first widebodies to join EAL; these were however sold in 1972, as the first Lockheed L-1011 TriStars came into the fleet. This seemed for EAL to be the ideal aircraft for its needs and the airline grew to be the third largest in the USA, with over 120 destinations both domestic and international. In 1973 with the takeover of CARIB-AIR, a regional company was acquired. Following deregulation, however, EAL headed into increasing financial difficulties. Even though over 35 million passengers were being carried each year, losses mounted. Recovery measures were introduced, but at the same time South American routes were bought from BRANIFF, expansion into Europe was envisaged, and the fleet was renewed with further Airbus A300s and Boeing 757s – all activities which increased the need for financial resources. The employees bought 25% of the

Boeing 757-200 N522EA in a special colour scheme. The aircraft type appears in large figures on the tailfin. (Josef Krauthäuser collection)

shares, in order to keep the airline flying. Following the financial participation of the Texas Air Corporation, under the leadership of its President, Frank Lorenzo, in 1966, the situation was little better. The staff thought that this could lead to massive cutbacks and redundancies. In November 1987 3,500 employees were indeed shed, the signal for the beginning of a long strike and a battle between the management and the unions and employees. In 1989 the company sought protection from bankruptcy under Chapter 11. From then on it was administered under a trusteeship. Strikes and further redundancies worsened the situation, and passengers were staying away as a result. Assets such as slots, terminals, shareholdings and aircraft were sold off in order to maintain liquidity. An end came suddenly to what had been a slow death of the company on 18th January 1991 with a cessation of operations, and the onset of bankruptcy proceedings. By then about 22,000 of what had at one time been 40,000 employees had lost their jobs, and in the collapse about 18,000 qualified employees became jobless. The debts of the company eventually amounted to about US$1.5 billion.

EASTERN AIR LINES had as many as 34 Airbus A300s in the fleet. N224EA was delivered on 9th October 1981 direct from the factory. After the collapse of EAL it went on to fly with CONTINENTAL. (Josef Krauthäuser collection)

EPA received this Boeing 737-200 CF-EPO in July 1970. After the merger with CANADIAN PACIFIC AIRWAYS and the further merger into CANADIAN AIRLINES INTERNATIONAL it flew on as C-FEPO. (Christofer Witt collection)

EASTERN PROVINCIAL AIRWAYS Canada

EASTERN PROVINCIAL AIRWAYS – EPA grew out of the small concern NEWFOUNDLAND AERO SALES AND SERVICE – NASS, which was founded in 1946 in Torbay by Eric W Blackwood and two partners. A Republic Seabee was used on utility flights to small coastal settlements. Expansion was needed but could not be financed, so NASS was sold to MCA – MARITIME CENTRAL AIRWAYS, but Blackwood set up EASTERN PROVINCIAL AIRWAYS as a new company, registered on 8th March 1949, so that he could continue his participation. With contracts for postal work and from the government for support flights to outlying areas the company prospered and further aircraft were acquired, including the second prototype of the de Havilland Canada DHC-3 Otter. In 1954 the base was moved to Gander. On behalf of the Danish government, survey, aid and utility flights were undertaken over Greenland with a PBY-5 Canso.

This contract lasted until the setting up of GRONLANDSFLY, who took over these tasks in 1965. Lockheed L-10s and Douglas DC-3 were bought by EPA during 1955-56 and used on scheduled services from Gander. Curtiss C-46s undertook freight flights from 1960 on behalf of various companies. EPA's strongest competitor, MCA was bought in 1963 and the fleet, routes and personnel integrated. Their Handley Page Dart Heralds and Aviation Traders Carvairs brought new types into the fleet for passenger and freight work respectively. On 1st June 1969 jet service was begun with a Boeing 737 between Montreal and St Johns and in 1972 EPA became a limited company, with quotations on the Toronto and Montreal exchanges. EPA abandoned its smaller aircraft and bush flying operations, which were taken on by newly-formed companies with former EPA employees and aircraft. In 1976 a move was

made from Gander to a new hangar at Hailifax, where the administrative headquarters would be next to the training and maintenance establishments. Boeing 737s and HS.748s formed the bulk of the fleet at this time, the 737s being also used for charter flights to Florida, on behalf of a separate tour company. In 1981 EPA gained operating rights for flights to Toronto, Canada's leading airport. Recession and business difficulties in Canada also brought crisis to EPA, as did management methods which were reminiscent of the situations at PEOPLEXPRESS or EASTERN AIRLINES. Massive staff dismissals and a month long battle with the employees weakened the once prosperous airline considerably. On 17th April 1984 CP AIR took over the Newfoundland Capital Corp., the holding company of EPA, for Can$ 20 million. On 12th January 1986 the merger was completed and EPA passed into history.

Fokker F.27-500 VH-EWT spent five years in service, principally from Brisbane. (Josef Krauthäuser collection)

EAST-WEST AIRLINES   Australia

EAST-WEST was founded as a private company in 1947. On 23rd June 1947, using an Avro Anson, the first route was opened, from Tamworth to Sydney. In 1953 EAST-WEST took over COAST AIRWAYS and introduced the Douglas DC-3. In 1959 it was one of the first airlines in the world to order and receive the new Fokker F.27 Friendship. This type was for many years the mainstay of the company and various different versions were used. Keeping it in the family, the Fokker F.28 Fellowship became the airline's first jet, and the route network was expanded correspondingly.

At the end of 1983 EAST-WEST AIRLINES was acquired by SKYWEST AIRLINES, but retained its own identity. Following a further sale to the ANSETT/TNT Group, EAST-WEST AIRLINES came out with additional routes but retained an autonomous management.

Boeing 727s were introduced, these being operated on behalf of

ANSETT. In the course of a fleet renewal, from 1989 BAe 146-300s arrived as replacements for the Fokker F.28s.

A reorganisation of the whole News Corporation, to whom the ANSETT/TNT Group belonged, brought the end for EAST-WEST AIRLINES in September 1993.

The integration of routes, personnel and aircraft into ANSETT AUSTRALIA meant that alongside EAST-WEST AIRLINES, ANSETT WA and ANSETT EXPRESS were also forced to give up their previous independence.

BAe 146-300 VH-EWI entered service with EAST-WEST in August 1990 and remained until it was absorbed into the ANSETT fleet.

The whole fleet of EUROBERLIN FRANCE/EUROBERLIN was rented from MONARCH AIRLINES. Here is Boeing 737-300 G-MONL at pushback at Berlin-Tegel. (Josef Krauthäuser collection)

EUROBERLIN   France/Germany

EUROBERLIN FRANCE was an airline which was established by AIR FRANCE and LUFTHANSA on 9th September 1988, in order to combat American competition in the Berlin market for air travel. From the end of the Second World War until the time of German reunification, only aircraft from the victorious nations, Great Britain, France, USSR and the USA, were permitted to fly to and from Berlin. Thus the companies of the three Western nations shared out the traffic from Western Germany to Berlin. between themselves. LUFTHANSA's objective was always to share in the Berlin traffic as soon as possible and other opportunities were explored; for example there was already a LUFTHANSA handling company in Berlin. So came about the idea for EUROBERLIN, whereby AIR FRANCE nominally held the majority of shares in this French company with its base in Berlin. Services began on 7th

November 1988 using leased Boeing 737-300s and linked Cologne, Düsseldorf, Frankfurt and Stuttgart several times daily with the German capital. Being linked into the LUFTHANSA and AIR FRANCE reservations systems, the company had a good base from which to grow and in 1989 flew over 600,000 passengers from and to Berlin. The unexpected opening of the Berlin Wall and the reunification of the two Germanys made EUROBERLIN FRANCE redundant, since with the achievement of 'air superiority' LUFTHANSA could now fly to Berlin in its own right. The company's shareholdings were altered and the 'France' in the title was dropped from 1990.

Until the leasing agreements ran off in 1994 EUROBERLIN flew on behalf of LUFTHANSA, but was more involved in charter work from Berlin. The dissolution of the company on 29th October 1994 was therefore only a formality.

89

BAe Jetstream 31 G-OEDC was one of six aircraft of this type with EURO DIRECT. (Josef Krauthäuser collection)

EURO DIRECT AIRLINES Great Britain

The new regional airline EURO DIRECT AIRLINES was founded in February 1994 by the former Manager of BRITISH WORLD AIRLINES, Neil Hansford. AIR KILROE of Manchester also had a shareholding in the company. Using four BAe Jetstream 31s, services began on 11th April 1994 from Bournemouth to Amsterdam, Brussels, Dublin, Leeds and Paris. The fleet was quickly enlarged; six BAe ATP and two more Jetstream 31s were leased in 1994. These were needed for new routes to smaller destinations which had previously not been served at all, or with poor frequency. Connections to London-Gatwick and the opening of a daily London-Berne service contributed to increased passenger boardings. Frequencies were increased on other routes, with Leeds for instance being served five times daily.

The end for this ambitious regional venture came only about a year after its inception. On 26th February 1995 EURO DIRECT ceased flying. The costs were too high in relation to the yields and further expected price increases in insurance premiums and airport charges. Furthermore, the places served by EURO DIRECT for the first time, having seen a rise in traffic, tended to want to raise their prices, which finally led to a reduction in passenger numbers.

Airbus A320-202 G-OEXC leased from GPA, seen on a charter flight at Graz, Austria. (Andreas Witek)

EXCALIBUR   Great Britain

Following the break up of the TEA Group (see page 189) a new charter company was formed in the Spring of 1992, known as EXCALIBUR AIRWAYS. Its headquarters and initial base were at East Midlands Airport. The participants in the company stemmed from TEA-UK and leased three Airbus A320s from Guinness Peat Aviation which began services from London-Gatwick. AIR MALTA was also a shareholder with a 30% interest in EXCALIBUR. A further Airbus A320 and a Boeing 737-300 were added for the 1994 summer season, in order to fulfil the numerous contracts.

A noteworthy number of flights were to Egypt and Israel, but of course there were also services to the traditional holiday resorts of the Mediterranean and North Africa. At the end of 1995 DC-10-30s flew to Florida and the Caribbean, and there was a reduced need for the Airbus A320s. As a result of a reorganisation of one of the most important customers, a medium-range tour operator, their business was more or less lost for the next season. As the company had no long-range aircraft of its own, and these could not be leased in quickly, sub-charters became the rule for these services. Indifferent performance by the airline attracted the critical attention of the British popular press, which made much of several everyday incidents.

On 26th June 1996 the company quickly declared bankruptcy, as travel operators withdrew their contracts.

Douglas DC-3 OB-R-676 served for many years with Faucett and was retired at the beginning of the 1970s. (Josef Krauthäuser collection)

FAUCETT

Peru

Elmar J Faucett, an expatriate US citizen and pilot, founded COMPANIA DE AVIACION FAUCETT SA with several Peruvian business people in May 1928. The government granted Peruvian operating permission on 4th June 1928, and the first service from Lima to Chiclayo followed, using a Stinson Detroiter on 15th September 1928. As a true aviation pioneer Elmar J Faucett scouted out a connection between Talara in the north of Peru and Arequipa in the south. Especially to the requirements of Faucett and in accordance with their plans, Stinson built the F-19. Thirty of these aircraft would be built under licence by Faucett and used on their services. The company gained financial support from American aviation industry interests. As well as being involved with the aircraft, Faucett concerned itself with the necessary infrastructure and built new airports, or expanded

existing ones. In 1938 AEROVIAS PERU was taken over. After the Second World War the Douglas DC-3 and DC-4 were successfully introduced to FAUCETT and remained in service for many years. In 1951 the airline's founder withdrew from the business and died in 1960. With the delivery of the first Douglas DC-6 in July 1960 FAUCETT also gained permission for international flights; however these were put on hold for the time being.

The delivery of a Boeing 727 in 1968 marked the first jet in the fleet, and in 1970 the operation of a freight service to Miami saw the international licence put into use for the first time.

Fleet expansion took place with the BAC 1-11, the first of which was delivered in 1971. From 1982 the Zanetti industrial family, who also owned AERONAVAS DEL PERU, became the major shareholders in FAUCETT.

Because of political differences

in the USA the sole route to Miami was suspended in 1984, or at least flown only as far as the Cayman Islands, from where passengers and freight were flown onwards to Miami by CAYMAN AIRWAYS. Since FAUCETT was particularly active in the freight business, Boeing 707s and Douglas DC-8s were also brought into service. When the Miami route was re-opened, it was with a Lockheed L-1011 TriStar, the most modern aircraft in an ageing fleet.

In 1994 FAUCETT flew services for APA in the Dominican Republic, as this airline had no aircraft of its own. The Lockheed L-1011 TriStar was also used from here, principally to Miami. Increasing losses and a decline in the previously important freight business compelled FAUCETT to cease operations in September 1997.

A Boeing 747-200F rolling from Frankfurt on the daily flight to New York. The whole FLYING TIGER LINE-fleet was integrated into FEDEX in 1989. (Josef Krauthäuser)

FLYING TIGER LINE – FTL USA

On 25th June 1945 a company was founded by Robert W Prescott as NATIONAL SKYWAY FREIGHT CORPORATION, which began transport services with eight Budd RB-1 Conestogas. These were quickly replaced with Douglas DC-3s and Curtiss C-46s. In 1946 the name was changed to THE FLYING TIGER LINE and Douglas C-54s were introduced on Pacific flights. This was to be a major feature of operations, with numerous flights being undertaken on behalf of the US Military Air Transport Service from Los Angeles to Tokyo, Okinawa and Manila. A busy freight schedule was in place on the US west cost by 1947.

From 1957 a total of 15 Lockheed L-1049 Super Constellations came into service, and connections were added to destinations from the west coast to the east coast. Alongside the freight work, passenger charters were not ignored. The airline was busy with numerous group charters to holiday areas. Canadair CL-44s, equipped with a swing-tail, were introduced from 1961 for specialist freight work and ended the era of the L-1049 Super Constellation, though the introduction of the Boeing 707 from 1965 heralded the changeover to an all-jet fleet. As the premier freight airline, FLYING TIGER opened schedules from Los Angeles to Tokyo, Osaka, Taipei, Seoul, Hong Kong, Singapore and Bangkok. For these routes the Douglas DC-8 came into service, supplanting the 707s from 1968 on account of its greater capacity. With the purchase of SEABOARD WORLD AIRLINES, which nominally took place on 1st October 1980, the two largest US freight airlines were merged. FLYING TIGER received more Boeing 747s and built up routes to South America and Australia. In the US market a dense freight network existed with direct and connecting services between business centres.

Boeing 727s entered the fleet, and smaller companies flew feeder service to hubs in Los Angeles, New York, Miami, Chicago, Atlanta, Houston and Anchorage. A passenger charter operation marketed as METRO-INTERNATIONAL AIRWAYS was suspended in 1983, in order to concentrate exclusively on freight work. Following the deregulation of air cargo flights in 1977, conditions were favourable to new companies such as FEDERAL EXPRESS and UPS, who entered the market with their own aircraft and were outstandingly successful. In1989 FEDEX quickly took over the majority shareholding in FLYING TIGER LINE and integrated the whole fleet from that time.

FORTUNAIR had a single Boeing 747-200 C-FXCE leased from AIR FRANCE. (Josef Krauthäuser collection)

FORTUNAIR CANADA   Canada

This new charter company began operations at Montreal in 1994, with the aim of offering flights from Montreal and Toronto to Fort Lauderdale, Paris, Nice and other destinations in Europe.

A Boeing 747-200 was leased from AIR FRANCE and arrived at Montreal on 24th May 1994. A few days later FORTUNAIR received its operating licence from the Canadian authorities, and the first charter flight to Paris took place on 30th June 1994. After only a few weeks, flights between Toronto and Europe were suspended and only departures from Montreal to Paris were continued.

On 19th August 1994 the company was grounded by order of a Quebec court, as the financial means to secure bank credits had not been forthcoming. A month later, the airline's licence was reinstated, as security had been put up by a tour operator. During the winter season flights were operated to destinations in Florida and the Caribbean, though continuing losses led on 23rd January 1995 to a temporary and voluntary surrender of the licence. The single Boeing 747-200 was returned to the lessor. Efforts to relaunch the company during the following months with a strengthened capital base were unsuccessful. Thus after only a short time, the life of another Canadian charter company was ended, its name having brought it little 'fortune'.

Lockheed L-188 Electra LN-FOH after landing at Amsterdam. After FRED OLSEN ceased flying operations in 1997 the Electra was sold to Austria. (Josef Krauthäuser)

FRED OLSEN   Norway

FRED OLSEN FLYSELSKAP A/S was set up in June 1946 as a subsidiary of the FRED OLSEN shipping line. In the beginning the airline specialised in freight work and flew contract charters for SAS on European routes. The first aircraft was a Royal Air Force surplus Douglas DC-3. Further contracts led to a need for more capacity and so the Curtiss C-46 Commando and the Douglas DC-6F came into service. However, not only freight work was lucrative, but also the charter and leasing of whole aircraft. Several Vickers Viscounts were leased long-term by FRED OLSEN to other companies such as AUSTRIAN AIRLINES. From 1973 the first of a fleet of Lockheed L-188 Electras were received. In time these became popular and replaced the DC-6s, as the turboprops were more economical and reliable. The Electras were also used to carry out group passenger charters, but the freight tasks still formed

the predominant part of the business. On behalf of the Norwegian government, survey and calibration flights were undertaken using a single HS.748, which was replaced in the mid-1990s with a de Havilland Canada DHC-8; these aircraft were not actually owned by Fred Olsen. From the early 1990s the Electras flew for DHL, UPS and other large freight companies from and to their european hubs and were used on services worldwide for these operators. However, in what was very much a surprising move, FRED OLSEN pulled out of the freight business in March 1997 and sold off the remaining Electras.

This Boeing 707-330C was delivered to LUFTHANSA on 11th March 1966 and moved on to GERMAN CARGO in May 1977 in this curry yellow colour scheme. TRANSBRASIL took over the aircraft in 1985, scrapping it after a landing accident in Manaus. (Manfred Winter)

GERMAN CARGO Germany

On 10th March 1977 a 100% owned subsidiary company of DEUTSCHE LUFTHANSA AG was registered as GERMAN CARGO SERVICES. With a single Boeing 707-330C, which was painted in an unusual and eyecatching curry yellow livery, flight operations were begun on 15th April 1977. By 1979 the Boeing 707 fleet grew to four examples. In 1984 the Boeing 707s were replaced with four Douglas DC-8-73s, re-worked with new, quieter engines. Though handling freight of all sorts and sizes, GERMAN CARGO gained particular experience in the handling of animals, and became a market leader in this sector. Regular charters were operated to Africa and to the Far East, though there was also capacity available for ad hoc charters. A further DC-8 was acquired in combi layout and was also used by CONDOR for passenger work. The colour scheme for the DC-8s was more conservative again and lost its individuality.

On 30th August 1990 the first of the Israeli-converted Boeing 747-200Fs arrived in Frankfurt, with further 747-200 Freighters following in November 1990 and at the beginning of 1991. In addition two Boeing 737-200s, converted from passenger aircraft to freight versions with side loading doors, were brought into service on European routes.

As a result of various re-organisations within the Lufthansa group, it was decided by management to integrate GERMAN CARGO into LUFTHANSA. It had a brief independent existence as LUFTHANSA CARGO , but the dissolution of GERMAN CARGO SERVICES followed inevitably on 1st May 1993.

MD-83 D-AGWA is seen here in GERMAN WINGS colours, about to leave Düsseldorf for another flight to the company's base airport at Munich-Riem. (Josef Krauthäuser)

GERMAN WINGS
Germany

The Kimmel brothers took a shareholding in 1983 in AIRFLIGHT, a small air taxi firm, and systematically built up the enterprise. By 1986 they had become the sole owners and the operating name fully changed over to GERMAN WINGS. Plans were in hand for bigger things and preparations were made for the entry into scheduled service operations. In February 1988 the appropriate permissions were received from the transport ministry, and on 10th April 1989 the new German airline started scheduled services. Initially four McDonnell Douglas MD-83s were used. These were fitted out with 114 (instead of the usual 172) seats and offered passengers an enhanced level of comfort. Furthermore, meals and drinks, not customarily available on other internal German services, and good on-board service were offered. These benefits and attractive fares, compared with the previous monopoly situation,

brought the company a lot of support from both fliers and non-fliers; German internal services needed the fresh momentum of a second operator.

Frankfurt, Cologne, Hamburg and Paris were served from Munich and further routes were requested. During the time before the airline began operations, and during the short existence of the second German scheduled airline, certain forces and competitors were working against the new company with all visible (and some less obvious) means. Thus there were legal arguments about interlining, (the acceptance by one airline of another's tickets) with the state monopoly, which went in favour of GERMAN WINGS. Also in the matter of slot allocations GERMAN WINGS was subjected to discrimination for not entirely comprehensible reasons. Since it was not Germany's will to have an open market and the monopoly holder was not inclined to give up its position willingly,

the experiment of customer-friendly service was doomed to early failure.

In an attempt to improve its position, GERMAN WINGS took on more MD-83s, which were used to increase frequencies; however the airline was losing its life-blood and its ability to repay bank loans which were to fall due on 30th April 1990. That also was noteworthy, in that powerful investors were behind GERMAN WINGS. Discussions with SAS, LUFTHANSA and BRITISH AIRWAYS with a view to them taking an interest were unsuccessful and thus on 30th April 1990 GERMAN WINGS became bankrupt. Thus for the lack of competition, German internal services again became grey and monotonous.

This Boeing 747-133 C-FTOA belonged to AIR CANADA and was only used by GLOBAL INTERNATIONAL AIRWAYS for the 1983 summer season. It is seen here at Frankfurt in a mixed colour scheme with GLOBAL titling. (Manfred Winter)

GLOBAL INTERNATIONAL USA

GIA – GLOBAL INTERNATIONAL AIRWAYS was founded in 1978 with its headquarters and base in Kansas City, Missouri; Boeing 707s were used for freight work. GIA applied for a passenger licence, but this was not granted until the beginning of 1981, after which further Boeing 707s were acquired for the new tasks. Europe was the destination for seasonal charter flights, with services to Amsterdam, Frankfurt, London and Paris. Charters to the Caribbean were offered using the Boeing 727 and ad hoc work was carried out for the US Army. Seasonal peaks in demand which occurred in 1983 were covered by the short lease of a Boeing 747. In the same year Farhad Azima took over as the owner of GIA, through Capitol Holdings, the owner of the financially afflicted CAPITOL AIR. Apparently he hoped to see some benefits from synergies between the two companies. Because of the differing fleets and capital

structures of the two airlines, this was however not possible and both companies had problems. In October 1983 GIA sought Chapter 11 bankruptcy protection and attempted a re-organisation. Net losses for 1983 alone came to more than US$ 5 million. The FAA withdrew the airline's licence

in December 1983, but this was reinstated early in 1994. CAPITOL AIR went into bankruptcy in November 1984, and this had consequences for GIA. There was no interest to be found for a sale of shares or an outright sale of the company, so that GIA also became bankrupt in 1985.

The Boeing 707 was the mainstay of the GLOBAL INTERNATIONAL AIRWAYS fleet. (Josef Krauthäuser collection)

Tupolev Tu-154 TC-GRA seen leaving Düsseldorf for another flight to Izmir. (Patrick Lutz)

GREEN AIR/ACTIVE AIR   Turkey

From 1980 Turkey has enjoyed an increasing popularity with tourists and that this boom has led to numerous set-ups of new airline companies is self-evident. GREENAIR, founded at the beginning of 1990, is just such an airline. AEROFLOT and TURKISH AIRLINES, with the support of other investors including business people from the former USSR, set up a co-operative venture, operating Soviet-built Tupolev Tu-154s principally from airports in Germany to destinations in Turkey. Paris, London, Milan and Amsterdam were however also served, carrying expatriate workers and holidaymakers to Turkey. Plans were in hand for the inauguration of scheduled services, using Tupolev Tu-134As from Istanbul to Moscow, but were at first not realised, though several Turkish internal destinations were served on a scheduled basis.

In December 1994 GREEN AIR ceased operations, but was reactivated in the Spring of 1995 as ACTIVE AIR. Again, the aircraft which came from the Soviet Union, were not popular amongst Western tourists. Especially after the collapse of BIRGENAIR, reservations about Turkish airlines increased and reached the proportions of hysteria, so that several tour operators suspended flights with Turkish companies. ACTIVE AIR was caught up in this whirlpool and had to give up flying at the end of 1996.

ACTIVE AIR Tu-154M TC-ACV leased from Russia's VNUKOVO AIRLINES with their colour scheme and logo on the tailfin. (Patrick Lutz)

Boeing 727-200 OB1301 belonged to Peruvian airline FAUCETT and from March 1989 to September 1994 was leased by HAITI TRANSAIR. Here it is leaving Miami for Port-au-Prince, wearing the basic colours of AIR MALTA, to whom it was originally intended to have been leased . (Josef Krauthäuser)

HAITI TRANSAIR   Haiti

Following many previous efforts in Haiti to establish an airline, mostly without success, a new attempt was made at the beginning of 1987.

Using a leased Boeing 727, HAITI TRANSAIR began scheduled and charter flights in the Caribbean and to the United States. Here Miami was the most important destination, with over 70% of all passenger and freight traffic concentrated at this city. A further Boeing 727 was received during 1988; this was configured as a combi version and so freight could be carried along with the passengers. From its home base at Port-au-Prince the airline served further important destinations such as San Juan or Kingston regularly and despite a problematic political situation, the company developed steadily. In 1992 a DC-8-61 was taken on and this allowed frequencies to be increased and further services to regional destinations to be added. The company was in a

position to offer multiple daily services to San Juan and Miami. However, the worsening political situation in Haiti caused tourists to stay away and one of the main sources of foreign exchange for the country was cut off. This had consequences for HAITI TRANSAIR, which at first reduced services and took a Boeing 727 out of service on cost grounds. In March 1995 the airline had to cease operations and the company went into bankruptcy.

de Havilland DHC-8 D-BOBY was bought from Rheintalflug and leased to HAMBURG AIRLINES. (Josef Krauthäuser collection)

HAMBURG AIRLINES   Germany

On 15th April 1988 Hamburg businessman Eugen Block founded this company. Operations began on 9th June using a Dornier Do 228 for flights from Hamburg to Rotterdam and Westerland. Following the delivery of another Do 228 in July 1988, Antwerp and Gothenburg were added as destinations. The advent of the de Havilland DHC-8, the first of which was delivered to Hamburg in October 1988, made possible a further expansion and following the opening of the Berlin Wall, flights to East Germany became a strong point of the airline. The leasing in of a Fokker 100 also opened the way for charter business with tourist flights to Ibiza, Palma de Mallorca, Alicante and Malaga. After German reunification several routes were taken over from TEMPELHOF AIRWAYS and a second base built up at Berlin-Tempelhof. From 1990 London-Gatwick showed in the schedule, and destinations such as

Kaliningrad and Riga also appeared. The undercapitalised and loss-making HAMBURG AIRLINES was sold on 5th January 1993 to SAARLAND AIRLINES, a charter company, which had been set up in 1991. The two companies operated independently, but when SAARLAND AIRLINES went into bankruptcy at the end of 1993 HAMBURG AIRLINES was naturally affected.

It was Eugen Block again who on 1st December 1993 set up the new HAMBURG AIRLINES LUFTFAHRTGESELLSCHAFT and using the old name, but with a completely new company, carried on the flying activities. In stark competition with LUFTHANSA CITYLINE, new and old destinations were served and with the BAe 146 a new aircraft type was introduced. This was used on both scheduled and charter services, including to Vilnius and Riga. Co-operation was established with AIR UK,

CROSSAIR and LTU and the company expanded its route network to include points in southern Europe. Operational disagreements led again to a change in management, but the yearly targets were not met and the company flew into losses again. Discussions about a possible sale with AUGSBURG AIRWAYS and LUFTHANSA faltered in Autumn 1997, whereupon Eugen Block decided to cease flying and to close down the airline. 21st December 1997 saw the last flight of HAMBURG AIRLINES, and the liquidation of the company followed.

First delivered to MAERSK, this Boeing 737-200 was taken on in 1985 from leasing company GPA and as EC-DXV flew with HISPANIA from November 1985 until November 1988. (Josef Krauthäuser)

HISPANIA   Spain

HISPANIA LINEAS AEREAS was set up in November 1982. About 80 former employees of the Spanish airline TAE-TRABAJOS AEREOS Y ENLACES, which had gone into bankruptcy, with the support of several banks and using their own capital, were able to bring together enough funds to bring the new carrier into existence. From the legacy of the no longer active airline TRANSEUROPA two SE 210 Caravelles were taken on, and flying commenced for the 1993 summer season.

As well as charter flights from Great Britain, Germany, France and other countries to Spain, internal Spanish charter flights were also carried out. Two more Caravelles were added in 1984 and in 1985 three Boeing 737-200s were additionally at the airline's disposal. For the 1987 summer season HISPANIA had an exclusively Boeing 737 fleet, as the Caravelles had been withdrawn from service and sold because of their high operating costs. During the 1987 season profits were made for the first time, and these were invested in new aircraft. With the delivery of the first Boeing 757 in Spring 1989, with a second following before the start of the summer season, HISPANIA had available so much capacity that for the first time over a million passengers were expected in the year. However, bankruptcy occurred in the middle of the season, quite unexpectedly to the travel trade. Flying ceased in July 1989. The background to this was a chaotic financial situation with liabilities accumulating to an extent that the banks judged themselves to be insufficiently secured.

Two modern Airbus A320s served only briefly with HOLIDAY. Here TC-GAA leaves Munich for Antalya. (Andrè Dietzel)

HOLIDAY AIRLINES   Turkey

Another of the numerous airlines that kept being set up in Turkey to service the tourist industry was HOLIDAY AIRLINES. It began services for the 1994 summer season using leased Airbus A320s. By the beginning of July, however, it was in trouble; the two A320s were grounded, because there were bureaucratic hurdles to be overcome. By the middle of July 1994 the necessary formalities were completed and HOLIDAY AIRLINES concentrated its activities particularly on the German tourist market. Seasonal use was made of Airbus A300s but these were only leased in on a short-term basis.

HOLIDAY AIRLINES temporarily halted services at the end of November 1994, after the leasing company repossessed the two A320s because of outstanding debts. However, by 1995 the airline was ready for the summer season's work with two Airbus A300B4s and from April began

services from numerous European airports to Turkey. Yakovlev Yak 42s, Tupolev Tu-154s and Boeing 727s were also to be found in the fleet, a situation which was also to be connected with the disastrous failure of the company. Following the BIRGENAIR crash in the Caribbean, the German media sweepingly characterised all Russian aircraft as fundamentally unsafe. Even though a TriStar and another Airbus A300B4 were rented in for the summer, on 10th September 1996 a refusal of permission to fly into Germany marked the end for HOLIDAY AIRLINES.

A newly formed 'Task Force' of the German aviation authority (often accompanied by cameras from private television stations) naturally and quickly found on several of the aircraft of HOLIDAY AIRLINES grounds for complaint and this led to a prohibition of flights into German airports.

The author notes however, that

the aircraft were able to fly out, and then to fly on with other airlines. With a high court decision in November 1996 the final end came for HOLIDAY AIRLINES, since its right to fly into Germany was irrevocably withdrawn and with the loss of its major market there was no prospect of it being viable.

The 'yellow bananas' of HUGHES AIR WEST were a regular sight in the airspace between Mexico and Canada. Here DC-9-31 N9343 is seen on approach to Las Vegas. (Manfred Winter)

HUGHES AIR WEST USA

On 31st March 1970 Hughes Air Corporation took over AIR WEST, which had been created in 1968 by the merger of BONANZA AIRLINES, PACIFIC AIRLINES and WEST COAST AIRLINES. This had been preceded by a soap-opera like takeover battle for the shares in this company. An initial offer to AIR WEST to purchase the company for US$90 million had been proposed by the Hughes Tool Company in 1968. The owner of the Hughes Tool Company was Howard R Hughes, who had a colourful life as film producer, aircraft manufacturer, pilot and financial juggler behind him. For many years he had been at the helm of TWA and had been responsible for the conception and building of the Lockheed Constellation and the 'Spruce Goose'. In 1968 Hughes sold his interest in TWA, but obviously had a penchant for a further involvement in the airline business and sought out AIR WEST as a target. Takeover offers

followed, put by Hughes himself to the directors of AIR WEST and their attorneys; apparently there were threats of a hostile takeover, and other financial acrobatics. It was quickly decided to form a new company, Hughes Air Corporation, which would take over AIR WEST without giving a majority of the shares directly to Hughes personally. He nominally owned only 22% of the shares, though he controlled 100% of the shares in Hughes Air Corporation. Following the takeover battle, the company changed its name in July 1970 to HUGHES AIR WEST, with a new management and a modern and striking corporate image, called 'Sundance'. Over 50 cities from Mexico to Canada appeared in the timetable and the fleet consisted over over 70 aircraft. Boeing 727s, Fairchild FH-227s and Douglas DC-9s came into service.

Howard Hughes died in 1975, but the ongoing legal process over the takeover of the WEST

AIR shares only came to an end in 1979, when the Summa Corporation as successor to the Hughes Tool Company, paid over another $39 million to the former shareholders. There was little argument when on 1st October 1980 REPUBLIC AIRLINES bought the whole of HUGHES AIR WEST and integrated it from 1981. It was a good commercial fit for REPUBLIC, which itself was later to be absorbed by its Minneapolis-based neighbour NORTHWEST.

An INDEPENDENT AIR Boeing 707 taking off from Frankfurt on a military charter flight. (Josef Krauthäuser)

INDEPENDENT AIR   USA

The ATLANTA SKYLARKS TRAVEL CLUB was founded in 1966 and used the Boeing 707-320 for its own club flights. From July 1966 these flights were managed and undertaken by INDEPENDENT AIR.

In 1984 an unrestricted licence for worldwide charter flights was granted, and the club was thus in a position to offer travel to non-members. This contributed to a better utilisation of the aircraft. A Boeing 727, which it was envisaged would be used for flights in the Caribbean area, was received in 1969. In association with Club International a tour operating company was set up for business in this region. INDEPENDENT AIR was also quite strongly engaged in military charter work on behalf of the US forces.

On 8th February 1989, following several attempts and broken-off approaches, one of the company's Boeing 707s crashed on the island of Santa Maria in the Azores, killing 144 people; this accident had an adverse influence on the future development of the company. The inauguration of a scheduled service from New York to Puerto Rico planned for 1990 was not realised, as following the accident, contracts with tour operators were ended and losses began to mount. This situation led to the suspension of flying in November 1990, and to the inevitable declaration of bankruptcy.

ATLANTA SKYLARKS Travel Club Boeing 707 N7229L which was used by INDEPENDENT AIR. (Josef Krauthäuser collection)

One of the three Airbus A310s used on INTERFLUG's route network from 1989. Seen here parked up at its home base of Berlin-Schönefeld after reunification, and already with its new registration of D-AOAA, this aircraft went on to serve with the Luftwaffe. (Lutz Schönfeld)

INTERFLUG

GDR Germany

When Germany became divided into two separate states after the Second World War, air transport also became a political matter. In 1955 DEUTSCHE LUFTHANSA Ost was set up in Berlin, and began services in September with the Ilyushin IL-14. On 10th September 1960 INTERFLUG GmbH was founded in Berlin, as DEUTSCHE LUFTHANSA Ost could not fly to various countries for political reasons. From 1st September 1963 DEUTSCHE LUFTHANSA Ost and INTERFLUG were merged, and the latter was to be the sole provider of air transport for the German Democratic Republic. Alongside the IL-14s, Ilyushin IL-18s, Antonov An-2s and An-24s were brought into use for domestic flights and for services to other Warsaw Pact member states.

With the introduction of the Tupolev Tu-134 from Autumn 1968 INTERFLUG received its first jet for middle-range routes, and

the IL-14s were disposed of. In April 1970 the first Ilyushin IL-62 came into service, for long-range flights; these were used to Havana, Hanoi and Maputo. Several routes were not commercially justifiable or sustainable judged by the traffic carried, but were served for political considerations.

As a state company INTERFLUG was organised in a similar way to the Soviet AEROFLOT model. Its responsibilities alongside the provision of passenger services included the operation of the airports and the provision of ground services. In addition there were agricultural flying duties and survey work. The co-ordination of helicopter activities and flight safety oversight were also entrusted to INTERFLUG.

When it placed an order for three Airbus A310s INTERFLUG became the first of the Warsaw Pact countries to embrace modern Western aircraft

technology. From 1989 these aircraft were used on services to Singapore, Beijing and Havana. 1989 was also the year in which the Berlin Wall fell, with the consequent radical changes in political and business circumstances. After the reunification of the two Germanys INTERFLUG became no more than a millstone on the established West German air transport scene.

Thus it came under the protection of the state trust institution and was 'wound down'. Merger discussions with several (apparently) interested parties came to nothing and there was no continuing political will to keep INTERFLUG in existence. In spite of all efforts on the side of the company's management and staff, it was found to be lacking on financial and national-interest grounds. On 30th April 1991 INTERFLUG finally ceased operations and the airline went into liquidation.

This Bristol Britannia 312 G-AOVF was only leased for a few months, but was fully painted in INVICTA colours. (Josef Krauthäuser collection)

INVICTA INTERNATIONAL AIRLINES Great Britain

In November 1964 INVICTA AIRWAYS was founded at Manston in Kent. Using two Vickers Vikings and two Douglas DC-4s, charter flights on behalf of tour operators were begun from March 1965. After the end of this first season, the fleet was enlarged with five further aircraft and charter services extended to serve other British airports. In 1966 INVICTA gained rights to serve the route from Manston to Ostend in Belgium. As well as passenger charters, freight charters were also flown. At the end of 1968 the last of the Vickers Vikings were retired and INVICTA AIRWAYS was merged with BRITISH MIDLAND.

However, the company's founder bought back some of the DC-4s in 1969 and set up INVICTA AIRWAYS 1969 Ltd, though in June of that year it was renamed INVICTA AIR CARGO. Using the DC-4s, freight contract work within Europe and to Africa and the Middle East was undertaken. Regular flights between Birmingham and Düsseldorf or Cologne/Bonn were operated to deliver components for car manufacturers. In 1970 the first Vickers Vanguard joined the fleet and replaced one of the older DC-4s. During 1971 two more Vanguards were added, but in passenger configuration. These were used extensively from London-Luton to Düsseldorf for military charter and student flights, using the name INVICTA INTERNATIONAL AIRLINES. Further destinations, though only during the winter, were Basle, Munich and Salzburg, which were served regularly for winter sports holidaymakers. At the beginning of January 1973 the whole of the Vanguard fleet was grounded on the orders of the leasing company which owned them, as there were obviously some difficulties in making the lease payments. The shipping company European Ferries took a 70% holding in the capital of INVICTA and leased the Vanguards back.

Flight operations were recommenced at the end of February, but were overshadowed by the crash in April 1973 of one of the Vanguards near Basle. Two Boeing 720Bs were acquired from the end of 1973, but only one of the pair saw service with INVICTA from the end of 1974, while the other flew for SOMALI AIRLINES. INVICTA took over more and more contracts for other airlines and in this year leased in two Bristol Britannia 312s, but then the whole concern was sold at the end of 1975 by European Ferries to UNIVERSAL AIR TRANSPORT SALES.

Douglas DC-9-15 I-TIGI was purchased by ITAVIA in 1972 from HAWAIIAN AIRLINES and crashed on 27th June 1980 into the sea west of Naples. (Josef Krauthäuser collection)

ITAVIA   Italy

Founded in April 1958 as Societa di Navigazione Aerea ITAVIA, services were begun from July 1959 using de Havilland Doves and Herons to several destinations within Italy.

However in 1961 all flights were cancelled and operations were suspended until May 1962. At the resumption, the ageing Herons were traded in or used as part-payment for Handley Page Dart Heralds. This second period of activity was to last for a shorter time than the first, as operations were again ceased in January 1965 as a result of financial problems. Obviously ITAVIA overcame these difficulties by August of 1965, as it was able to start up again after a refinancing. From 1969 the first of the Fokker F.28s were introduced, and these were supplemented from 1971 with Douglas DC-9s. The departure points for most of the regional scheduled services were Rome and Milan, but the airline also undertook charter business

successfully and had seasonal routes throughout Europe. On 27th June 1980 there was a spectacular crash of one of the airline's DC-9s which for unknown reasons fell from a cruising altitude of about 27,000 feet into the sea off Naples. This affected the reputation of the airline so much that it ran into financial difficulties, and several aircraft were grounded by the authorities on safety grounds. Several years later it became known that the probable cause of the accident was a mistake on the part of the military. A misdirected missile hit the aircraft during an exercise and caused it to crash. This fact was covered up and denied over many years after the accident.

This later knowledge did not help the company, since by 10th December 1980 ITAVIA was finally forced to give up all services and seek bankruptcy.

This Boeing 727-100 N837N was rented from SOUTHAIR American Aircraft Leasing from April 1984 until JETAIR's bankruptcy. (Josef Krauthäuser)

JETAIR   Germany

Set up in Munich in 1982 by two former BAVARIA GERMANAIR pilots, JETAIR at first developed without owning its own aircraft, but great plans were hatched for the routes and goals of the company. In order to do this the provision of capital was needed, which was raised by the issue of bonds and shares. However, the capital thus raised was not sufficient to acquire the originally envisaged new Boeing 737-200 and the airline had to turn to the used aircraft market. Thus operations began in May 1984 using a Boeing 727 which had been acquired from AIR PANAMA, but flights were sporadic and restricted to one-off charters only. For the current season there were no more contracts to be had from tour operators, who had made their block bookings well in advance. To see the airline through the lean period until the next summer season, only one, instead of two, Boeing 727s was leased. In the 1985 summer season, which was destined to be the last for JETAIR, the aircraft were well booked, but at prices which did not accord with the profitable running of the airline. As a newcomer, the demands of the tour operators had to be accepted, or no contracts would be won. The high expenses set against poor receipts, and in the light of the meagre capitalisation, were simply too much and the banks were unwilling to extend credit. In December 1985 it was decided to liquidate the airline and it went into bankruptcy. Several years later there was a legal postscript, whereby the founders of JETAIR received prison sentences, as the state solicitors took action to show that the bankruptcy had been fraudulent, to the detriment of the shareholders.

This Boeing 707-329C was built for SABENA in 1968 and at first leased by JET CHARTER SERVICE in 1982, but was purchased in the same year and re-registered in the USA as N3238N. (Josef Krauthäuser collection)

JET 24 USA

JET CHARTER SERVICE was established in August 1979 in Miami and began charter services from December 1981 under the name JET 24. The initial freight-only flights were from Miami to Caracas and used the Boeing 707. Two more Boeing 707s were bought, of which one was a combi version and so could be used on either passenger or freight work. The latter was leased out from time to time, as the airline had no licence for passenger traffic.

After JET 24 did obtain a passenger licence in 1983, two Douglas DC-10-40s entered the fleet in the same year to supplant the ageing 707s and to operate flights to South America and to Europe. Alongside its own charter work on behalf of various tour operators, the airline also flew sub-charters for other operators. JET 24 established its own scheduled service in May 1985 from Miami via San Juan to Madrid; further destinations in

Europe were Paris and Zurich. Further expansion was planned during this year and an option was obtained for two used DC-10s. In South America, Bogota in Colombia was served on a scheduled basis with departures from Miami. In August 1985 JET 24 was obliged to seek Chapter 11 bankruptcy protection, as the scheduled services had not performed as well as had been hoped. The airline rapidly reached a state of financial distress, as there was not sufficient funding available to allow the routes to become established. As the situation was fundamentally not improving and more credit was clearly not going to become available, the company had no alternative but to declare bankruptcy in October 1985. Flight operations ceased from this time, and even an attempted restart, this time with Boeing 747 equipment, fell through at the beginning of 1986.

DC-8-51 OH-KDM was in service with KARAIR from 1972 to the end of 1984. This colour scheme and titling was current in the mid 1970s. (Manfred Winter collection)

KARAIR OY

Finland

The three Karhumäki brothers made their living by running an aircraft workshop in Keljo, Finland. They were noteworthy in that they developed their own aircraft and undertook modest licence production. In 1933 the company Avion Yhtiö Veljekset Karhumäki was registered. As well as under-taking contracts for the Finnish Air Force, a small flying service was operated. After the Second World War, scheduled services were begun for the first time; these emanated from Helsinki to Joensum and were operated with a de Havilland DH.89 Dragon Rapide. In 1952 these were turned over to a Lockheed Lodestar, and in 1954 several Douglas DC-3s were taken over from SAS and the company's base moved to Helsinki. The change of name to KAR-AIR OY followed late in 1956. Convair 440s and Douglas DC-6s were to be the last piston-engined types for KARAIR, before it got into business difficulties in 1962. It

was rescued by FINNAIR which took a 51% shareholding.

After the DC-6, the DC-8 followed in 1972. These were used especially on charter work and from 1987 replaced by two Airbus A300B4s. In 1988 FINNAIR bought the remaining shares. KARAIR remained operationally

independent and built up a substantial regional network on FINNAIR's behalf. In 1990 ATR 42s were introduced.

At the end of 1993 FINNAIR decided on a full merger of KARAIR into FINNAIR and from 1994 the integration was gradually undertaken.

Airbus A300B4 OH-LAB on approach to Palma de Mallorca, wearing the final version of the KARAIR colour scheme. (Manfred Winter)

Boeing 727-100 N28KA was taken on in 1965 by UNITED AIR LINES as the 119th aircraft of the series and came via ALLEGHENY AIRLINES in 983 to KEY AIRLINES. (Josef Krauthäuser collection)

KEY AIR USA

The story of KEY AIR began in the early 1970s when SUN VALLEY AIR and KEY AIRLINES brought together their respective regional services from Salt Lake City as KEY AIRLINES. In 1972 TIGER AIR became the new owner and built up the airline and its route network with Convair 440s. Yet another sale in 1983 saw a further change in circumstances and the arrival at the new Las Vegas base of the airline, of the first Boeing 727, in a new colour scheme and with KEY AIR titling. Charter activities were also expanded and the programme included flights to Miami, the Caribbean and to Mexico. The advent of deregulation in the United Sates led to a rash of airline sales and purchases. KEY AIR was disposed of to PRESIDENTIAL AIRWAYS in 1986, but business was carried on independently of the new owners. After only a year there was a further sale, this time to WORLD AIRWAYS, but the independence of operation was

again maintained. However KEY AIR did take over various charter contracts and several Douglas DC-10s from WORLD AIRWAYS. Flights were conducted to Europe and Asia and a new hub in Savannah, Georgia was established in an attempt to set up more new routes. This all expended a lot of money, but in the early stages brought in little return and so in 1992 KEY AIR was once again sold. The financial base had in the meantime been so depleted that KEY AIR sought a partner. After the failure to consummate a planned merger KEY AIR went into bankruptcy protection under Chapter 11 in February 1993. With a reduced fleet, several of the ten older Boeing 727s being sold, a new start was attempted. Though two new leased MD-80s were added, a final cessation of operations came on 10th May 1993. The accumulated debts were so high and the chance of future success and thus

emergence from Chapter 11 so small that bankruptcy was the only logical consequence.

BAC 1-11 G-AVYZ belonged to the Laker fleet from the beginning of April 1968 and was used to European destinations, such as here at Munich-Riem. (Josef Krauthäuser collection)

LAKER AIRWAYS

Great Britain

Frederick Alfred (Freddie) Laker founded the airline which bore his name in February 1966. He had already been actively engaged in the Berlin Airlift in 1948 and had for several years been in charge at BUA. LAKER AIRWAYS received its first Bristol Britannia at the beginning of March 1966 and commenced operations from London-Gatwick on 29th July 1966. Ad hoc charters and flights on behalf of other airlines were undertaken. Two BAC 1-11s were received early in 1967, of which one was leased out to AIR CONGO. Laker's ideas brought new innovations to the traditional British travel industry. Charter flights at fixed times and at seasonally adjusted prices brought Winter utilisation for the aircraft. In association with hotel chains in Spain, attractive inclusive package prices were offered. LAKER AIRWAYS also benefited from the failure of TREFFIELD INTERNATIONAL, in that it was able to take over

several contracts. This entailed departures from Castle Donington during the summer season. LAKER also took over a Liverpool-based tour operator and thus enlarged its radius of operations. In 1969 the Bristol Britannias were exchanged for two Boeing 707s, thus turning LAKER over to be a jet-only operator. During 1969 the company received rights for charters to the USA, and was active from Berlin on behalf of a German tour operator. In 1970 charter flights to the USA were commenced and Laker reorganised his previously numerous companies under the umbrella of Laker Airways International Holdings. In addition to LAKER AIRWAYS this had a 49% shareholding in another airline, INTERNATIONAL CARIBBEAN AIRWAYS, and numerous shareholdings in travel operators in England and Spain as well as hotel companies. The Barbados-Luxembourg route was served weekly by LAKER

AIRWAYS Boeing 707, and Barbados-Gatwick was begun in 1971. Here LAKER AIRWAYS gained its first successful experiences as a low-price operator, so that four flights a week were to follow from Gatwick. A first application to run such cheap flights between London and New York was turned down, but the authorities obviously underestimated Freddie Laker. He turned to the courts and pursued his aims unendingly against the British government, who wanted to protect their own national airline from competition and eventually received his permission, though this was helped by the new deregulation politics of the newly installed Carter administration in the USA. During 1972 LAKER AIRWAYS received its first DC-10. This type was used at first to destinations in the Mediterranean area, but also for ABC-charters to the USA and Canada. For the airlines in the closed IATA cartel, the

Douglas DC-10-10 G-AZZD carried the 'Skytrain' logo before the official launch of the service, while it was being used for European charter work. It was also used for pilgrim flights to Jeddah. LAKER had a total of eleven DC-10s in the fleet. (Manfred Winter)

inauguration of Laker's 'Skytrain' cheap flight service on 27th September 1977 came as a shock, showing the whole pricing policy of the cartel to be absurd. For these flights, just like on the trains, a longstanding booking was not necessary; passengers just turned up, bought their tickets at the airport and boarded the aircraft. Simple, easy and cheap was the motto. The ticket price was markedly cheaper than the cheapest IATA ticket, though no greater comfort was offered and in flight meals were not included. A model for LAKER AIRWAYS was the 'Ponta del Gada' shuttle operation between Rio de Janeiro and Sao Paulo in Brazil, which had been run successfully on similar principles since 1959. After a year the 'Skytrain' service was extended to a new route to Los Angeles and more DC-10s and Airbus A300s were ordered. The Airbus A300s were intended for a european 'Skytrain' service, and there were

further thoughts about future 'Skytrain' connections to Hong Kong and Australia, when LAKER AIRWAYS began to feel the effects of economic recession. The immense acquisition costs for the new aircraft were financed by bank borrowings expressed in US dollars, against which the British pound at this time was substantially weakened. When LAKER AIRWAYS ceased flying on 5th February 1982, not only did thousands of passengers who had paid for their tickets lose their money, and thousands more were left stranded at their holiday destinations, but over the course of time an unfathomable swamp of corruption and conspiracy, never before seen in the airline industry, became apparent. Established european customers of McDonnell Douglas had threatened to order no more aircraft, should MDD give support to LAKER AIRWAYS, and the engine manufacturer General Electric received similar threats.

Anti-trust processes were begun in the USA against airlines, who were themselves in danger of collapse, but who had come together to try to bring about the downfall of Laker's 'Skytrain'. It was a long drawn out affair, lasting until 1985 when the final end of the 'Laker affair' was reached with compensation being paid by the guilty parties. It is to Sir Freddie's credit that a high-handed, self-serving and consumer-unfriendly cartel was broken. However some of the unorthodox methods which he used to achieve his goal were not always those of a gentleman and his aversion to trades unions did not win friends for him in some quarters. It is clear though, that the whole airline business was greatly influenced by his activities and many other airlines later successfully took up elements of his 'Skytrain' ideas, including SOUTHWEST AIRLINES, VIRGIN ATLANTIC and others.

LA TUR used this McDonnell Douglas MD-83 XA-TUR principally on routes to the USA, but it was in use for only a very short time before passing on to Aviaco in Spain. (Josef Krauthäuser collection)

LA TUR   Mexico

LA TUR was set up in 1988 by a hotel chain and the Mexican pilots union. The background to this was that efforts to develop the Mexican tourist market which, particularly in the United States, had been declining. Using three McDonnell Douglas MD-83s, operations were begun in Autumn 1988 and developed satisfactorily during the first season. The first Airbus A300-600 was introduced in August 1989, with a second following in December and these were used on routes to Europe. In an effort to achieve a homogeneous fleet, four Airbus A320s and two Airbus A321s were ordered as replacements for the McDonnell Douglas MD-83s. A shortage of bookings however led to overcapacity and an A300-600 was thus leased out.

The deepening business crisis, the rapid fall in the worth of the Mexican currency against the dollar in which the leasing costs had to be paid, and the full deregulation of Mexican air transport, led to the failure and bankruptcy of LA TUR on 18th December 1991. Numerous new airlines had been established in Mexico following deregulation and this resulted in bitter competition. At the beginning of 1992 the remaining LA TUR staff and routes were taken over by another Mexican airline TAESA. It also took on the Airbus A300-600 and the MD-83 and integrated these into their own fleet. The already agreed charter series to Europe were also taken over by TAESA and flown with the Airbus A300 or other aircraft.

LEISURE AIR used leased Airbus A320s on behalf of numerous tour operators. Here N315RX is ready to roll from Fort Lauderdale. (Josef Krauthäuser)

LEISURE AIR   USA

World Wide Aviation Services set up in1992 its own airline company, LEISURE AIR with its headquarters in Washington, DC. Its home base however was Winston-Salem. Using five leased Airbus A320s, two DC-10-30s and later Boeing 757s as well, holidaymakers were flown from the colder parts of the northern United States to California, Nevada, Arizona, Mexico and the Caribbean. LEISURE AIR also flew exclusively for one tour operator from Los Angeles and San Francisco to Hawaii. As the Airbus A320 was not suited to this route, the company acquired two second hand DC-10s. From 1994 these were also used for the first time to service European destinations, with a weekly route from San Francisco to London-Stansted. In a move designed to capitalise on their differing busy seasons, LEISURE AIR and TRANSLIFT of Ireland reached an agreement for the temporary exchange of A320s for the winter and summer months.

The American aviation safety authority, the FAA, discovered massive shortcomings in the maintenance records of the DC-10s and withdrew the operating licence for these and for the Boeing 757s. With the fleet reduced to only three A320s, it was possible for operations to be continued, but only until 4th February 1995, when Chapter 11 bankruptcy protection was sought and operations ceased.

LEISURE INTERNATIONAL AIRWAYS Airbus A320 G-UKLL brings skiers from Gatwick to Innsbruck, Austria, which was regularly served during the winter sports seasons. (Uwe Gleisberg)

LEISURE INTERNATIONAL AIRWAYS Great Britain

In April 1988 AIR UK set up an independent subsidiary company called UK LEISURE. From the outset it operated independently and began its first summer season with three leased Boeing 737-400s from its home base at London-Luton. During the winter the aircraft were leased out, as there was otherwise little work available for them. Over time the fleet grew to seven aircraft, used to the traditional destinations on behalf of larger tour operators. In1996 the company was sold to tour operator Unijet.

LEISURE INTERNATIONAL AIRWAYS began as a sister company of AIR UK LEISURE in April 1993, operating from London-Gatwick with two Boeing 767s on longer range routes to the Caribbean and the USA. In 1997 LEISURE received three Airbus A320s, before the operations of the two companies were sensibly merged in 1997 under the LEISURE name and the base established at Luton in preference

to Gatwick. The first Airbus A321 was delivered in time for the start of the 1998 summer season.

In Autumn 1998 Unijet was sold out to its competitor First Choice, which already had its own inhouse airline AIR 2000. The types in the fleets were already matched, and the airlines merged under the name of AIR 2000.

AIR UK LEISURE Boeing 737-400 G-UKLC at Hamburg preparing to take off for London-Luton. This aircraft was delivered new by Boeing to UK LEISURE in June 1990 and sold in 1996 to KLM. (Patrick Lutz)

Boeing 707-300B ZP-CCG joined LAP from PAN AMERICAN WORLD AIRWAY in 1980 and stayed with the airline until it was taken out of service in 1988. (Josef Krauthäuser collection)

LINEAS AEREAS PARAGUAYAS – LAP Paraguay

Set up in 1962 as a national airline and as a practical development of TRANSPORTES AEREO MILITAR, the domestic service organised by the Paraguayan Air Force, LAP began services in August 1963. Using three Convair 240s bought from AEROLINEAS ARGENTINAS, services were flown initially to Rio de Janeiro, Buenos Aires, Montevideo, Santa Cruz and Curitiba. A co-operation was set up with CRUZEIRO DO SUL. To replace the Convair 240s three Lockheed L-188 Electras were acquired from EASTERN AIR LINES. These were to remain in service with LAP for over twenty years, and in 1975 established a route over the Andes to Lima in Peru. From PAN AMERICAN in 1978 came two Boeing 707s, which were used on the Lima service and further, to Miami. A third Boeing 707 was added and this allowed the commencement of services to Europe from 2nd November 1979 to Madrid,

Brussels and Frankfurt. The 707s were replaced in 1984 and 1988 by twoDouglas DC-8 series 60s. The first and only widebody, a DC-10-30, for European services came into the fleet in 1992.

The intention to privatise LAP, by a new government which wanted to put the deeply indebted country into a more sound financial shape after nearly 40 years of dictatorship, failed, as investors were not forthcoming, because the prospects of a lucrative outcome from airline operation in Paraguay were not good and furthermore LAP was heavily in debt. No further government money was to be made available, and so at the beginning of 1994 operations were ceased on financial grounds.

Fokker F.28 Fellowship SE-DGO was received by LINJEFLYG on 28th November1982. It is seen here at Salzburg Airport being prepared for its return flight to Gothenburg. It remained in the fleet after the SAS takeover, received SAS colours and the name 'Odd Viking'. (Gottfried Auer)

LINJEFLYG   Sweden

LINJEFLYG was founded in April 1957 by AEROTRANSPORT AB and SAS in order to take over the services of AIRTACO, an airline which flew regional services as well as postal and newspaper flights. LINJEFLYG used Douglas DC-3s at first; these were replaced from 1960 by the larger Convair 440. In 1973 LINJEFLYG received its first Fokker F.28, a type which built up to a fleet of more than twenty aircraft by 1989, in which year a fleet renewal was begun with the delivery of the first of the replacement Boeing 737-500s. LINJEFLYG had a dense domestic network in Sweden and also served neighbouring Scandinavian countries. In addition, charter services were operated to many European points, both in summer and winter.

A re-organisation of the whole SAS-Group saw the end of independence for LINJEFLYG. In March 1993 SAS took over the company and integrated it into its own operations.

LINJEFLYG took over Boeing 737-500 SE-DNA from GPA in April 1990. Following the takeover it flew with SAS until 1994. (Josef Krauthäuser collection)

This Douglas DC-8-63 was leased from SEABORD WORLD AIRLINES for each summer season from 1970 to 1977 by LOFTLEIDIR. After rebuild as a series -73C the aircraft was used by CONDOR and GERMAN CARGO as D-ADUC. (Christofer Witt collection)

LOFTLEIDIR   Iceland

In 1944, while war was raging in Europe, LOFTLEIDIR was set up by three Icelandic pilots on 10th March. As early as 7th April, casual work was being undertaken with a Stinson Reliant. This brought the beauty of Iceland closer to the American military personnel who were in the country. A regional route network was built up and a Douglas DC-3 was used for services to destinations with prepared runways, while some western coastal points were served using flying boats. In 1946 LOFT-LEIDIR received its first DC-4 for flights to Glasgow and on to Copenhagen. A year later, London was being served regularly. DC-4s were likewise used from Copen-hagen via Reykjavik and Gander to New York; this service was opened on 25th August 1948 after agreement had been given by the US, but. it was suspended after only two years as the operating costs for such a route were simply too high. However LOFTLEIDIR was dependent on the New York

route and from 1952 tried again under unusual circumstances. The airline marketed itself as a cheap price alternative, with tickets costing much less than those of the airlines in the IATA cartel. Travellers had to take into account the longer flights in the DC-4s, compared with the IATA companies who had already invested in faster Douglas DC-6 and DC-7s and Lockheed Constellations; thus LOFTLEIDIR opened up the Scandinavian market to a less well-off public. LOFTLEIDIR was the pioneer of discount flights to the USA and was successful, with the result that from 1957 connections from other European cities via the crossroads at Reykjavik to New York were introduced. Alongside Copenhagen, London, Oslo and Stockholm, there was a special role for Luxembourg. From here developed a strong flow of traffic with passengers coming from the whole of Western Europe. DC-6s entered service from 1960, but it

was another ten years before the first jets – Douglas DC-8s – were to be introduced. In 1964 LOFTLEIDIR received the first of four Canadair CL-44 turboprops, later brought up to CL-44 J standard and thus longer than the original model and suitable for freight traffic. New destinations were added at Baltimore and Chicago, from where subsidiary company INTERNATIONAL AIR BAHAMA provided connections via Miami to Nassau in the Bahamas. A further subsidiary company, CARGOLUX, took over the CL-44s when it commenced freight operations in 1970. The Icelandic government, following the first oil crisis, decided that for business reasons, Iceland's two international airlines LOFTLEIDIR and ICELANDAIR should merge from 1st August 1973. Under the aegis of a holding company called FLUGLEIDIR the two continued independent operations until 1979 when LOFTLEIDIR was integrated into ICELANDAIR.

In the original light blue LTS colours is Boeing 757-200 D-AMUR. In 1987 it was rented out to Spanish subsidiary LTE. (Josef Krauthäuser)

LTS/LTU-SÜD

On 25th August 1983 LTS-Lufttransport Süd Geschäftsführungs AG was founded in Munich.

Likewise in Munich another enterprise was founded on 5th December 1983, LTS LUFTTRANSPORT SÜD AG & Co Fluggesellschaft with only one shareholder, LTS-Geschäftsführungs AG. This somewhat complicated prelude to the setting up of LTS made the intention clear, that here would be built up an independent non-scheduled airline, under the sponsorship of LTU.

On 25th May 1984 the first Boeing 757-200 arrived at Munich wearing the light and dark blue colours of the new airline. Operations began in June 1984, but after a few days the aircraft flew through a severe hailstorm on approach to Munich and was seriously damaged. LTS received two more Boeing 757-200s during 1985 and 1986. On 1st November 1987 the former independence of

LTS was set aside and it became known as LTU-SÜD. The colour scheme of the aircraft was altered to reflect the change, and LTU-SÜD flew in the red and white of its parent.

As part of a cost reduction exercise, the thoughts of LTU in

Düsseldorf moved towards a bringing together of the two companies LTU and LTU-SÜD. After lengthy negotiations with the appropriate authorities both within and outside LTU, the path to merger was put in place in 1997 and completed in 1998.

After the change of name to LTU-Süd the aircraft were repainted in the colours of LTU. (Josef Krauthäuser)

This Boeing 737-300 N690MA flew with AIR EUROPE from 1989 until their collapse and was then bought by MARKAIR. Here it is seen on the move at Las Vegas for a flight to Seattle and onwards to Anchorage. (Josef Krauthäuser)

MARKAIR

USA

MARKAIR came into existence in 1947 as INTERIOR AIRWAYS in Fairbanks, Alaska, with the same aim as many bush flyers, to fly diverse tasks using small aircraft. In summer the aircraft were equipped with floats and in winter with skis. Beech 18s, Douglas DC-3s and Curtiss C-46s were then employed as larger aircraft for the carriage of freight, equipment and occasionally passengers. About 350 miles north of Fairbanks at Sagwon, INTERIOR had its own airport which during the time of the oil boom developed into one of the liveliest in Alaska.

During this time Lockheed L-100 Hercules with much larger freight volume were introduced and the name of the airline was changed in 1972 to ALASKA INTERNATIONAL AIR; worldwide charter flights were being offered.

At the beginning of 1984 under the new name MARKAIR scheduled passenger service between Fairbanks and Anchorage, as well as from Fairbanks to Barrow and Bethel were introduced. Boeing 737s came into service and the company quickly widened its activities. Thus at the end of 1984 a further expansion came about by the acquisition of the route licences, aircraft and airport facilities of WIEN AIRLINES. Under the name MARKAIR EXPRESS the activities of smaller operators were brought together, producing a dense regional network of feeder services to the larger airports. MARKAIR first got into difficulties in 1992, after it embarked on a senseless and expensive price war with ALASKA AIRLINES. At the end of 1992 Chapter 11 bankruptcy protection was sought and the airline was reorganised. After emergence from Chapter 11 it looked at first as if all was going well, yet an obviously flawed company policy changed everything again. The airline offered bargain price services to such destinations as Denver, Las Vegas, Chicago and Newark, yet provided the full traditional cabin service. The company headquarters was then moved to Denver, when the FAA placed a ban on flights because of maintenance deficiencies on the aircraft fleet. From April 1995 operations were resumed on a reduced basis, and again under the protection of Chapter 11, until Boeing and the leasing companies started to repossess aircraft, on which the payments due had not been forthcoming.

At the end of October 1995 MARKAIR was finally out of business and bankrupt.

Using luxuriously appointed aircraft MGM GRAND AIR operated a scheduled service between Los Angeles and New York. This DC-8-62 is seen parked at the airline's own terminal at Los Angeles ready for its next departure. (Josef Krauthäuser)

MGM GRAND AIR   USA

Luxury flights were the objective of the 1987 enterprise MGM GRAND AIR founded by multi-millionaire Kirk Kerkorian. A door-to-door service, finest food and wine service, as well as a luxuriously outfitted aircraft cabin, were intended to attract a corresponding clientele. Service was offered between New York and Los Angeles, on a scheduled basis. It was also possible to rent the company's Boeing 727, and this facility was taken up by stars of the film and pop music world as well as by various baseball or ice hockey teams. Three DC-8-62s with new Stage III hushkits and 79 seats in luxurious cabin surroundings were added to the Boeing 727 from 1990. A chartered DHC-6 Twin Otter was used for feeder flights from Orange County or Palm Springs to Los Angeles. An application for international flights from New York to London was made. However luxury has to be paid for, and there were simply not

enough potential customers to achieve a profitable result from the aircraft on scheduled services. Thus on 31st December 1992 the schedules between the two conurbations of New York and Los Angeles were ceased and the airline flew on as a charter only operator. With a newly-acquired Boeing 757 the airline busied itself making contact with tour operators, pursuing the possibility of offering holiday flights for the less well-off. Flights were carried out to Mexico and to the Caribbean, but also to Las Vegas and other destinations within the USA.

In 1994 the scheduled service from Los Angeles via Las Vegas to New York was reintroduced, before on 31st December 1994 the airline and its aircraft were sold off.

MID PACIFIC AIR YS-11 N109MP in the initial colour scheme when it was in use on the Hawaiian inter-island services. (Josef Krauthäuser collection)

MID PACIFIC AIR   USA

MID PACIFIC AIR had its origins in Hawaii, having been set up there by former Hawaiian Airlines staff in August 1979. Using Japanese-built NAMC YS-11s the Inter Island Service was begun on 15th March 1981 and straightaway a full-blown price war broke out between the incumbent Aloha Airlines, Hawaiian Airlines and the newcomer. Fundamentally MID PACIFIC AIR had the lowest operating costs and continued to offer attractive ticket prices. 130 daily flights between three islands from the hub at Honolulu, using 22 YS-11s, was the outcome by 1983. Using a leased Boeing 707 the airline also briefly operated from Honolulu to Pago Pago. MID PACIFIC AIR received the first of its own jets from 1985. Fokker F.28s were obviously the right choice and also allowed the airline to build up an intra-Hawaiian freight network. Early in 1985 a share of the business to the mainland USA was also claimed, with the inauguration of

a 'low-fare' service to the western cities. A further investment was also made in building up a feeder company in Texas. Both of these activities led to substantial losses and to a sale of the airline to KOA Holdings. The F.28s were returned to the lessors, but cost-reducing measures came too late to avoid

bankruptcy in January 1988. This however only affected passenger services, since the freight side was separated out and moved to Lafayette, Indiana from where it continued to fly the YS-11s. A BAe 146 was also flown on behalf of TNT but by 1995 MID PACIFIC AIR finally gave up operations.

Another YS-11 N113MP which after the bankruptcy in 1988, was used on freight services from a new hub at Lafayette, Indiana in a revised colour scheme.

This DC-9-30 was built for EASTERN AIR LINES and delivered in August 1968. MIDWAY AIRLINES received the aircraft in 1989 from the Aviation Sales Company. The registration N8964E did not change as a result of the sale. (Josef Krauthäuser collection)

MIDWAY AIRLINES   USA

MIDWAY AIRLINES was founded on 13th October 1976 with its base at Chicago's second airport, Midway, from which it took its name. The 1978 deregulation of air transport in the USA, seemed to offer some attractive opportunities and MIDWAY was one of the first of the new airlines to be set up. Using Douglas DC-9s, scheduled service was commenced on 1st November 1979 from Chicago to Cleveland, Detroit and Kansas City. These services were marketed as MIDWEST-Metrolink Service and with considerable advertising support. The network grew quickly and the airline expanded with daily flights to Dallas in Texas and New York-La Guardia and over the course of time also opened up to Las Vegas, Los Angeles and to several destinations in the Caribbean. Alongside the schedules, charter flights were also undertaken. From 1983 MIDWAY AIRLINES changed its status and became a

low-fare carrier. As well as the routes, which now served about 60 points, the fleet was also expanded and had reached 60 aircraft after only a few years of operation. In 1984 MIDWAY EXPRESS was founded as a subsidiary company, taking over AIR FLORIDA, which had gone into bankruptcy, along with its route network and aircraft. During 1989 route licences and the Philadelphia hub were bought from the troubled EASTERN AIR LINES. In this way, eighteen aircraft, mostly DC-9-30s, came into the MIDWAY fleet from EASTERN. By the acquisition of smaller companies including Fischer Brothers with their Dornier Do 228s, the company had by 1987 built up its own feeder service, which became known as MIDWAY CONNECTION. All these measures served to increase passenger numbers at MIDWAY AIRLINES, but major financial efforts were necessary to stave off the mounting competition. In

March 1991 the company was obliged to seek the protection of Chapter 11 and tried until November of that year to bring about a reorganisation.

However, no stronger financial investor could be found, nor did efforts to find another airline with whom to merge meet any success, and so MIDWAY AIRLINES ceased operating on 14th November 1991 and filed for bankruptcy.

Douglas C-117 (Super DC-3) C-GGKG was used by MILLARDAIR during the mid 1980s principally for the transport of automotive parts. (Josef Krauthäuser collection)

MILLARDAIR   Canada

This family-owned company was set up in 1963 by Carl Millard and began operations with the Douglas DC-3. Millard had been a pilot for many years with Trans Canada Airlines and had been involved in aircraft sales and servicing through his own company Carl Millard Ltd, which he had set up in 1953. In this connection the company was already active with casual charter work for the automobile industry, using a Beech 18. Millard's own airline was therefore a logical development, especially as Carl Millard's son, who had already attained his pilot's licence at the age of 17, could be employed as pilot for the Beech 18. Using this aircraft, the Millards flew principally automotive parts and this part of the business was to be a feature of their operations for many years. In 1970 MILLARDAIR bought more DC-3s, several in passenger configuration and these were brought into use during the great air traffic strike of 1972, when flights in Canada could only be carried out under visual conditions and jet traffic came to a standstill for weeks. Also, over 10,000 Canadian schoolchildren improved their geography in the course of educational/sightseeing flights on board MILLARDAIR DC-3s. In 1972 came the first of a total of eight Douglas DC-4s; these were used for freight only. In the mid-1980s the DC-3s were exchanged for C-117s (Super DC-3s). This larger version of the DC-3 had extended wings and vertical tailfin and had principally served with the United States Navy.

In 1990 MILLARDAIR gave up its base at Toronto International Airport, because there were problems in obtaining arrival and departure slots, which was making life difficult for a standby charter carrier. The aircraft were gradually sold off and MILLARDAIR operations were ceased on 31st May 1990, the company shrinking to become only a pilot training organisation. The hangar at Toronto International Airport was rented long-term to CANADA 3000.

McDonnell Douglas MD-83 in the colours of MINERVE. This type replaced the SE.210 Caravelle on European routes. (Josef Krauthäuser collection)

MINERVE   France

The privately owned airline MINERVE was established in June 1975. Using the proven SE 210 Caravelle, charter flights were begun in November 1975 from Paris-Le Bourget. During 1983 MINERVE obtained permission to fly to the USA. For the routes to New York and Los Angeles Douglas DC-8s and at times Boeing 747-200s were also brought into service. Further destinations were in the French overseas territories, as well as in the Caribbean, Pacific and the Indian Ocean. The European holiday season in the Mediterranean area and in North Africa also played a role in the airline's charter operations. The fleet of six Caravelles were exchanged for more modern MD-83s from 1987.

A subsidiary company was set up as MINERVE CANADA and likewise flew the Douglas DC-8. This company however succumbed to bankruptcy after only a short time, and this had an effect on the French parent company. The acquisition of shareholdings in JET ALSACE and JET FRET led to a chronic lack of liquidity, but this was to some extent helped by the acquisition of 50% of MINERVE's share by the tour operator Club Mediteranee.

A further expansion in the capital resources of Club Mediteranee was expected and the airline ordered three McDonnell Douglas MD-11s, in order to strengthen its ability to provide long-range services.

During 1992 there were negotiations with AIR OUTRE MER, which initially had the goal of a shareholding being taken. However at the end of 1992 there emerged an amalgamation of the two companies as AOM FRENCH AIRLINES.

One of a total of eight Convair 990 Coronados which saw service with MAT. (Josef Krauthäuser collection)

MODERN AIR TRANSPORT USA

MODERN AIR TRANSPORT – MAT was registered in New York as a charter company in 1946. The Martin 2-0-2 was the aircraft chosen as the airline's first equipment, with larger DC-4s coming in the mid 1950s. These were in turn replaced in 1961 by the Lockheed L-049 Constellation. During 1963 Douglas DC-7s were added. The airline held licences for flights within the USA, but also flew occasionally to Canada and Mexico, but when the company was taken over by the Gulf America Land Corporation-GAC, things changed. GAC flew customers interested in buying their land in Florida and Arizona, as well as charters in those states. The headquarters and base was moved to Miami in 1966. In order to modernise the fleet five Convair 990 Coronados were bought from AMERICAN AIRLINES. The first of these was introduced in January 1967 and flown in a single-class layout. Later the seating capacity was

increased from 139 to 149. For financial reasons, only three of the five aircraft on order were actually taken on, and two were leased in 1968 to NORDAIR. Following a reorganisation and new management things were making progress a year later. Using the Coronados MAT entered the transatlantic charter market. Having taken on a further two CV-990s, Berlin was established as a second base. From a still divided city of Berlin MAT flew principally to the Mediterranean, but also to Bangkok and Johannesburg. At the beginning of the 1970s, with a total of eight, MAT had the largest fleet of Coronados, which were maintained in Miami. To this end MODERN AIR TRANSPORT had a large maintenance hangar at Miami International Airport. A little ingenuity helped MAT to survive the oil crisis. The Coronado's cruising speed was reduced from Mach 0.85 to Mach 0.78 and other modifications were made to

the jet engines. This markedly increased the range for little use of fuel. MAT caused a stir with several round-the-world flights when a CV-990 became the first commercial aircraft to land in the Antarctic at the ice airfield of McMurdo Sound. Because of the deepening recession in 1971 MODERN AIR TRANSPORT withdrew from Berlin and restricted itself to charters to Berlin from the USA. However, business was not running so smoothly in the USA either and several Coronados were sold off.

When in 1971 GAC itself was forced into bankruptcy, the charters for land investors also ceased. In 1974 all flights to Germany were suddenly stopped and GAC sold these rights to AEROAMERICA. On 6th October 1975 the CAB withdrew the operating licence of MODERN AIR TRANSPORT and all the aircraft were grounded.

Boeing 737-200F D-ABFF seen here at Hamburg ready for handover to MODILUFT. The colour scheme is not too far removed from that of its former operator, LUFTHANSA. (Patrick Lutz)

MODILUFT   India

With support from and with a shareholding investment by the German airline LUFTHANSA this freight airline was set up in 1993 in India. The partners were the Modi-Group of Indian businessmen and Deutsche Lufthansa AG. Using Boeing 737-200s, supplied by LUFTHANSA and retaining much of their former livery in the colour scheme of the new airline, services were begun. However there were soon sharply differing opinions about the way the airline was set up and was to be developed, accompanied by financial irregularities. The problems and differences in business mentality between the two parties were obviously insurmountable, since lawyers were soon busy with the leasing contracts for the aircraft and making settlement claims from MODILUFT for broken contracts.

To replace the LUFTHANSA aircraft Boeing 737-400s were acquired at the beginning of April 1996. Co-operation between western-cultured companies and those in developing countries was not fundamentally destined to failure, but were obviously going to have to be ruled by different considerations, where government and administrative influences would play a substantial role. Thus it proved to be at MODILUFT, a joint venture which had taken time in the planning, but which lasted only for a short and unsuccessful time, for in 1996 the company was wound up.

Boeing 707-138B OE-IRA first served with QANTAS and came via BRANIFF to MONTANA in 1976. It finished up in Arizona as a parts donor for the USAF KC-135E tanker programme. (Josef Krauthäuser collection)

MONTANA AUSTRIA   Austria

This airline was set up in 1975 by Captain Hans Stöckl. Using two leased Boeing 707s, a privately-owned Austrian airline was offering intercontinental services for the first time in many years. However a lot of bureaucratic hurdles and a policy of hindrance from the national monopoly carrier had to be overcome before it was possible, in November 1976, to operate the first Vienna-Baghdad-Bangkok service.

The route network was built up steadily and was principally to destinations which were either not served or could not be served by other Austrian carriers. Both freight and passenger services were offered. In 1977 MONTANA received another Boeing 707. Subcharter for other companies and wet leasing were also a lucrative part of the business. Recession and the increasing price of fuel following the first oil crisis, coupled with a fall in prices on routes to the Far East and the

USA as a result of an unprecedented price war, led to mounting difficulties in the utilisation of the aircraft. Activity was reduced more and more and eventually only New York was left as a regular schedule. The emphasis moved increasingly to freight charter work, where even some dubious contracts were obviously not turned down. So it was that in May 1981 in Houston, Texas, a Boeing 707 was impounded for the illegal transportation of weapons. The stricken company sought to get its finances back on a firm footing, or a refinancing, but the Austrian government responded by taking away its operating licence. The German leasing company called in all amounts due in June 1981 and had bailiffs attach the business accounts. MONTANA was thus without resources to continue and in the middle of July 1981 declared bankruptcy. More than 2,000 passengers were stranded in the

United States and at various points in Europe.

MORRIS AIR Boeing 737-300 N734MA on the move at Las Vegas for another flight. The aircraft was passed over to SOUTHWEST AIRLINES in the course of the takeover. (Josef Krauthäuser)

MORRIS AIR   USA

June Morris was the founder of a travel bureau in Salt Lake City and quickly came to specialise in organising her own tours. Since she had no licence of her own, the flights to Hawaii, Las Vegas, Los Angeles and Mexico, were undertaken by various other airlines.

RYAN INTERNATIONAL, AMERICAN TRANS AIR and SIERRA PACIFIC all flew these routes regularly for Morris. She had however sought to have her own licence for a long time, and this led in 1992 to a situation where there were up to 300 charter flights a week which could not be operated on their own account, but these could be organised as scheduled flights. With eleven leased Boeing 737-300s in their own colours a significant route network was soon being built up. MORRIS AIR faced considerable competition from established companies, but was able to fly at more attractive prices.

Within a year MORRIS AIR already had 21 Boeing 737-300s in service and was in the black from the outset. This meteoric rise led to a takeover offer from SOUTHWEST AIRLINES worth over US$ 130 million, which MORRIS AIR eventually accepted. Until the end of 1994 MORRIS AIR remained more or less independent and built up the route network further for SOUTHWEST. During 1995 the merger of the companies took place and SOUTHWEST was again without competition.

Boeing 707-300 9V-BBA on approach to Frankfurt. On 28th May 1968 MSA received the aircraft from Boeing; after retirement from SIA it saw service with AIR LANKA and TRADEWINDS AIRWAYS. In 1982 it was broken up for spares and the remainder scrapped. (Manfred Winter)

MSA MALAYSIA-SINGAPORE AIRLINES Malaysia & Singapore

The establishment of this airline goes back to political initiatives, following a split in the Malaysian Federation into Malaysia and the city state of Singapore. Until this time Singapore was the most important business centre for the whole region, with a well developed airport. A further centre was at Kuala Lumpur, where the infrastructure was in place from British colonial times. After the Second World War, air traffic had developed here and MALAYAN AIRWAYS had been founded. Using the Airspeed Consul, scheduled services were begun in 1947; DC-3s followed quickly and these were used for services to neighbouring countries. In 1959 using a leased QANTAS Douglas DC-4, a route was inaugurated from Singapore to Hong Kong, providing the first direct connection between South East Asia's two most important cities. On 4th December 1962 MALAYAN AIRWAYS used a de Havilland Comet 4 to open up a

Singapore-Kuala Lumpur-Bangkok route. Fokker F.27 Friendships replaced the elderly DC-3s on the most important routes between Kuala Lumpur and Singapore. In 1963, with the founding of the United States of Malaysia, independence from Great Britain was achieved and the airline name changed to MALAYSIAN AIRWAYS. During the same year four more Comets were received, but then in 1965 came the breakaway of Singapore into a separate state, but one without an airline. The two countries thus decided to rename MALAYSIAN AIRWAYS as MALAYSIA-SINGAPORE AIRLINES (MSA), whereby the two states each held 38% of the airline, with the rest of the shares being taken over by the Sultanate of Brunei and by BOAC and QANTAS.

With a rapid expansion of the fleet and route network MSA became one of the region's most respected airlines. Routes were opened to Australia, Japan and

the Philippines. Using Boeing 707s, the longest route via Bombay, Bahrein and Rome to London was opened in 1971. Regional services were expanded significantly and for these routes Britten-Norman BN-2 Islanders were brought into use for services to minor destinations, and Boeing 737s replaced the Comets on medium length routes. Year on year, profits increased, yet the differences between the two governments over the wider politics of the company were also increasing. On 27th April 1971 negotiations began over a splitting of interests, with the aim of creating two independent airlines. From 1st October 1972 MSA was dissolved and its successors SINGAPORE AIRLINES took over the 707s and 737s for international routes, whilst MALAYSIAN AIRWAYS SYSTEM took the Fokker F.27s and BN-2s, as well as the still to be delivered new Boeing 737s for the extensive regional network.

Boeing 727-200 N4731 seen here at New Orleans flew for a long time with the name 'Margie', as in a major advertising campaign NATIONAL aircraft were bestowed with the names of female staff members. (Manfred Winter)

NATIONAL AIRLINES   USA

Theodore Baker of Chicago was the owner of two Ryan Monoplanes, which he bought in 1929 after setting up his NATIONAL AIRLINES AIR TAXI SYSTEM. His passengers were overwhelmingly American nationals who wanted to fly to Canada, in order to be able to drink whisky and other alcoholic beverages legally in a time of prohibition. Beginning in 1934, with the granting of the new air mail licences, Baker applied for the postal routes from Cleveland to Nashville and St Petersburg to Daytona Beach. He received permission for the latter on 25th May 1934. Following the grant of a licence, the firm now known just as NATIONAL AIRLINES took to the air on 15th October 1934 on the route St Petersburg-Tampa-Lakeland-Orlando-Daytona. During 1936 the Ryans were exchanged for Stinson Trimotors and using the capital of the dormant GULF AIRLINES, NATIONAL became a company. NATIONAL was

granted licences for further postal routes, for the first time including New Orleans. Further development was signalled in 1944 with the opening of a route from Jacksonville to New York, though this was against great competition from EASTERN AIR LINES. Douglas DC-4s, DC-6s, DC-7s and Lockheed Constellations came into service on this route over the years, until in 1958 the Boeing 707 began the first American domestic jet service. During 1946 NATIONAL moved headquarters from Jacksonville to Miami and flew into neighbouring Cuba for the first time. The propensity of NATIONAL AIRLINES staff to go on strike was noteworthy; until 1948 Baker had refused to allow the staff to organise trades unions. Only after the government had pressured Baker with dissolution and compulsory administration, did he give way after a long strike. At the beginning of the 1950s NATIONAL concluded an agreement with hotels in Miami

Beach, allowing year-round attractive prices to be offered for hotel-inclusive vacations. Night-time fares followed on the New York-Miami route, which also attracted new passengers. Older Convairs were replaced by Lockheed L-188 Electras and later by Boeing 727s. These were also used to extend the route network westwards to San Francisco. On 15th June 1970 the first flight from Miami to London took place, operated by the DC-8, but by Autumn 1970 the first of the Boeing 747s were delivered and took over on this route. During 1971 the first of the DC-10s were also added. Amsterdam and Frankfurt were served on a regular basis from 1978. NATIONAL had an extensive network within the USA and in 1978/79 PAN AMERICAN quickly emerged as the winner of a takeover battle. NATIONAL was merged into PAN AM in 1980 and their colourful aircraft received the blue and white PAN AM livery.

Previously used by EASTERN AIR LINES, JAPAN AIRLINES and CAPITOL AIR, this ill-fated Douglas DC-8-61 C-GMXQ was taken on by NATIONAIR in December 1984. (Josef Krauthäuser collection)

NATIONAIR CANADA Canada

NATIONAIR CANADA had its headquarters in Montreal and in 1984 started flights to the Caribbean, Florida and Mexico. Using Douglas DC-8s holiday-makers were flown from the winter cold of Canada to sunny destinations including for example Port-au-Prince, Barbados, Cancun, Fort Lauderdale and Varadero.

For the summer season of 1985 destinations in Europe also appeared in the timetable. London, Paris and Frankfurt were served with regular charter series. On 3rd May 1987 NATIONAIR began a scheduled service linking Montreal with Brussels. With sensationally low prices, a round trip costing as little as $299, battle was commenced with other operators on the European routes.

A year later, from 2nd May 1988 London-Gatwick followed; however the departure point was Hamilton, some 100 km to the west of Toronto.

Scheduled licences for Manchester were sought and granted. As elsewhere, there was a business recession in Canada at the end of the 1980s and NATIONAIR at first benefited from the collapse of ODYSSEY INTERNATIONAL and WORLDWAYS CANADA and took over not only passengers but also Boeing 757s. Alongside DC-8s of series 61 and 63, the fleet also embraced Boeing 747-100s and 200s. Troop transport flights to Europe were operated on behalf of the Canadian military and there was considerable sub-charter business for other airlines such as AIR ALGERIE, SUDAN AIRWAYS, HISPANIA and for the annual Hadj flights to Saudi Arabia. On 11th July 1991 the pilot of a DC-8-61 encountered hydraulic problems after take-off at Jeddah and a loss of cabin pressure. An emergency return to the airport was unsuccessful, and C-GMXQ crashed with 261 fatalities. Investigations by the authorities

led to a temporary cutback of services and to several DC-8s being taken out of service. The financially troubled company disposed of several of the aircraft which it owned itself and withdrew from the scheduled service market on the grounds that the very low prices were simply not profitable. In March 1993 NATIONAIR entered protection from creditors, but a month later ceased flying and succumbed to bankruptcy.

BAe Jetstream 31 PH-KJF of NETHERLINES being readied for its next flight. The complete company name is presented on the fuselage above the front three cabin windows. A total of six Jetstreams saw service. (Josef Krauthäuser collection)

NETHERLINES   Netherlands

NETHERLINES AIRLINES FOR EUROPEAN COMMUTER SERVICES BV, as the company was fully known in the register of businesses, was established in April 1993 by Leen P Jansson. The first route between Amsterdam and Luxembourg was started in January 1985 with BAe Jetstream 31s. From this time also, Groningen, within the Netherlands was also served. From the outset NETHERLINES co-operated with NLM CITYHOPPER. It took over from NLM routes which they were unable to operate economically with their Fokker F.27s or Fokker F.28s. KLM was a shareholder in NLM and NETHERLINES used the KLM reservation system. For a small company like this, it was a distinct advantage, as travel was bookable via major hubs at through-fare tariffs. The Jetstream 31 was able to seat 18 passengers and was thus suited to smaller airports Eindhoven, Enschede, Groningen or

Rotterdam, from which there was only a modest demand for direct services. Cologne/Bonn and Münster/Osnabrück in Germany, Lille and Strasbourg in France and Birmingham, East Midlands and Luton in Great Britain were all brought into the network with direct flights from the early part of 1996.

For a route from Amsterdam to Hamburg NETHERLINES leased in a Dornier Do 228 of HOLIDAY AIR, and with the addition of Vienna, this became the longest route. Two more Jetstreams were added to the fleet in Spring 1986 and the airline continued to expand.

From the outset, Rotterdam was the home base of the airline, but another hangar was established at Eindhoven and the management also moved there. After KLM re-organised its regional-level activities in the mid 1980s and completely took over NLM, it made a corresponding offer to take over NETHERLINES.

On 1st January 1989 NETHERLINES was merged with NLM as part of the new KLM-CITYHOPPER branding.

DC-9s and MD-80s were the workhorses at NEW YORK AIR and thanks to their bright red colour scheme, were always conspicuous at airports. (Christofer Witt collection)

NEW YORK AIR USA

NEW YORK AIR was a well-known part of the 'Lorenzo-Airline-Monopoly' and had its origins in 1979 when TEXAS AIR set up the company with its fine-sounding name, in order to compete head-on with the established EASTERN AIRSHUTTLE between New York and Washington.

The low-fare service began on 19th December 1980 with flights between New York-La Guardia and Washington-National. Compared with EASTERN SHUTTLE, seats were pre-booked, reserved and passengers received a small meal pack. A fleet of DC-9-30 and MD-80 jets came into service. On 15th February 1981 a second route between New York and Boston was established. Alongside these shuttle flights which operated on an hourly basis, services were operated to other cities such as Detroit, Orlando, Raleigh-Durham, Tampa and New Orleans, and at weekends there was intensive charter work to Florida. During

the infamous air traffic controllers strike the airline moved operations from La Guardia to Newark and here was in direct competition with PEOPLEXPRESS. In the first year of service 1.5 million passengers were carried, but the losses sustained amounted to more than US$11 million.

Under a new management, a completely different approach was taken in the following years, and an attempt made to distance the airline from that of cheap flights. Business travellers especially were regaled with wine and meals. Despite this the deficit rose to $23 million; in the second year of operation only 1.7 million passengers flew with NEW YORK AIR. Further reorganisation followed and the Newark hub was abandoned. Washington-Dulles Airport became the new hub and a north-south route network was established from there. COLGAN AIRWAYS functioned as NEW YORK AIR CONNECTION with regional feeder services. The New

York-Washington and New York-Boston shuttle services were sold to PAN AM on 1st October 1986; this sale was a condition imposed by the regulatory authorities following the purchase of EASTERN AIR LINES by Lorenzo's Texas Air Corporation. With CONTINENTAL, PEOPLEXPRESS and NEW YORK AIR, Texas Air Corporation now had three airline companies whose routes, fleets and markets were from time to time competing with each other. A merger of all three companies was therefore in the offing. Boeing 737-300s, which had been ordered by CONTINENTAL, came into service with NEW YORK AIR from 1986. From 1st February 1987 the expected and logical merger took place with NEW YORK AIR and PEOPLEXPRESS being fused into CONTINENTAL AIRLINES.

The Boeing 737-200 was used by NAC for domestic services in New Zealand. This example ZK-NAK , a model -214, came to NAC from Pacific Southwest in 1973, remaining in New Zealand until 1986. (Christofer Witt collection)

NEW ZEALAND NATIONAL AW CO – NAC New Zealand

NAC, as it was habitually abbreviated, was set up by the New Zealand government by an Act of Parliament on 7th December 1945. It brought together the operations of three inland operators to form a national domestic airline. In August 1946 UNION AIRWAYS and COOK STRAIT AIRWAYS were bought, followed in 1947 by AIR TRAVEL NEW ZEALAND. All three companies had been active since the 1930s and had built up regional networks. NAC took over all their routes and aircraft and expanded quickly. The Douglas DC-3 was the preferred type for internal services, with routes encompassing both North and South Islands. There were direct connections between Auckland, Wellington, Christchurch and Dunedin. Using Short Sunderland flying boats there were also services to islands in the Pacific such as Norfolk Island or Fiji. DC-3s were also used to Samoa, Tonga and the Cook Islands.

However these international routes were taken over from 1950 by TEAL – TASMAN EMPIRE AIRLINES. On 3rd February 1958 NAC received the first of four Vickers Viscount 807s. Two years later in February 1960 the first Fokker F.27 Friendship also arrived and by and by these replaced the DC-3., which were used for freight services for some years; from 1966 SAFE AIR flew freight services more and more on behalf of NAC. When the decision came to replace the Vickers Viscounts, the Boeing 737 was chosen for short and middle range routes. On 18th September 1968 the first Boeing 737 arrived in New Zealand and was ready to operate the airline's first jet schedules from the end of the month. During 1972 came the takeover of SAFE AIR, which was flying Bristol 170s and Armstrong Whitworth Argosy freighters. NAC also took on a 15% shareholding in MOUNT COOK AIRLINES. As a result of the first oil crisis, fuel

prices rose dramatically in New Zealand and the consequences of the worldwide business recession were evident. The New Zealand government decided by a further Act of Parliament to merge the international airline AIR NEW ZEALAND (formerly TEAL) with NAC to form a new company, NEW ZEALAND NATIONAL AIRWAYS CORPORATION which became effective from 1st April 1978.

Boeing 727-200 TC-AFB with the name 'Vatan', formerly with AIR FRANCE, belonged to SBG Overseas Leasing and is seen here departing on a charter flight to Istanbul. (Josef Krauthäuser)

NOBLE AIR   Turkey

Using two leased Boeing 727s the Turkish airline NOBLE AIR first appeared on the scene in 1989. It was a Turkish/British joint venture company and initially flew for the travel company with the same name and ownership. During the first year NOBLE AIR was primarily engaged in flying British holidaymakers from London to Turkey. In March and June 1990 four more Boeing 727s were acquired and during the summer season flights were operated from other European airports.

Additionally NOBLE AIR was awarded scheduled service rights between London and Istanbul. Likewise, within Turkey schedules were flown, from Antalya to Ankara and Istanbul.

Increasing competition in the Turkish holiday flight market and poor passenger loads on the scheduled services led to mounting financial difficulties, which could not be catered for within the airline's own capital structure. Services were terminated at the end of 1991 and the company liquidated in 1992.

NORCANAIR received its first Fokker F.28 Fellowship in 1986. C-GTEO is seen here in the company's colours; it joined the fleet of TIME AIR in 1987, when TIME AIR bought NORCANAIR. (Josef Krauthäuser collection)

NORCANAIR   Canada

NORTH CANADA AIR Ltd or NORCANAIR for short was founded in August 1947 as SASKATCHEWAN GOVERNMENT AIRWAYS – SASKAIR. The provincial government had since the beginning of 1947 been the owner of another airline M & C AVIATION and since 1945 had also had aircraft in use by its Department for Natural Resources. These activities were taken over by SASKAIR and the scheduled services expanded. During the early years there was a very mixed fleet in use, including such types as the Beech 18, PBY-5A Canso, Douglas DC-3, Bristol 170 Freighter, DHC-2 Beaver and smaller Cessnas. Scheduled services ran to over 20 destinations in the province, with departures from the base at the main city of Prince Albert. Several aircraft were fitted with floats in summer and ski undercarriages in winter, in order to be able to

operate in otherwise inaccessible areas. The government invested large amounts of money in the airline, but following a change of administration in1964 it was nevertheless sold and renamed as NORCANAIR. Government work was guaranteed for the first year. Modern turboprop aircraft were acquired for the busiest routes from the beginning of 1970, the first type being the DHC-6 Twin Otter. The first Fokker F.27 Friendship arrived in 1972. NORCANAIR took over the Regina-Prince Albert route from TRANSAIR and thus linked the two most important centres in the province, and the first strike at NORCANAIR, so that by 1981 the company was being offered for sale and the provincial government wanted to take it over again. Political considerations however led to a sale in 1982 to HIGH LINE AIRWAYS, though continuing to fly under the NORCANAIR name.

During 1984 the fleet was modernised and Embraer Bandeirantes took over various routes. In 1985 NORCANAIR provided the first direct connection between Saskatoon and Minneapolis, USA. With the advent of the Fokker F.28 in 1986, NORCANAIR received its first jets. A year later the airline entered into an alliance with CP AIR, which meant that NORCANAIR was active flying feeder services from Calgary, Edmonton and Winnepeg. As a result of the takeover of CP AIR by PWA, the situation changed and in March 1987 NORCANAIR was likewise taken over by TIME AIR, in which PWA had a holding of 45%.

NORDAIR Boeing 737-200 C-GNDS at Fort Lauderdale, a favourite winter destination for Canadian tourists. NORDAIR flew to Florida from 1963 with Douglas DC-6s, DC-7s, Super Constellations, DC-8s and Boeing 737s. (Josef Krauthäuser collection)

NORDAIR
Canada

NORDAIR had its origins in MONT LAURIER AVIATION founded on 25th February 1946 and BOREAL AIRWAYS set up in 1948. The latter had a financial stake in MONT LAURIER AVIATION and merged the two companies on 24th May 1957 to form NORDAIR with its headquarters in Montreal. Using a Douglas DC-4, services were operated on former Canso flying boat routes Montreal-Robervale-Fort Chimo (today known as Kuujjuaq)-Frobisher (now Iqualit). Contracts for the energy ministry were also taken over in the Quebec's Arctic regions.

During 1960 NORDAIR took over the route licences and aircraft of WHEELER AIRLINES with routes to Val d'Or, Cape Dyer and Barter Island. The Curtiss C-46 was brought into service on these important routes for which NORDAIR received a government subsidy. Likewise in 1960 the licence of SARNIA AIRLINES was bought and flights continued Windsor-Sarnia-London-Toronto

using the Douglas DC-3 which was also taken over. In 1961 a Handley Page Dart Herald was acquired as a DC-3 replacement and from 6th August 1961 NORD-AIR operated the first scheduled service to Resolute Bay.

Using the Douglas DC-6 NORDAIR entered the holiday charter market in 1963. During 1964 four Lockheed Super Constellations were added, and used for charter and scheduled services as well as flights to the Arctic. In 1968 a Conviar 990 was leased from MODERN AIR TRANSPORT for charter work; this was the airline's first jet. In the same year NORDAIR received the first of its own Boeing 737s, with four more following by 1969. The first international scheduled service was from Hamilton to Pittsburgh in the USA in 1972. For this route the Fairchild FH-227 joined the fleet. This type also took over all of the Arctic work and acquitted itself well, as did the Boeing 737s equipped for

operations from unprepared gravel and ice runways. During 1972 three specially-equipped Lockheed Electras were received; these were used for maritime patrol and ice watching duties for the government. Using a Douglas DC-8 delivered in 1974 winter charters to the Caribbean, Florida and Mexico were flown, until James Tooley, the owner of NORDAIR put it up for sale in 1977. There had been increasing disputes between the French- and English-speaking authorities and politicians wanted to interfere with the sale. At first AIR CANADA took a majority holding, but was obliged to give this up. QUEBECAIR also took over a portion of the NORDAIR stock, but became bankrupt and the NORDAIR staff picketed a francophone investment firm. In 1986 CP AIR quickly took over the majority holding in NORDAIR and in January 1987 the ten-year takeover pantomime ended with the integration of NORDAIR into CP AIR.

NEA – NORDIC EUROPEAN/NORDIC EAST took over several Lockheed L-1011 TriStars from CATHAY PACIFIC and used them on charter work. Here SE-DPX is seen on approach to London-Heathrow. (Frank Schorr)

NORDIC EUROPEAN AIRLINES Sweden

Set up in 1991 as NORDIC EAST AIRWAYS in Stockholm, the airline succeeded in taking to the air in August of that year. A Douglas DC-9-41 was used, with two MD-80s added a year later. Charters – both series and ad hoc – were flown, predominantly to the Mediterranean region.

NORDIC EAST was also particularly active in the charter of its aircraft to other companies, who suffered from seasonal capacity shortages. In 1994 Boeing 737s, with longer range than the Douglas types, were added. Thus in the summer of 1994 a Boeing 737-400 flew exclusively for the German airline LTU. The DC-9 and the MD-80s were returned to their lessors and further Boeing 737s brought into the fleet, again working exclusively for a large German tour operator. Using a DC-8 NORDIC EAST operated briefly in the freight market to the Middle East. The airline also operated in close co-operation with

TRANSWEDE AIRWAYS for whom some schedules were flown.

Lockheed L-1011 TriStars from CATHAY PACIFIC were taken over in 1995 and enlarged the available fleet. Now long-distance charter work was possible, and the heavily frequented mass destinations of Palma de Mallorca or Tenerife could also be served with the widebodies. At the end of 1996 came a change of name to NORDIC EUROPEAN AIRLINES – NEA and the airline made efforts to position itself more in central Europe.

1997 was a critical year for the company, as fewer charter contracts could be negotiated, which led to NEA running into financial difficulties. In February 1998 it announced a suspension of some activities and tried to re-organise, offering some aircraft for sale. On 8th March 1998 operations finally ceased altogether and the company went into liquidation.

Two Convair 580s are seen on the departure ramp at Chicago O'Hare, with an AMERICAN AIRLINES 747 just showing in the background. The Convair 580 N90854 served with NORTH CENTRAL from 1968 and was sold to KEY AIR after the merger. (Manfred Winter)

NORTH CENTRAL AIRLINES USA

The beginnings of NORTH CENTRAL AIRLINES went back to 1944, when on 15th May WISCONSIN CENTRAL AIRLINES was founded in Madison. As the name suggests, the initial offering was a regional network in the state of Wisconsin, commenced with an inaugural flight on 24th February 1948. Three Lockheed L-10A Electras formed the initial fleet. From 1951 Douglas DC-3s flew to points outside the state and offered connections to the major cities of Chicago, Minneapolis and Detroit in the neighbouring states. In 1952 a new route was opened to North and South Dakota and to reflect this increased radius of operation the company was renamed as NORTH CENTRAL AIRLINES. The headquarters of the company was also moved to a new home in Minneapolis in the next state of Minnesota. The company grew steadily and more modern and larger aircraft such as the Convair 340 were added from 1959. As

loads increased these were in turn supplemented by up-to-date Convair 440s and in 1967 by the Convair 580, the first turboprop type in use on the schedules. The older Convair aircraft were not retired, but modernised and with the fitment of turboprop engines brought up to the Convair 580 standard. During 1957 the longer routes were turned over to operation by the first jets, Douglas DC-9-31s, the first of which was delivered in August. The route network now extended as far as Boston and New York in the east. The airline also operated to Toronto and Winnipeg in Canada, and as far as Denver as the most westerly point on the route network. More than 60 aircraft – Convair 580s and DC-9-31/32s were in service with NORTH CENTRAL by 1978, when there were serious changes afoot. Following deregulation of air services in the USA, mega-carriers were being built up, better able to cope with the new

open market conditions. NORTH CENTRAL AIRLINES thus merged in 1979 with the Atlanta-based SOUTHERN AIRWAYS to form the new REPUBLIC AIRLINES, which in turn was later to be absorbed into NORTHWEST.

NORTHEAST Vickers Viscount 806 G-AOYH, a former BEA machine, in the latest colour scheme at Heathrow, operating the daily Leeds-London service. (Manfred Winter)

NORTHEAST AIRLINES Great Britain

On 12th October 1951 Messrs Barnby, Keegan and Stevens, together with chief pilot Falconer, took their leave of CREWSAIR and set up CREWS-AIR ENGINEERING. They took their financial share in the form of a Douglas DC-3. BKS AERO CHARTER was a further company, set up on 7th February 1952 by the three above-named gentlemen (taking the name from the first letters of their respective surnames) and it used the DC-3 on diverse charter and freight flights. They carried engines and replacement parts for stranded ships, ships crews, racing pigeons, students, and anything else which could be loaded into a DC-3. CREWSAIR ENGINEERING became BKS Engineering. Unlike other companies which stored their aircraft in winter, BKS carried its first ski holidaymakers from London to Innsbruck. Flights were also undertaken on behalf of other companies to Berlin and in 1953 the company received its

long-awaited licence for scheduled services from Newcastle to the Isle of Man and Jersey. During 1954 Vickers Vikings were added and these were used during the summer season for services to Malaga. In 1955 BKS opened a Leeds-Düsseldorf scheduled service and during 1956 many relief flights were operated to Austria, in connection with the Hungarian refugees; these were operated without pay by the crews. The fleet and the work grew steadily. In 1958 several Airspeed Ambassadors were taken over from BEA, and these were fitted out in a high-density 55-passenger configuration. More scheduled services to Basle, Belfast, Bilbao, Dublin and Santander were added in 1958, and the airport at Leeds built up as a base. The most profitable route from Newcastle to London was first served in May 1959, later being served several times daily. A Bristol 170 Freighter was used for

freight work, and was available for all sorts of charters. During 1960 several routes were exchanged with BEA and this brought the two companies closer together. In 1961 the Vickers Viscount was leased for the Leeds-London and Newcastle-London routes, while the first HS.748 was introduced in 1962. During 1964 and 1965 the larger Bristol Britannia followed; a total of three aircraft of this type were used. Jet service began in March 1969 with the HS.121 Trident, after BRITISH AIR SERVICES had bought shares in BKS in 1967. The change of name to NORTHEAST AIRLINES followed in 1970, with a new predominantly yellow colour scheme for the Viscounts and Tridents, while the Britannias were taken out of service. The company was more and more engaged in work on behalf of what had now become BRITISH AIRWAYS and was quickly integrated into the national airline in 1976.

On account of their striking colour scheme, NORTHEAST's aircraft, such as this Boeing 727-95 delivered new to the airline in October 1967, were also known as 'yellowbirds'. (Josef Krauthäuser collection)

NORTHEAST AIRLINES USA

This company had its origins in BOSTON-MAIN AIRWAYS, which was founded in 1931. On 19th November 1940 it came together with other smaller airlines to form NORTHEAST AIRLINES and bought the most modern aircraft available in the form of the Douglas DC-3. During the Second World War NORTHEAST was involved in Lend-Lease and ferried Douglas C-47s to Europe; other government work was also undertaken during this period.

Post-war the airline steadfastly built up its own route network and in 1946 introduced the larger DC-4. Convair 240s were added in 1949, but still no permission was forthcoming for routes to Florida. This was eventually to come in 1956 from the CAB, which was not in the habit of awarding such routes readily to smaller airlines. Using the DC-6 NORTHEAST opened up the route from Boston to Miami on 9th January 1957. In the same year the first of the airline's Vickers Viscounts were

delivered, and using this type, the New York-Boston route became successful as passenger figures rose sharply. During 1960 NORTHEAST received six Convair 880s and worked closely with TWA. Howard Hughes, who at the time was the dominant figure within TWA, bought 55% of the NORTHEAST shares and wanted to merge the two. However this move was torpedoed by EASTERN AIR LINES and NATIONAL AIRLINES. NORTHEAST ran into serious difficulties in 1962, when the CAB would not renew traffic rights to Florida. Massive objections to the US congress and a petition with the support of 250,000 voters, brought the CAB to its senses and resulted in an unlimited licence being awarded.

In 1965 the Storer Broadcasting Company took over the former Hughes shares and invested several million more dollars in NORTHEAST. New aircraft in the form of Boeing 727s, Douglas DC-9s and Fairchild FH-227s

were ordered and with the delivery of the first FH-227, there was a change in the appearance of the NORTHEAST fleet. The famous 'Yellowbirds' swiftly became a familiar sight in the skies of the north-east of the USA. During 1968 services were added to Nassau and Freeport in the Bahamas. The first transcontinental route from Miami to Los Angeles was started in 1969. In this year also, several other airlines were showing an interest in NORTHEAST. NORTHWEST AIRLINES wanted to make a takeover, but this failed because of CAB objections; they would only allow a sale of a part of the route network. TWA and EASTERN AIR LINES then also planned to take over the more attractive routes, but eventually DELTA AIR LINES made a successful bid.

On 23rd April 1971 the merger of NORTHEAST with DELTA AIR LINES was announced, becoming effective from 1st August 1972.

With this brightly painted Boeing 727 – a sister ship flew in blue with clouds – NORTHEASTERN put their New York-originating passengers in the right mood for their flight to sunny Florida. (Christofer Witt collection)

NORTHEASTERN INTERNATIONAL AIRWAYS USA

NORTHEASTERN was established in 1980 as a 'low-fare' company with the object of offering scheduled flights from the north-eastern states of the USA to the Florida resorts. Permission for charter operations was granted in December 1980, but it was decided to defer the commencement of operations until a scheduled service licence was forthcoming, and this eventually was awarded at the beginning of 1982. Services began on 12th February 1982 using Douglas DC-8s. Flying from Long Island McArthur Airport, near Islip, the first services were to Fort Lauderdale and St Petersburg/Clearwater. A further route linked Hartford with Fort Lauderdale and Orlando. As a result of the strong demand for their attractively-priced flights, the company was able to expand quickly and was to receive four more DC-8s in the course of the same year. In 1983 four Boeing 727-100s were added, as were flights to other sunspots – Las

Vegas and San Diego. The Boeing 727s stood out because of their 'clouds' colour schemes and helped the airline to have a high public awareness. During 1984 NORTHEASTERN began a special programme to rapidly expand the company by the purchase or lease of further aircraft. Freddie Laker was taken on as an advisor to the company and was expected to take a share in further expansion. Several Airbus A300s were leased in, making the airline only the second American company (after EASTERN AIR LINES) to use the European type. These were in use from February 1984, after pilots and cabin staff had undertaken training in France. New York, Los Angeles and San Francisco were new destinations and during the summer season, flights from the US west coast to Europe were operated for the first time. The ambitious targets for 1984 were however not achieved and towards the end of the year

came the first financial crisis. The four Airbus A300 were returned by October and reductions made in the route network. An arrangement with BRANIFF for the lease of ten Boeing 727s for the winter season, failed because of legal objections and these aircraft were returned to BRANIFF. Further cutbacks, both in routes and the aircraft fleet were put in place at the beginning of 1985, and staff numbers drastically reduced. With a debt mountain of $48 million, NORTHEASTERN placed itself under Chapter 11 bankruptcy protection from 8th January 1985, whereby a reduced operation would be maintained until 4th March 1985. On 21st June 1985 a further restart was made following another re-organisation, at first with two aircraft and again from Islip to Fort Lauderdale. This new start was short-lived however, as on 5th November 1985 the airline finally declared bankruptcy and was liquidated during 1986.

Boeing 737-400 G-BOPJ on its way to the runway at Salzburg for a flight to Manchester. Regular charter flights for skiers were operated during the 1989/90 winter season. (Gottfried Auer)

NOVAIR   Great Britain

Following the failure of LAKER AIRWAYS the Rank Organisation suddenly found itself in the Spring of 1982 as a large tour operator with no aircraft for its summer programme, but with firm bookings sufficient for two DC-10s. BRITISH CALEDONIAN came to the rescue by taking over two of the DC-10s and former LAKER personnel and operating them with their own support services. The season's work was completed to the satisfaction of both parties, with the outcome that BRITISH CALEDONIAN CHARTER was then founded. The Rank Organisation was a share-holder. In autumn 1985 the name was changed to CAL AIR INTERNATIONAL, with its own callsign and a new colour scheme. However, CALEDONIAN's lion motif still appeared on the tailfin.

Following the takeover of BRITISH CALEDONIAN by BRITISH AIRWAYS in 1987, BA became a shareholder. In order to make a clean break, BA sold its shares in May 1988 to the Rank Organisation, which on 7th December 1988 again changed the name, this time to NOVAIR. Using three DC-10s, the airline specialised in long-distance work; however in 1989 two Boeing 737-400s were added and were used for routes in Europe, to North Africa and to the Canary Isles. Obviously though, the airline management had misjudged the state of the British tourist market, since at the beginning of 1990, the two underutilised 737s were sold. On 5th May 1990 NOVAIR ceased operations and the company was dissolved.

A striking shot of DC-10-10 G-GCAL in January 1990 at Munich-Riem. This was also used for charter flights for skiers and winter holidaymakers in the German and Austrian Alps. (Christofer Witt)

McDonnell Douglas MD-83 with temporary Spanish registration EC-642 and an interim colour scheme. This aircraft was fully registered as EC-FEB at the end of 1991. (Josef Krauthäuser)

OASIS   Spain

ANDALUSAIR was founded in Malaga, Spain in 1986 and the airline operated briefly in 1987 using the McDonnell Douglas MD-83. After a few months the OASIS hotel group took a shareholding in the company and not only took a majority of the shares, but also installed a new management team. The name ANDALUSAIR also fell victim to the change of circumstances and OASIS was introduced instead.

Using further MD-83s, acquired mostly under lease arrangements, many charter series were operated during the 1988 summer season from Great Britain, Scandinavia and mid-Europe to Spain.

In order to have a chance in participating in transatlantic charter work, OASIS bought the majority of the capital of the Mexican airline AEROCANCUN and received its first Airbus A310-300 in 1991. This was however used initially by AEROCANCUN. More Airbus A310-300s followed

from 1992 and up to five were in use. MD-80s were also exchanged with AEROCANCUN on a seasonal basis, in order to gain best use of the aircraft at peak times. Additionally OASIS had shareholdings in the Cuban charter company AEROVARADERO as well as AEROCANCUN, and using leased Airbus A300-600s or Airbus A310-300s took part in the booming Cuban tourist market. During 1995 OASIS was granted routes licences to the USA, and these were used in conjunction with partner Apple Vacations for flights from Madrid. Via this American partner OASIS also had an interest in the American airline PRIVATE JET. A reduction in demand and the entry into Spanish internal scheduled services, against heavy competition from other Spanish companies, led to mounting losses and brought the company into financial difficulties, which led to bankruptcy at the end of 1986.

147

In the tradition of WARDAIR, ODYSSEY INTERNATIONAL gave generally excellent service and on-board catering; here is their Boeing 757-200 C-GAWB. (Josef Krauthäuser collection)

ODYSSEY INTERNATIONAL Canada

In October 1973 Brian Child set up OWEN SOUND AIR SERVICES (OSAS) to the north of Toronto and from May 1974 was initially active as a flying school and charter company. The profits from a government contract in East Africa were reinvested in Canada. In 1977 the company succeeded in establishing operations from Toronto International Airport, with initial participation in the express packet market. Using a Fairchild Metro flights were undertaken for PUROLATOR from 1980, and two DC-3s were in service for AIRBORNE EXPRESS and Emery. During 1984 SOUNDAIR took over AERO TRADES WESTERN and in doing so not only took on its DC-4, but also a licence to carry on airfreight work on its own account. From 1986 Convair 580s replaced the DC-4 and Fokker F.27s supplanted the DC-3s.

From 1988 all of these freight and courier flights for various companies were brought together under the SOUNDAIR EXPRESS

banner. Already in 1984, as COMMUTER EXPRESS, a direct service had been started with Fairchild Metros from Toronto to Columbus, Ohio, in the neighbouring USA and these cross-border flights were built up successfully. During 1987 COMMUTER EXPRESS became a partner of AIR CANADA and took on the name AIR TORONTO, with BAe Jetstream 31s arriving as replacements for the Metros in July 1988. In mid-June 1988, the charter airline ODYSSEY INTERNATIONAL was founded as the third member of the group. Flights began on 3rd November 1988, using a leased Boeing 757 from Toronto to Las Vegas.

For this first season, the destinations were those typical for the Canadian winter, almost exclusively to the Caribbean.

The summer season however saw flights to some smaller airports such as Leeds/Bradford or Newcastle in England. Two Boeing 737-300s were leased

from AIR EUROPE for use on shorter routes and those under development where traffic did not yet justify use of the larger 757. More 757s were added during 1989. In order to provide full employment for the aircraft, SOUNDAIR took over Thomas Vacations Canada Ltd. The acquisition took place at a time when not only in Canada, but also in many other countries, there was business recession. A new headquarters building with maintenance complex at Toronto's Lester B Pierson Airport, the setting up of their own fuelling company and of a leasing company at this time, combined with a fallback in passenger boardings at AIR TORONTO, and the loss of a freight contract all led to liquidity problems at SOUNDAIR and rapidly to the cessation of all services by all three companies on 27th April 1990; the parent company had declared bankruptcy, leaving behind it debts of Can$65 million.

Using Boeing 737-200s such as this one, G-BHVH, ORION AIRWAYS served most areas in Europe, North Africa and the Canary Isles. (Josef Krauthäuser collection)

ORION AIRWAYS   Great Britain

Having no connections with an earlier British charter airline of the same name which had existed from 1956 to 1960, this ORION AIRWAYS was set up in 1980 by tour operator Horizon Travel.

Services were operated from its base at East Midlands Airport and from other points in the English industrial cities such as Liverpool, Birmingham, Leeds, Newcastle, and in addition from Glasgow, Edinburgh, Cardiff and Gatwick.

Boeing 737s were the ideal aircraft to operate profitably from smaller airports. Holidaymakers were carried on behalf of Horizon Holidays and Broadway Holidays to Italy, Spain, Portugal, North Africa, Greece and to the Canary Isles. On 28th March 1980 the first flight took place, using a leased 737 from East Midlands to Pisa. As the number of destinations increased, so the fleet also grew, and in 1983 over a million passengers were flown for the first time, and alongside the Boeing 737-200s in 1985

came Boeing 737-300s, the first of this new model to be used in Europe. In order to meet growing passenger demand, especially during the summer, ORION AIRWAYS also leased in Airbus A300s, while during the winter aircraft were leased out.

A consolidation of businesses

in the British inclusive tour market led in 1988 to a takeover of Horizon by Thomson Travel. Thomson already had BRITANNIA AIRWAYS, the largest British charter company, as its in-house airline, and logically ORION AIRWAYS was merged into the larger operator in mid 1989.

Airbus A300B4 G-BMZK came to ORION AIRWAYS via LUFTHANSA. After the merger with BRITANNIA AIRWAYS it passed into the ownership of IBERIA. (Josef Krauthäuser collection)

149

To celebrate the 200th anniversary of the founding of the United Sates of America, this ONA Douglas DC-8 N1776 was painted in a special colour scheme. The registration is significant in reflecting the year of foundation of the USA. (Josef Krauthäuser collection)

OVERSEAS NATIONAL AIRWAYS – ONA USA

ONA was a charter company which carried freight as well as passengers. In June 1950 it was set up in New York, starting operations from what was then Idlewild Airport (now Kennedy) with five Douglas DC-7s. Services were principally troop transport charters, or carrying families for visits to US military personnel stationed in Europe. For special freight tasks, a DC-7F was also available.

In 1964 the company voluntarily went into bankruptcy and ceased all operations in order to effect a re-organisation. This was successfully completed by October 1965 and new financial backers found, so that flights could be resumed. ONA was granted an unrestricted licence in 1966 for flights to the Caribbean, Europe and to India. Again it was with a Douglas-built aircraft, this time the DC-8, that ONA resumed operations. During 1968 the first of a total of 11 Lockheed L-188 Electra freighters

arrived. These were used in the Caribbean and within the USA, while the DC-8s found use on the transatlantic routes. IT-Charters, freight work and again, military contracts took the aircraft to London, Paris, Brussels, Amsterdam, Frankfurt and Zurich.

The fleet of Lockheed Electras was retired relatively quickly, when in 1967 the first Douglas DC-9 arrived as a replacement. After the licence was extended to include Hawaii, ONA received two combi DC-10s, one each in April and June 1973. However, both were damaged beyond repair in accidents and had to be replaced by other DC-10s. During the mid-1970s a planned merger with ALASKA INTERNATIONAL failed to materialise. It had been hoped that this would lead to a better market position. As a result of financial difficulties and the tightening business opportunities in the charter market ONA – OVERSEAS NATIONAL AIRWAYS ceased flying in October 1978

and went into bankruptcy. Several former employees of ONA had set up UNITED AIR CARRIERS in 1977, and from the beginning of 1979 this was renamed as OVERSEAS NATIONAL AIRWAYS, but had only the name in common. In turn, after the collapse of NATIONAL AIRLINES, the name was changed again in 1983 to NATIONAL AIRLINES after the rights to use the name had been bought from PAN AM. Again this was no more than a re-use of the name and this company too went into bankruptcy in 1985.

OZARK AIRLINES DC-9-31 N987Z was built in 1968 and came to OZARK in March 1974 after service with NORTHEAST AIRLINES and DELTA AIR LINES. (Manfred Winter)

OZARK AIR LINES   USA

In September 1943 four business-men from Springfield, Missouri set up OZARK AIR LINES and thus complied with the wishes of the US transport minister that smaller towns and cities should have air links with larger centres of population. On 10th January 1945 a regular service was begun between Springfield, St Louis and Kansas City. Single-engined Beech 17 Staggerwings were used, being replaced over time with twin-engined Cessna Bobcats. In this way OZARK AIR LINES proved that it had the will and the financial ability to maintain an air service. At that time, this was a prerequisite for the granting of a licence by the CAB. As this was in prospect only for 1947, operations were ceased for the time being in November 1945. A competitor for the sought-after CAB licence was PARKS AIR LINES, to whom a licence was granted, but because of financial difficulties had to defer the start of operations. It was quickly decided

that OZARK AIR LINES would take over its competitor PARKS AIR LINES including its staff and several DC-3s. This action placed the airline in the position of being able to operate its renewed flight on 26th September 1950 from St Louis to Chicago and thus be back in business again. By 1955 15 DC-3s were in service to over 25 destinations and the company was growing. Modern turboprops, Fairchild F.27s, were brought into service from January 1960; these were faster and larger than the DC-3s. To further increase available capacity, several Convair 240s were also acquired in 1961.

During 1964 a spectacular fleet exchange took place with MOHAWK 1964, when OZARK AIR LINES took on 14 Martin 4-0-4s and in turn gave up six Convair 240s. This led to a unification of the fleet and to a significant increase in seating capacity. 1966 was also a significant year for fleet renewal. The first Douglas DC-9-10 was

introduced and new Fairchild FH-227s replaced the older F-27s and Martin 4-0-4s.

New destinations for the jets were Denver, Indianapolis, Louisville, Nashville. Washington, New York, Miami, Tampa and Orlando. OZARK flew its last FH227 service in October 1978, after which only DC-9s and from 1984 MD-82s were used. The local rival in St Louis was for many years TWA, which flew directly in competition on several routes. In 1985 TWA gained a new management team with Carl Icahn at the head, and he had had his eye on OZARK AIR LINES. A hostile takeover bid was launched in February 1986, with TWA offering over $224 million and this led to a merger which was approved by the government in August 1986. OZARK AIR LINES brought 4,000 employees, 50 aircraft and an extensive route network into TWA. The last flight under the OZARK name was carried out on 27th October 1986.

Douglas DC-9-81 N924PS was named 'The Smile of Burbank' in November 1984 by PACIFIC SOUTHWEST AIRLINES – PSA when it was delivered from the manufacturers. It continued to fly with US AIR after the merger. Note the 'smile' painted on the nose. (Josef Krauthäuser collection)

PACIFIC SOUTHWEST AIRLINES – PSA USA

This airline was set up in 1945 in San Diego by Friedkin Aeronautics as their own airline. Using a single leased DC-3, PSA began services in May 1949 from San Diego to Los Angeles and a year later also to San Francisco and Oakland. The potential on these routes was so good that PSA bought more DC-3s. In 1955 the DC-3s were supplemented with two DC-4s which replaced the DC-3s on the San Francisco route. Since PSA operated only in California, ticket prices were regulated not by the national authority, the CAB, but by the state of California. They were about 20% under the prices of the national companies and naturally that attracted a lot of passengers. In November 1959 a brand new aircraft came into service. The Lockheed L-188 Electra, a four-engined turboprop, took over the several times daily services from San Diego to Los Angeles and San Diego-San Francisco. The airline's first jet, the Boeing 727,

was introduced in June 1965.

PSA was however not only active in the airline business, but also had a well-known flight school, especially for 727 and DC-9 training, to which its own pilots were sent. Further PSA activities were in the hotel business, broadcasting and television and in aircraft leasing. Boeing 737s were introduced in September 1968, and the first widebody, the Lockheed L-1011 TriStar in July 1974. After the deregulation of air transport the first route outside California was added, from Oakland to Reno, Nevada. Further routes along the Pacific coast were also opened, with destinations in Mexico being served with MD-80s and BAe 146s. The modern and quiet BAe 146 were used especially at airports which had particularly strong prohibitions concerning noise. Principal amongst these was the airport at Orange County, today known as the John Wayne International Airport. In the course

of the hectic airline merger scene of the 1980s, PSA suffered a similar fate to that of its main California competitor AIR CAL, which was absorbed by AMERICAN.

The US AIR Group bought PSA on 29th May 1987. With the merger and the integration of PSA into US AIR from 9th April 1988 the 'Smiliners' of PSA ('smiles' had been painted onto the noses of the aircraft) disappeared forever.

This DC-8 of PACIFIC EAST AIR is seen here stored after the bankruptcy, and awaiting further employment. (Josef Krauthäuser collection)

PACIFIC EAST AIR   USA

Hawaii is a classic holiday destination for mainland Americans, and it is therefore hardly surprising that over the years there have been more and more airlines coming along to provide services to this destination, mostly from Los Angeles or San Francisco.

Former WESTERN AIRLINES employees set up PACIFIC EAST AIR in 1982 and began services on 14th June of that year using a Douglas DC-8-61 from Los Angeles to Hawaii. The price for a one-way ticket on this route was only $99, which passengers naturally found very attractive. The airline was also quickly able to offer services from Chicago to Los Angeles and from San Francisco to Honolulu. In order to fill the aircraft, combination tickets were allowed, which had not been the case until that time. DC-10s and more DC-8s were leased from different companies from time to time, in order to be able to meet the demand, and

during 1983 over 230,000 passengers were carried. A further route from New York to Hawaii was introduced in time for the 1983/84 winter season, and for 1984 the situation with bookings looked positive, and yet the airline suffered from unfavourable reports and got into financial difficulties.

The authorities often had grounds to take action against the company, as it was too often overbooked and it took a long time to pay refunds for tickets, or even failed to make these payments at all and the travellers were offered no alternative. In anticipation of the closure of the airline and the withdrawal of its operating licence by the authorities, the company declared insolvency on 9th May 1984 and took refuge under the protection of Chapter 11. From this date there was no flying activity. As a reorganisation was not found to be possible, owing to the debts of $10 million, a lawyer was

successful in petitioning to have the company liquidated in August 1984.

Boeing 737-200 C-GUPW in mixed colour scheme with the final PWA colours and new CANADIAN titling. (Josef Krauthäuser collection)

PACIFIC WESTERN   Canada

On 1st July 1945 CENTRAL BRITISH COLUMBIA AIRWAYS was set up by Russ Baker in Fort St James, initially flying for the forestry administration. Junkers W34s and Noorduyn Norsemans were used on various tasks and fire-fighting operations. In order to be able to maintain these contracts during the following years, more aircraft were acquired by CBCA, which also expanded its operations to include mining support flights and planned on a large industrial project in Kitimat. From 1950, modern aircraft in the form of the DHC-2 Beaver were added and two smaller competitors were swallowed up. On 30th May 1953 a new name, PACIFIC WESTERN AIRLINES, was introduced, when the airline bought three more companies which already operated from Vancouver along the Pacific coast to the north. The company had no qualms about setting its plans into action and a route from Calgary via Edmonton, Regina, and Saskatoon to Winnepeg was

pushed through, though this initially entailed the dumping of tickets at low prices to see off a competitor. This airline, QUEEN CHARLOTTE AIRLINE merged in 1954 with PWA, thus increasing the total of aircraft and the routes.

As PWA itself had no contracts in connection with the construction of the DEW-Line, Russ Baker seized the chance in 1955 of buying ASSOCIATED AIRWAYS, which at that time had DEW contracts but no longer had a licence. At the beginning of 1986, PWA was using 85 aircraft to serve 112 points in the west and north of Canada. DC-3s, DC-6s and Curtiss C-46s were the larger types in use, all of the others being single-engined bush flying types. Several routes were taken over from CPAL and thus services were expanded as far as Yellow-knife. Russ Baker died in 1958 and the management of PWA passed into new hands. A changeover to turboprop types was not allowed by the transport

ministry and so the airline continued with its old pistons.

A long fostered plan to operate an Air Bus service between Edmonton and Calgary was able to be fulfilled in 1963 with three daily DC-4 flights each way. Now PWA was a 'real' airline and plans were made to withdraw from the bush-flying operations. In 1964 PWA was the first regional company to organise charter flights to the Cayman Islands using a DC-6 and then with further DC-6s and DC-7s, there was a good transitional period until the arrival of the first Boeing 707 in 1967. These were also brought into use on services to Europe, where London and Frankfurt were served. PWA was able to secure only 6% of the charter business from Canada however, with the Boeing 707s also serving Honoluiu, Mexico and the Caribbean. More Lockheed C-130 Hercules were needed from 1970; the first had been received in 1967 in order to fulfil a long-

PACIFIC WESTERN also used several Lockheed Hercules for freight work, including this example C-FPWN. (Christofer Witt collection)

term contract for the modernisation of the DEW-Line. Over the years the Hercules took part in many relief flights in Angola, Bangladesh, Ethiopia and the Sudan on behalf of the United Nations.

In 1970 a Vancouver-Victoria-Seattle route marked PWA's first venture into the USA, and more important routes in the west were taken over from the unpopular AIR CANADA. During 1972 with the delivery of the first Boeing 737 came a change, with older propeller-driven types including the DC-3 and DC-4 being retired, but with two Lockheed L-188 Electras being taken on for freight. The Victoria-Vancouver Shuttle was served with Convair 580s. On 1st August 1974 the Province of Alberta bought PWA for barely Canadian $39 million and moved its headquarters to Calgary. During 1977 TRANSAIR took over 72% of the shares and there were difficult discussions with the central government and AIR CANADA concerning the

reduction of the state carrier's monopoly by the granting of new route licences. In 1980 PWA was able to fly to Toronto and in the same year acquired a 24% holding in AIR ONTARIO. During 1983 Boeing 767s were introduced, allowing the airline to compete directly with AIR

CANADA. The climax of this war of strength came however with the takeover on 1st February 1987 of CP AIR by the nominally smaller PWA and the merger of the two companies from the beginning of 1988, to operate in the future as CANADIAN AIRLINES INTERNATIONAL.

While the Hercules above still wears the 1960s colour scheme, this Boeing 737-200 already has the more modern livery. (Josef Krauthäuser collection)

The striking, bright red colour scheme of PALAIR MACEDONIAN's aircraft might have been chosen on safety grounds, as it operated principally from the airport at Skopje under visual flight conditions. Fokker 100 F-DGGB leaves Munich in December 1993 on such a flight. (Albert Kuhbandner)

PALAIR MACEDONIAN   Macedonia

When the Yugoslavian airline JAT – YUGOSLAV AIRLINES was obliged to cease operations as a result of a United Nations resolution in 1991, PALAIR MACEDONIAN was founded in that same year in the Yugoslavian province of Macedonia.

Using a Tupolev Tu-154 the most important routes to Western Europe were maintained. The Tu-154 was supplemented with a Fokker 28 and Fokker 100, which were used on routes within Yugoslavia, to Turkey and to Greece. These services were important, since because of the war in Bosnia, road and rail routes in Croatia and Herzegovina were blocked. In spite of a failing infrastructure at the airport at Skopje, traffic there increased enormously, but operations also became more and more dangerous, leading to the crash of a PALAIR MACEDONIAN Fokker 100 on 5th March 1993. PALAIR MACEDONIAN leased two more Fokker 100s in October 1993, which likewise were used on services to Western Europe. Services to New York and Sydney were also considered, using a DC-10-30, but this idea was abandoned on cost considerations. An entry into the planned scheduled market did not reach fruition, as in September 1996 PALAIR MACEDONIAN ceased operations, after UN sanctions against Yugoslavia were eased and JAT was able to fly again. An airline which had owed its existence to political considerations was no longer needed and its financial basis was withdrawn. The aircraft were returned to their respective lessors.

A Boeing 747 lifts off from Frankfurt Airport in 1987 towards an uncertain future. PAN AM was already facing financial difficulties by this time and was selling off routes and aircraft. (Josef Krauthäuser)

PAN AMERICAN WORLD AIRWAYS USA

PAN AMERICAN AIRWAYS Inc was formed on 14th March 1927 in New York as a joint-stock company, by a group of investors led by Peter Paul von Bauer, J K Montgomery, Richard Bevier and G G Mason. They were in the race for the postal route from Key West to Havana, with another investor group led by Juan T Trippe, who had set up the AVIATION CORPORATION OF THE AMERICAS on 25th June 1927. Also in the running was a third group, with Richard Hoyt, who had set up SOUTHEASTERN AIR LINES on 1st July 1927. Under dubious circumstances it was Trippe who initially managed to get the postal contract, but additionally a co-operation was struck between all three interested groups, who came out in favour of the PAN AMERICAN AIRWAYS name for their joint venture. The first flight took place on 19th October 1927 using a rented flying boat. Under the leadership of its President, Trippe, the company received

massive political support from the outset and because of that financial support also. For many years PAN AMERICAN AIRWAYS was an element of power in the background of the United States in seeing through its plans. As well as many moves which were proved to be pioneering in nature, there were also some negative aspects in their dealings with competition and especially in their acquisitions or partnerships with other airlines. Thus it was with NYRBA, taken over in 1930, with the founding of PAN AMERICAN GRACE and the taking of shareholdings in several national airlines such as AERONAVAS DE MEXICO, PANAIR DO BRASIL, CUBANA, WEST INDIAN AIRWAYS, and SCADTA. Flights from the US west coast via Hawaii, Midway and Guam to Manila with Sikorsky S.42, Martin 130 and Boeing 314 flying boats were both historically significant and relevant to the future development of air transport.

These services, begun in 1935, were extended to Hong Kong in 1938 and from 1940 New Zealand was served via Hawaii. Alongside the flying boats however, a large number of Douglas DC-3s came into service with PAN AMERICAN and its associated companies. During the war PAN AMERICAN took over the formerly German-influenced companies in South America. The company was also actively engaged in logistical support for the war and flew many transport aircraft. PAN AMERICAN personnel ferried DC-3/C-47s for the Allied forces via Brazil and North Africa to Europe. After the war, over 90 DC-4s came into the PAN AMERICAN fleet, which had now changed into a land-based operation. Transatlantic services were set up as early as 1946 with Lockheed L-049 Constellations, followed by luxurious Boeing 377 Stratocruisers. During 1949 AOA – AMERICAN OVERSEAS AIRLINES was taken over with their routes to

157

Boeing 727-21 N329PA was delivered in 1966 and used in Europe and on the internal German services; it passed on to AVIANCA in 1975 as HK-1804. (Josef Krauthäuser collection)

Scandinavia and Germany, including their internal services to and from Berlin. From Berlin further european routes were also set up. PAN AM, as the company was also now known, had a world-spanning service in place by 1951. DC-6s and DC-7s came at the beginning of the 1950s until in late 1958 they began to be replaced by the new Boeing 707s on long-range routes. It was PAN AM which in 1955 ordered 20 of these jets and 25 Douglas DC-8s, thus opening the door to a 'jet boom', with many airlines placing orders for the new technology. PAN AM was the first airline in the world to fly the Boeing 707, and likewise later the 747 in commercial service. The latter was introduced on the prestigious New York-London run on 22nd January 1970, and thus ushered in a new era for civil aviation, mass transport. Again, PAN AM was the first to operate non-stop from Los Angeles to Tokyo, this time on 25th April 1976 using a Boeing 747SP.

However, PAN AM was active not only in air transport but had hotel interests and other shareholdings such as a 25% share of NATIONAL AIRLINES. For Caribbean and internal European routes PAN AM received Boeing 727s from 1965, replacing DC-6s and DC-7s also to Berlin, an important hub for PAN AM. By purchasing NATIONAL AIRLINES outright in 1979 PAN AM gained an internal US network which it had previously lacked. After deregulation PAN AM lost its previous position of strength on international services. Immediately after the merger with NATIONAL, financial problems set in. PAN AM sold its own headquarters building, some routes and rationalised its fleet. At the beginning of 1980 Lockheed L-1011 TriStars were introduced on the less well patronised long-range routes. The DC-10s taken over from NATIONAL were the first to be sold, with the Boeing 747SPs and the L-1011s likewise disposed of until 1986. These were replaced

from 1984 by new Airbus A300s and A310s from 1986. These were leased, cheaper to operate and more profitable than the first generation widebodies. Despite all these economy measures, which also affected the staff, PAN AM was not able to escape from its loss-making situation. After the fall of the Berlin Wall, the German routes were sold off to LUFTHANSA and on 8th January 1991 PAN AM sought the bankruptcy protection of Chapter 11. On 11th July 1991 PAN AM sold all its European routes and the PAN AM Shuttle to DELTA AIR LINES. Only the profitable Caribbean routes remained, but these could not support the mounting debts. After only a few months PAN AM had to give up flying on 4th. December 1991 and file for bankruptcy. The rights to use the PAN AM name were sold on by the liquidator, and have since passed on through more than one further incarnation.

Boeing 707 D-ALAL was acquired from AMERICAN AIRLINES on 4th November1970 but was used for only a small number of flights by PANINTERNATIONAL. (Christofer Witt)

PANINTERNATIONAL   Germany

Set up in 1969 as GERMANIA Fluganlage GmbH, the company was obliged to change its name to PANAIR even before services began, as a result of legal pressure from GERMANAIR in case the companies might be confused. In the absence of its own charter licence, operations were started on 5th February 1969 using an SE 210 Caravelle of TRANS-UNION. When the first BAC 1-11-500 was delivered from the manufacturer on 13th June 1969, the necessary operating permits were granted and the summer season business got off to a good start. As was common practice at that time, the aircraft were acquired and financed by investment bonds which had tax advantages. From 1st January 1970 PANAIR changed its name again to avoid possible confusion which might be to the detriment of PAN AMERICAN, who demanded the change, to PANINTERNATIONAL. Immediately before the 1970

summer season the company received two more BAC 1-11-500s, and the operational base was moved from Düsseldorf to Munich, the location also of the company's headquarters. Aircraft maintenance was carried out in Dublin. In August 1970 PANINTERNATIONAL planned to enter the long-distance tour market and bought two Boeing 707s from AMERICAN AIRLINES. These were ferried to London in December and readied for service. The planned delivery in January to Düsseldorf caused problems, since the aircraft had no permits to fly into Germany; these were not forthcoming until March. During this three-month waiting period, aircraft from other companies had to be sub-chartered to operate the long-range services on behalf of PAN-INTERNATIONAL, a situation which meant that costs were doubled since the inactive aircraft were also costing money. On 12th March 1971 a further BAC

1-11-500 arrived, but there was not sufficient capacity for the contracted charters and yet again other companies had to be called upon to operate sub-charters. The losses mounted and after the unfortunate emergency landing by a BAC 1-11-500 on 6th September 1971 on the autobahn near Hamburg, the airline was the subject of much discussion. Tour operators withdrew contracts, and the Boeing 707s, which had not been paid for, were returned to AMERICAN in October. The BAC 1-11s were grounded and several thousand holidaymakers were stranded at their resorts, when PANINTERNATIONAL was obliged to cease flying on 6th October 1971. At the beginning of 1972 PANINTERNATIONAL was granted a restricted licence but BAC took back the three remaining aircraft because of outstanding payments. Formal bankruptcy for PANINTERNATIO-NAL came in March 1972.

Up to 12 Douglas DC-3s were used by the Southern division of PBA, including N32PB seen about to touch down at Miami. (Josef Krauthäuser collection)

PBA – PROVINCETOWN-BOSTON AIRLINE USA

What can be seen as a precursor of today's regional or commuter airlines was PROVINCETOWN-BOSTON AIRLINE, or simply PBA, founded in the state capital of Massachusetts in 1949 by John C Van Arsdale. Since 1946 he had been proprietor of CAPE COD FLYING SERVICE and operated a flying school. Provincetown to Boston, a five hour car journey, but only half an hour by aircraft, was the staple route of the airline which began its first schedule on the route with a Cessna Bobcat on 30th November 1949. By 1953 several Lockheed Electras were being used on the route and the airline was looking for ways to keep the aircraft employed outside of the busy summer season. This led in 1957 to the establishment of a co-operation with NAPLES AIRLINES of Naples, Florida. Using PBA aircraft, a scheduled service was operated to Miami from November through to April. During 1959 PBA took over the financially stricken firm.

NAPLES AIRLINES & PROVINCE-TOWN-BOSTON AIRLINE as the company became known, expanded particularly in Florida, opening new routes. Larger aircraft – Douglas DC-3s – were acquired in February 1968, and alongside these operated some Piper Aztecs which were used to maintain route licences outside the high season. As further routes in Massachusetts were also opened, two Martin 4-0-4s were added to the fleet in 1975 and 1976. By 1980 the sizeable fleet included 12 DC-3s, 4 Martin 4-0-4s and a number of smaller Cessnas and Pipers. On 30th April 1980 John C Van Arsdale passed over the company to his two sons, who were happier to take risks and thus expanded strongly both in the North and in Florida. Embraer Bandeirantes came into service from 1980 in Florida and when the airline succeeded in driving the larger AIR FLORIDA out of the regional market, some of their scheduled routes were also taken

over. An interline agreement was concluded with DELTA AIR LINES, and later the airline moved closer to EASTERN and joined their computer reservations system. In Summer 1982 the Island Shuttle from Boston to Martha's Vineyard was begun and larger NAMC YS-11 took over on the route to New York-La Guardia. During 1983 PBA was converted into a joint stock company, and during 1984 AIR DOLPHIN, MARCO ISLAND AIRWAYS, AIR VERMONT and TRANS EAST INTERNATIONAL were all taken over in order to strengthen the airline. Because of technical and administrative shortcomings, the FAA ordered PBA to suspend operations in November 1984. Permission was given to restart at the beginning of December, but the crash of a Bandeirante on 6th December 1984 saw PBA criticised again.

In 1986 PEOPLEXPRESS took over the majority of the shares in PBA in order to strengthen its own position in Florida.

Ex-LUFTHANSA Boeing 737-100 D-ABEU in full PEOPLEXPRESS livery but with its new American registration N414PE temporarily covered over, begins its delivery flight to the USA. (Manfred Winter)

PEOPLEXPRESS   USA

The history of PEOPLEXPRESS and its founder Donald C Burr illustrates well the upswing and fall of the whole industry at the time and gives an insight into the roles of the various players. After a rapidly rising career on Wall Street, Burr had at the age of 30 become President of the National Aviation Corporation, from where he was wooed by Frank Lorenzo for his TEXAS INTERNATIONAL AIR. He embraced the Deregulation Act of 1978 and set up his own company on 7th April 1980. Two former TIA managers joined him in the venture. His unorthodox management style led to short-term success: the provision of plenty of capital and absolute rock-bottom prices for the flights. Freddie Laker's 'Skytrain' was one of the models on which his system was based. Burr looked to the greater New York area and the densely populated areas of the US east coast for his activities and made his first hub at a terminal at Newark which was otherwise fit for

demolition. On 24th October 1980 Burr received his CAB licence for internal flights and at a stroke his new company, PEOPLEXPRESS ordered 17 Boeing 737-100s which were being retired from the LUFTHANSA fleet. With plenty of former airline employees looking for work, there was no difficulty in building up the staff numbers quickly, though a condition was that there would be no unions allowed. Every employee became a shareholder and had the title 'manager'. On 30th April 1981 services were begun from Newark to Columbus, Buffalo and Norfolk. As more aircraft came on line, PEOPLEXPRESS expanded. While the passengers seemed to be accepting Newark and PEOPLEXPRESS, the outbreak of the US air traffic controllers' strike had catastrophic consequences, when they were all sacked. It was complete chaos and the FAA cut 50% of flight frequencies. By using unusual routings, some of the bottlenecks could be avoided,

and it was possible to maintain some sort of service. Instead of Miami the airline flew to Sarasota, lowered the ticket price to $59 and the masses streamed in, even to Sarasota. After all, the sun shone there as well, and that was what the people wanted. Competition came from NEW YORK AIR, which had also moved out to Newark. In order to finance further growth, a new share issue was made in August 1982 and these shares were quickly taken up. There were tough competitive battles between EASTERN, NEW YORK AIR and PEOPLEXPRESS at Washington, to which all three flew, but where PEOPLEXPRESS offered the best price.

In 1983 came a decisive change as far as international flights were concerned. With the collapse of LAKER AIRWAYS on 5th February 1983 there was no longer a cheap-fare operator on the transatlantic routes. On 23rd May 1983 PEOPLEXPRESS sold its first tickets for $149 one way,

For transatlantic services to London-Gatwick and Brussels Boeing 747s came into service. N604PE is seen here pushing back at Gatwick. (Manfred Winter)

and began services three days later from Newark to London. For the next two months all flights were sold out within 24 hours. Boeing 747s were used for this new venture. Internally, the route network was built up to the west and with the addition of Houston moved into Lorenzo's home market. By 1984 the route network spanned the whole of the USA from east to west: a ticket from Newark to Los Angeles or San Francis cost $119. Some 70 aircraft made up the steadily growing fleet in 1985. In Florida in the meantime, nine destinations had been added and with the purchases of FRONTIER AIRLINES in 1985 and a year later PBA – PROVINCETOWN-BOSTON AIRLINES expansion continued. BRITT AIRWAYS was likewise taken over and Burr's acquisitive appetite seemed insatiable. Even though the practice of job-rotation amongst the staff often led to mistakes and bad decisions, things continued to progress and

many people flew where they might previously have taken the bus. In spite of this, losses were made for the first time in 1986 and FRONTIER went into bankruptcy. Thus rival Frank Lorenzo, who had acquired EASTERN AIRLINES in the

meantime, came onto the scene.

In a huge buy-out TIA acquired the whole of PEOPLEXPRESS on 15th September 1986, and merged the airline with CONTINENTAL AIRLINES and NEW YORK AIR from 1st February 1987.

Out in the wilderness in Nevada! Several PEOPLEXPRESS Boeing 737s were surplus to requirements after the merger with CONTINENTAL and parked up at Las Vegas. In the foreground is N417PE, also an ex LUFTHANSA aircraft (Manfred Winter)

Fokker F.28 N290N taking off from Fort Lauderdale on another of its daily services to Charlotte. With over 40 F.28s PIEDMONT was the largest user of the type in the USA. (Josef Krautháuser collection)

PIEDMONT AIRLINES   USA

Based in Winston-Salem, North Carolina, PIEDMONT AIRLINES INC was founded on 1st January 1948 by Piedmont Aviation, which in turn had been active since 1940 as an aircraft handling and service company. The first scheduled service, naturally using the Douglas DC-3 which was the staple aircraft at this time, was from Wilmington to Cincinnati. On this route many intermediate stops were made. The build-up of the route network was continued and larger Martin 4-0-4s were introduced. From 1958 PIEDMONT received its first turboprops in the form of the Fairchild F.27 , which took over the duties of the DC-3s and the Martin 4-0-4s.

Later aircraft in the fleet were the Japanese-built NAMC YS-11 and the Fairchild FH-227, a more modern turboprop for the regional routes. In 1967 came the first Boeing 727 jets, followed by the Boeing 737 in 1967. During the following years the 737 became

the workhorse at PIEDMONT and no less than 65 Boeing 737-200s were in PIEDMONT service in 1985. When the Fokker F.28 was acquired for less busy routes in place of the YS-11s and the FH 227s also retired, the PIEDMONT fleet consisted only of jets. After deregulation PIEDMONT broke free from its regional origins and widened its route network extensively. Charlotte in South Carolina was the central hub with 150 departures each day, but other hubs were at Baltimore and Dayton. Some 60 destinations were served until 1983 when the route network was further expanded by the takeover of HENSON AIRLINES, an established regional carrier. A year later JETSTREAM INTERNATIONAL AIRLINES became another takeover candidate. From the mid 1980s PIEDMONT also flew international services to Canada, Nassau in the Bahamas and London, using Boeing 767s. In 1966 huge orders

were placed for the new Boeing 737-300 in order to further modernise the fleet. A year later US AIR bought the substantially larger PIEDMONT AIRLINES and the airlines were merged as US AIR by the beginning of August 1989.

Boeing 727-214 N409BN was leased by PRIDE AIR from 1st June to 13th November 1985. It had been with FRONTIER and BRANIFF, and went on to serve with ARROW AIR and the new BRANIFF amongst others. It is now in Canada as C-GOKF with Kelowna. (Josef Krauthäuser collection)

PRIDE AIR   USA

In 1984 a group of former CONTINENTAL employees, having lost their jobs, set up their own airline, PRIDE AIR, using their own and outside capital. The American aviation authorities viewed their plans positively and quickly granted a licence for the planned US internal scheduled services. The original intention to operate from a hub at Kansas City could not be realised, as there were problems with TWA, who already had their base there, and so the airline chose instead to fly from New Orleans. Using three Boeing 727s, operations began from 1st August 1985 to destinations including Los Angeles, Sacramento, Miami, Fort Lauderdale, Orlando, San Diego, San Jose, Tampa and West Palm Beach.

However, the services which had begun so enthusiastically failed to reach the expectations of the owners and creditors, as the demand for flights with PRIDE AIR was much less than anticipated.

When the search for further bank credit or a new investor failed in November 1985, the end came quickly for the company after only three months. Flying operations were suspended from 15th November 1985 and the trip to the bankruptcy lawyers followed on 2nd December 1985. The short history of this company again demonstrates how difficult it is, even with a highly motivated team, to sustain the start-up period of an unknown airline and gain sufficient market share, without extensive capital resources.

164

PRINAIR Convair 580 N5599J on approach to St Maarten. The CV 580s came into service with the company from 1980 and were used principally on group charter work. (Martin Bach collection)

PRINAIR

Puerto Rico/USA

PONCE AIR, founded on 4th July 1964 and named after the town of that name in the south of the island Of Puerto Rico, grew to be one of the largest regional airlines in the Caribbean. From Ponce, the airline at first served the capital San Juan an an on-demand basis using four-seat aircraft. In 1966 the company received a de Havilland Heron, moved its base and company headquarters to the international airport at San Juan and renamed itself as PUERTO RICO INTERNATIONAL AIRLINES, which in practice was usually shortened to PRINAIR.

Using the de Havilland Heron, a small feederliner with two crew and carrying up to 17 passengers the San Juan-Ponce route was operated on a scheduled basis. Mayaguez and the neighbouring islands of St Croix and St Thomas were soon added as destinations. During 1967 and 1968 further Herons joined the growing fleet. These and all future aircraft of the type were converted with

Lycoming engines and were ideal aircraft for PRINAIR. The route network to neighbouring islands was further expanded to include St Maarten, St Kitts and Nevis and routes to the Dominican Republic. PRINAIR's success was down to providing high frequency flights between its major destinations San Juan-St Thomas, San Juan-Mayaguez and San Juan-St Croix, sometimes at only twenty minute intervals. There was also the advantage that a Boeing 707 or Douglas DC-8 coming from the USA, could not land on the smaller islands, and all passengers for the American Virgin Islands needed to transfer via San Juan. At peak times up to 28 Herons were in use, making up to 130 flights a day. Passenger boardings increased correspondingly, with over 900,000 carried in the last year of service. From 1980 four Convair 580s were employed on the routes to Santo Domingo or Port-

au-Prince and to the larger airports. These were also used regularly for charter groups from San Juan to Punta Cana. In 1982 some of the ageing Herons were retired, and replaced by a new type, the CASA C.212 Aviocar, a 26-passenger turboprop, which could also be converted for freight work. Options were also held for the larger CASA type, the CN-235 with delivery intended from 1986. In PRINAIR underwent a change of ownership. The new owner was the Caribbean Basin Investment Corporation, a firm with diverse interests. It was therefore unusual that this flourishing company declared bankruptcy in 1985 and surprisingly ceased operations.

Leased McDonnell Douglas MD-83 EI-CEK flew with PRIVATE JET for several months in 1991 and then again from November 1992 until March 1993. (Björn Kannengiesser)

PRIVATE JET   USA

PRIVATE JET EXPEDITIONS was set up as a travel club in 1989 and began operations with a luxuriously appointed Boeing 727 to exotic charter destinations. As early as 1991, though, PRIVATE JET was disposed of to Apple Vacations, who in turn brought its Spanish partner OASIS into the picture.

Taking over several MD-83s from the OASIS fleet, the airline expanded strongly and entered the scheduled service business. From 1993 the airline flew from Chicago and Atlanta to Miami, until 1994 when the name was changed to NATIONAL for these services. In October 1994 these schedules were abandoned because of poor demand and on 11th October 1994 Chapter 11 bankruptcy protection was granted. The whole company was sold to NAL Holdings, but the new owners failed to take over the important contracts of the former owners for the long term. so that PRIVATE JET was left without work for the current season. By renting out aircraft the company was able to keep its head above water for a short time, but at the beginning of 1995 it was obliged to declare bankruptcy and finally ceased operations on 28th March 1995.

QUEBECAIR Boeing 737-200 C-GQBB was not in service for very long, as compared with the BAC 1-11 the type was not found to be so flexible in use. (Josef Krauthäuser collection)

QUEBECAIR   Canada

Several Quebec business people set up RIMOUSKI AIRLINES in 1947. Pierre Lapointe, a pilot, organised the setting up of services and bought from the old QUEBEC AIRWAYS/CPA the route licences to Mont Joli and Sept Iles. In 1953 RIMOUSKI AIRLINES merged with GULF AVIATION to form QUEBEC-AIR. Beech 18s, DHC-2 Beavers and DC-3s were all in use for the government in connection with the building of the DEW-Line and these contracts ensured the safe development of the airline for several years. Montreal was first introduced into the timetable from 1957. A year later three DC-3s were destroyed in a hangar fire; these were replaced with Fokker F.27s which proved a great success. Larger aircraft – leased Convair 540s – appeared on the major route from Montreal and Quebec during 1960-62 . Several other aviation companies were taken over between 1965 and 1969, MATANE AIR SERVICE and NORTHERN WINGS in 1965,

FECTEAU AIR SERVICE in 1968 and ROYALE AIR in 1969. In this year also the first of the BAC 1-11s arrived, and immediately put into use between Toronto and Montreal, at a time when AIR CANADA was strikebound. There were quarrels again with AIR CANADA over traffic rights, especially for the lucrative route between Montreal and Toronto where AIR CANADA had a monopoly. On behalf of SEJB-Société d' Energie de la Baie James QUEBECAIR operated five Convair 580s. In 1974 two Boeing 707s were bought for charter work and a Boeing 727 for planned services to New York. Charter destinations were Florida, the Caribbean, Europe and Hawaii. However in 1979 this charter activity was given up, and the 707s sold. New Boeing 737s entered service during the year and in 1981 scheduled service rights between Montreal and Toronto were finally granted. Disputes between the English-speaking management of

the company and the French-speaking separatist politicians brought mounting difficulties, especially after the separatists won the election in Quebec. A francophone management was installed and QUEBECAIR became something of a political status symbol. The F.27s and the BAC 1-11s left the fleet in 1981. In this time of recession the company was making losses and the government took over a large part of the shares. Fleet policy was changed in 1983 with the disposal of several Boeing 737s and the re-introduction of the BAC 1-11. The charter market was also re-entered in 1984. Two Douglas DC-8-63s came into service, but when in 1985 the most important customer went into bankruptcy, the provincial government again sustained losses. These losses continued to increase and in July 1986 QUEBECAIR was taken over by CP AIR. The DC-8s and BAC 1-11s were sold off, with only 737s passing into the CP AIR fleet.

RENO AIR McDonnell Douglas MD-82 N822RA on approach to Las Vegas, the second important destination in Nevada. (Josef Krauthäuser)

RENO AIR   USA

RENO AIR, formed in 1990 with its headquarters in Reno, Nevada, received operating permission for flights from Reno to Los Angeles in April 1992 and began service on 1st July 1992 using a single McDonnell Douglas MD-82. The bargain ticket prices combined with full on-board service soon caught the attention of the public, who were attracted at the weekends to the casinos in the gaming resort of Reno.

With the delivery of further MD-80s the route network was quickly increased. By the end of 1992 seven aircraft were already in service; this total doubled by the end of 1993 and over 1.5 million passengers were carried during that year.

A second hub was established at San Jose, California, the nearest airport to Silicon Valley with its numerous high-tech companies. Here RENO AIR benefited from the partial withdrawal from the western USA by AMERICAN AIRLINES. A co-

operation agreement was set up with AMERICAN AIRLINES and RENO AIR became a partner in its frequent flyer programme. Unprofitable routes were dropped by the airline in favour of new routes. Thus services to Chicago, Seattle and Orange County all came about. The first of ten new McDonnell Douglas MD-90s was brought into service.

RENO AIR was a joint stock company, acquiring its capital by the issue of shares tradeable on the stock exchange. During 1995 new shares with a nominal value of US $25 million were issued. These served to finance the acquisition of the MD-90s and the further build-up of the route network. The whole fleet consisted of some 30 aircraft, all McDonnell Douglas types, which unified maintenance and kept costs to a minimum. The airline had its own maintenance facility at its base at Reno-Cannon and in co-operation with RENO AIR EXPRESS a feeder service using

BAe Jetstream 31s was built up from 1996.

In November 1998 AMERICAN AIRLINES bought RENO AIR for $124 million and from the Spring of 1999 began to integrate operations and the MD aircraft into its own fleet which already included more than 200 MD-80s.

This Boeing 727 N719RC still wears the former colours of NORTH CENTRAL AIRLINES with its bird emblem on the tailfin and the blue and turquoise cheatline. (Josef Krauthäuser collection)

REPUBLIC AIRLINES   USA

From the 1979 merger of NORTH CENTRAL AIRLINES and SOUTH-ERN AIRWAYS emerged a new airline known as REPUBLIC AIRLINES. It had its headquarters in Minneapolis-St Paul and upon formation became the USA's sixth largest airline. The operations and timetables of the two companies were quite complementary, with little duplication or overlap in their services. Many new routes were opened up and carried out using the world's largest DC-9 fleet, with more than a thousand flights a day. As well as the DC-9s many Boeing 727s were also in service. The signs pointed to further growth, and in 1980 REPUBLIC acquired HUGHES AIR WEST for $38.5 million. The whole fleet, also consisting of DC-9s and Boeing 727s was integrated, and again then route network was largely complementary. The new combined route network stretched throughout the USA and into Mexico, Canada and the Caribbean.

Further hubs were established and a shareholding taken in SIMMONS AIRLINES, which, operating as REPUBLINK was used to establish a regional feeder service. A new corporate identity was needed, to give the aircraft a unified appearance. This was put into action in 1984 but was never

fully completed before a merger of REPUBLIC with NORTHWEST AIRLINES took place in 1986. NORTHWEST AIRLINES bought REPUBLIC, which was then barely seven years old, for $884 million on 29th July 1986 and thus became one of the largest airlines in the USA and the world.

In the new corporate colours which were being introduced in the mid 1980s is Boeing 727 N275RC, seen on approach to Chicago. (Josef Krauthäuser)

A RICH INTERNATIONAL L-1011 TriStar at Fort Lauderdale. The Miami-based company had eleven TriStars and four DC-8s in use for services to Europe, the Caribbean and Mexico as well as internal US services until operations were ceased in September 1996. (Josef Krauthäuser)

RICH INTERNATIONAL   USA

This private company was founded in 1970 in Miami and began operations with freight flights to the neighbouring Caribbean using Curtiss C-46s and Beech 18s . Douglas DC-6s, again fitted out as freighters, were quickly added and initially the airline flourished. RICH increased its capacity still further with the purchase of a Douglas DC-8-62. During 1982 application was made for permission to operate passenger charters also. The first group charters were flown during the same year from Florida to the Caribbean, but it was from other departure points in the USA that flights were undertaken to Hawaii and to Europe. In June 1983 RICH INTERNATIONAL AIRWAYS went into Chapter 11 protection from bankruptcy, though continuing operations. However in the Spring of 1984 the Federal Aviation Administration found serious maintenance deficiencies at RICH INTERNATIONAL and withdrew the operating licence.

A financially strong partner was quickly found in the form of George Batchelor, who also had a leading role with ARROW AIR, and it was possible for the Chapter 11 protection to be lifted.

From then on the company expanded and in 1991 put its first Lockheed L-1011 TriStar into service for European routes, supplementing the DC-8s. Over the course of the next few years, ten aircraft of this type came into service with RICH INTERNATIONAL and from 1994 these flew in a new, more modern colour scheme. However, problems with the upkeep and maintenance of the aircraft recurred, leading to many complaints from the FAA and finally in September 1996 to the cessation of operations by RICH INTERNATIONAL. In order to avoid the impending bankruptcy, Chapter 11 protection was again resorted to in November 1996, while an attempt was made to sort out the problems. Agreement was

reached with the FAA for an operating permit for February 1997, but the Department of Transport was not in agreement and made the award of a new licence dependent on numerous further conditions. RICH INTER-NATIONAL succumbed to bankruptcy and was thus liquidated, with the aircraft and the whole inventory being put up for auction in July 1997.

Boeing 737-200 HR-SHI with the small titling which was altered after the merger with TAN, so that the whole colour scheme still remained attractive. (Josef Krauthäuser collection)

SAHSA   Honduras

With support from PAN AMERICAN WORLD AIRWAYS, which held 40% of the shares, Honduran businessmen founded SERVICIO AEREO DE HONDURAS SA (SAHSA) in 1944. Using a Douglas DC-3, services were begun in October of that year. SAHSA took over TACA DE HONDURAS in 1953 and in 1957 also acquired ANSAH, a smaller airline, which in future would operate regional services.

During 1970 PAN AMERICAN disposed of its shares in TAN-AIRLINES, and this holding was taken on by SAHSA. Alongside the DC-3, Convair 440s, Convair 580s, Curtiss C-46s and Lockheed L-188 Electras all came into service. TAN and SAHSA however operated independently until 1991. From this time on the two companies were combined and continued operations under the SAHSA name. SAHSA's first jet, a Boeing 727, was delivered in 1980, and from the mid 1980s Boeing 737s replaced some of the older propeller-driven types. Suddenly on 15th January 1994, services were terminated for economic reasons.

Lockheed Hercules N12ST in the colours of SATURN AIRWAYS. After the takeover the aircraft went on to fly with TIA/TRANSAMERICA.
(Josef Krauthäuser collection)

SATURN AIRWAYS   USA

In 1948 ALL AMERICAN AIRWAYS was founded in Oakland, California. At first freight charters and civil contracts were flown, as well as work for the US military. The well-proven C-46 Curtiss Commando was used, and over the course of the years the airline would use up to 23 examples of this transport. During 1960 SATURN AIRWAYS was adopted as a new name, and in the same year larger aircraft, Douglas DC-6s also came on the scene. These were supplemented at the end of 1963 by DC-7s. After SATURN AIRWAYS was granted its long-awaited certificate for transatlantic charter flights on 3rd March 1964, regular flights to Europe were undertaken.

AAXICO AIRLINES, based in Miami, Florida and also known under the name of AMERICAN AIR EXPORT AND IMPORT was taken over in November 1965. SATURN thus had a new base in Miami and moved its headquarters there. With the C-46s and DC-6s

ready for retirement SATURN AIRWAYS decided, with an eye to military charter work for MAC, to equip with Lockheed Hercules. Using up to 17 of these, both civil and military-configured versions, SATURN AIRWAYS became the largest civil user of the type. The first jet was introduced with the Douglas DC-8-61CF in 1967. As a combi version this offered the possibility of being used to enter the passenger charter business. More DC-8s were added in 1968 and 1969.

In 1972 SATURN AIRWAYS gained a contract for MAC along with nine Lockheed L-188 Electras. These were taken over in less than a week, along with the MAC contract, from UNIVERSAL AIRLINES which had become bankrupt. The aircraft, initially leased, were bought outright in 1974. SATURN AIRLINES itself was then bought very quickly. In 1976 the Trans-america Corporation made an offer for SATURN AIRWAYS, and

from 30th November 1976 SATURN AIRWAYS was merged with TRANS INTERNATIONAL AIRLINES-TIA. TIA was also owned by Transamerica Corporation. The merger brought into being the largest freight charter operation of its type in the world.

The SCANAIR colour scheme as seen on Douglas DC-10-10 SE-DHY resembles closely that of SAS. The 'SunJet' titling and the logo were taken over from TRANSAIR SWEDEN which was liquidated in 1981. (Josef Krauthäuser collection)

SCANAIR
Denmark, Norway, Sweden

SCANAIR A/S was originally a Danish company, which was set up on 30th June 1961. 45% of the capital came from the Scandinavian airline SAS, the rest coming from aircraft and car manufacturer SAAB and from a Norwegian and Swedish shipping company. Douglas DC-6s were leased from SAS for charter flights to Spain and North Africa. Some group charters were also offered to the USA. On 1st October 1965 a reorganisation of the company took place and the three participants in SAS – ABA, DDL and DNL – took over seventh shares of SCANAIR in the ratio 3:2:2. The headquarters and the operating base were moved to Stockholm, and from this time on all the aircraft were supplied by the SAS group. Four DC-8s from SAS and two Boeing 727s from TRANSAIR formed the basic fleet, but at peak periods the airline could call on further SAS aircraft. SCANAIR quickly grew to become a market leader and the

largest player in Norway and Sweden. The traditional holiday resorts for the Scandinavians are the Canary Islands and SCANAIR had contracts with over 20 tour operators. In addition, North Africa, mainland Spain, the USA, Canada and destinations such as Sri Lanka and Thailand were served with DC-8s. Charter series were conducted during the winter ski season to Austria, Switzerland and Germany. Airbus A300s were brought into service during the mid 1980s, but because of range restrictions had only a short career with SCANAIR. The whole fleet was turned over in 1989 to the Douglas DC-10, allowing non-stop service with full loads from Scandinavia to the Canary Islands. Each year about two million passengers flew on their holidays with SCANAIR, but even for SCANAIR increasing costs and competition became a mounting problem. A merger with the Danish airline CONAIR was thus decided upon, effective from

1st January 1994, resulting in the formation of a new charter airline PREMIAIR, which has since become closely aligned with the British tour operator Airtours.

SEABOARD WORLD AIRWAYS Douglas DC-8 N865F at Frankfurt am Main, where the company flew weekly scheduled services and numerous charters on behalf of MAC. (Manfred Winter)

SEABOARD WORLD AIRWAYS USA

SEABOARD & WESTERN AIRLINES was founded on 16th September 1946 as an independent freight company. Based in New York, the company began operations with a single Douglas DC-4 on 10th May 1947.

In the same year it became the first private freight airline to operate transatlantic freight charters to Europe. More DC-4s and from 1954, Lockheed Constellations also, strengthened the fleet. In 1955 SEABOARD & WESTERN received a licence to allow scheduled freight services from New York, Philadelphia and Baltimore to destinations in Europe. These freight services were begun in 1956 with Lockheed Constellations and routed to London, Paris, Frankfurt, Hamburg and Zurich. Numerous aircraft were leased out to other companies. Thus the Irish flag carrier AERLINTE EIREANN was able to open up a new route from Dublin to New York with SEABOARD &

WESTERN Super Constellations. From 1961 the Constellations were retired in favour of new Canadair CL-44s. This aircraft was specially constructed for freight work, with a swing-tail, which made loading a lot easier. During 1961 the company name was changed to SEABOARD WORLD AIRLINES, in order to better reflect the changed nature of its operating spectrum. Other airlines were invited to forward freight by taking 'blocked space agreements' on their scheduled services. BOAC, LUFTHANSA and SWISSAIR all participated in this arrangement, as at the time none of these airlines had suitable dedicated freighters of their own.

When the scope of its licence was broadened in 1966, even more European points were served on a scheduled basis. Amsterdam, Basle, Brussels, Geneva, Glasgow, Copenhagen, Milan, Munich, Nurenberg, Stuttgart, Rome and Stockholm

were brought on line, which necessitated more aircraft. DC-8 freighters were the first jet type, which supplemented the CL-44s from 1964. The airline's own freight services were augmented with work for the US military, especially during the time of the Vietnam conflict when aircraft were especially active on behalf of Military Airlift Command. In July 1974 SEABOARD became the first freight airline to use the Boeing 747. From time to time these were operated for other companies such as SAUDIA or VIASA. Tiger International, the holding company of FLYING TIGER LINE, took over the majority of the shares in SEABOARD WORLD AIRLINES from 1979 and merged the two specialist airfreight companies in 1980. The SEABOARD aircraft, which still consisted of DC-8s and Boeing 747s, were comfortably integrated into the FLYING TIGER LINE fleet.

Using Airbus A300B4 PK-JIA seen here at Perth, destinations in South-East Asia and Australia were served. by Sempati Air. (Uwe Gleisberg)

SEMPATI AIR

Indonesia

PT SEMPATI AIR TRANSPORT was founded by the PT Tri Usaha Bhakti company on 16th December 1968. Services began in March 1969 using a Douglas DC-3, providing staff transport for international oil companies.

Following the purchase of more DC-3s and Fokker F.27s regional flights were begun, to Singapore, Kuala Lumpur and Manila. Using a leased Boeing 707 from 1975 to 1978 scheduled services were also offered from Jakarta to Tokyo. However, this lucrative route was then handed over by the government to the national airline GARUDA. Between 1977 and 1984, the still robust DC-3 was phased out following the purchase of more Fokker F.27s and the fleet consisted of this single type only as a result of restrictive measures in place against private airline operators. By the end of the 1980s SEMPATI was in a position to acquire jet aircraft. New shareholders came on the scene,

several of whom were members of the clan which controlled the government, and this meant that the airline had the means to acquire Fokker 100s, Boeing 737s and Airbus A300B4s. As new services were started to points in South-East Asia and Australia, the name was changed in 1996 to SEMPATI AIR. However, the government withheld permission for planned flights to Europe. The business situation in Indonesia at the beginning of 1998 led to a massive reduction in the demand for air services. International services were suspended because of a lack of foreign exchange and the collapse of the Indonesian currency. The aircraft were either sold or returned to their leasing companies. Despite massive economies and other special measures, operations had to be ceased in June 1998, and the path taken to the bankruptcy lawyers.

Boeing 737-200 N671MA came from MARKAIR to SKYBUS and flew several charters to Las Vegas and sub-charters for other companies. (Josef Krauthäuser collection)

SKYBUS

USA

The existence of this airline turned out to be only brief and began in Autumn 1984, when the newly formed company contracted to operate from a secondary airport in the Atlanta area. The idea behind this was that passengers would move rapidly from their cars to boarding the aircraft, thus avoiding possible delays at the vast and busy Atlanta-Hartsfield international airport. The concept had already been tried at other major centres of population in the USA and had led to a redistribution of traffic. However, in the area of Fulton County Airport there were those who opposed the plan and after the appropriate authorities refused the airline's application, the owners of SKYBUS decided to acquire an existing licence for flying operations. They struck lucky quite quickly in January 1985 with Frontier Holdings and acquired FRONTIER HORIZON AIRLINES of Denver, Colorado.

Charter flights were begun from here to Las Vegas and there were future plans, but these were not fully developed. Several Boeing 727s were bought and the route network of the former airline given up without concrete plans for service to new destinations; initially SKYBUS involved itself in sub-charter work for other companies such as FLYING TIGER and NEW YORK AIR.

A projected route from Denver, where the company now had its base and headquarters, via Miami to London using DC-10-30s was not taken up. A new location for the airline was sought, as Denver was not really well suited to SKYBUS's plans. The fleet was a mixed bag consisting of Douglas DC-9s, Boeing 727s and Boeing 737s.

As it was not found possible to build up a new route network of its own without further capital investment which was not forthcoming, operations were ceased in November 1986.

Built as a Convair 480, this aircraft was upgraded as a Convair 600 and joined the SMB STAGE LINE fleet in 1988 as N94258. (Josef Krauthäuser collection)

SMB STAGE LINES   USA

SEDALIA-MARSHALL-BOONVILLE STAGE LINES Inc was established in 1930 in Des Moines, Iowa. Bus schedules and road transport services were the domain of the company for the next 30 years, but in 1950 the company was awarded a contract by the postal authorities for the transport of letters and packages. However, the company did not start its own flying service until September 1967, at first transferring postal work to air transport, but then quite quickly offering passenger service also. Beech 18s were the ideal aircraft for this type of work.

SMB-STAGE LINES quickly grew to become a large commuter company in Iowa, and across the state borders into the whole of the American Midwest, being active in freight transport as well as passenger work. Douglas DC-3s supplemented the Beech 18s.

In 1968 SMB STAGE LINES received a licence for scheduled services and built up the route network as far as Dallas, Texas. More than 30 Beech 18s or its improved development the Hamilton Westwind III, alongside several DC-3s were the pillars of the business. Following the deregulation of air transport in the USA, SMB STAGE LINES changed its business strategy and withdrew from passenger transport. The conversion to Convair 600 turboprops in 1978, with a larger capacity and a higher take-off weight, was a consequence of the sale of the company to a new owner in Dallas, Texas.

The arrival of the Convairs made it possible to phase out the DC-3s and older Beech 18s. The company then operated as a night freight specialist, airfreighting everything including post, but also ad hoc services for the automotive industry or specialist freight companies. The airline was no longer restricted to the Midwest, but active in the whole of the continental United States and Canada. A hub was accordingly set up at Dallas/Fort Worth and up to 16 Convairs were in service. During 1990 Landa Industries, the owner of SMB STAGE LINES, went into bankruptcy and the company was liquidated.

Boeing 707-300 60-SBS on approach to Frankfurt., which was familiar territory to the aircraft which had served for many years with LUFTHANSA as D-ABUL and then with CONDOR. In April 1984 the former 'Duisburg' was sold to Somalia. (Josef Krauthäuser)

SOMALI AIRLINES Somalia

SOMALI AIRLINES was set up in 1964 by order of the government and was established with technical aid and financial support from the Italian national airline ALITALIA; the Italians have traditionally had influence in Somalia. Initially it was envisaged that internal services would be operated and for these several small Piper aircraft were bought; these could also be used for pilot training purposes. Fokker F.27s later replaced these.

Using a leased Boeing 707 SOMALI AIRLINES began services in 1974 from Mogadishu via Cairo to London. From 1975 Frankfurt also came into the timetable and many passengers used the connection via Mogadishu to reach Johannesburg. SOMALI AIRLINES used a total of seven Boeing 707s, these being replaced from 1989 by the Airbus A310. Along with two Dornier Do 228s which were delivered, these were to represent a complete fleet

renewal. The political unrest in Somalia led SOMALI AIRLINES to a cessation of international services at the beginning of 1991 and the return of the A310s.

As the unrest developed into a state of civil war, operations were ceased completely at the turn of the year 1991/92, since which time there has been no return to normal government in the country.

Up to ten Lockheed L-100s, the civil version of the C-130 Hercules, were in service with SOUTHERN AIR TRANSPORT including N906SJ seen here on approach to Frankfurt. (Josef Krauthäuser)

SOUTHERN AIR TRANSPORT USA

This undertaking was set up in 1947 in Miami and began freight services in the same year using Curtiss C-46 Commandos. Throughout the year the main sphere of operations was the nearby Caribbean which provided heavy freight loads. There were regular services between San Juan in Puerto Rico and Miami, and the American Virgin Islands including St Thomas were also served on a scheduled basis.

Douglas DC-3s and DC-6s supplemented the Commandos, with the DC-6s being used particularly on new routes to Colombia and Venezuela. The civil version of the Lockheed C-130 Hercules freighter was brought into service from the mid 1960s and replaced the older propeller-driven types.

SOUTHERN AIR TRANSPORT was entrusted by the US government, or more exactly by the CIA, with special freight tasks during the Vietnam conflict; these contracts were very secret and

details only came to light some years after the event during research into the conduct of the war. SOUTHERN AIR TRANSPORT sometimes had more than two thirds of its fleet committed to Military Airlift Command and gave good service during the war.

The proven Boeing 707 came into service for such contracts and in 1973 the airline received a licence for worldwide freight operations on its own account. Scheduled freight services were quickly built up; these stretched across the Pacific as far as Hong Kong, and charter work was also expanded. In 1984 as a result of the worldwide recession, the scheduled services were dropped. The first Boeing 747Fs were brought into use during 1995 and the company headquarters was moved from Miami to Columbus, Ohio, where there seemed to be better opportunities for expansion.

From 1997 the company had to combat serious difficulties, with

the result that the four Douglas DC-8-71s were disposed of and five Lockheed L-100s were taken out of service. The possibilities of a sale, or of shareholdings, were explored with many other companies and were drawn out until 1998. However, as no agreement was reached with the interested parties, SOUTHERN AIR TRANSPORT ceased operations on 25th September 1998 and filed for bankruptcy because of its indebtedness.

SOUTHERN AIRWAYS DC-9-15 N96S was delivered in June 1968, passed to REPUBLIC on the merger and then on the further sale moved on to NORTHWEST where it remains in service. (Josef Krauthäuser collection)

SOUTHERN AIRWAYS USA

SOUTHERN AIRWAYS, based in Atlanta,Georgia was founded in July 1943. At first it was granted only a restricted licence and flew only some regional charter and freight operations. In 1949, using a DC-3, SOUTHERN opened its first scheduled service from Atlanta to Memphis. During 1951 a new route southwards to New Orleans and Mobile was added and it was not long before more than ten DC-3s were in use on an extensive network. Larger Martin 4-0-4s were well suited to be intensively used for the predominantly short routes. More southern states as far as Florida and to the north New York, Chicago and Washington DC were added to the timetables. By 1967 service extended to over 50 cities, with the concentrations in Tennessee, South Carolina and Alabama. Atlanta and Memphis formed the hubs of the route system. The first Douglas DC-9-10 was introduced in May 1967, expanding the existing fleet, and

marking the introduction of the airline's first jet type. A new route from Atlanta via Miami to the Cayman Islands and Grand Cayman endowed SOUTHERN AIRWAYS with international status in 1974. The larger DC-9-30 was brought into use for the first time on this service, and with further deliveries of this type the last of the DC-3 and Martin 4-0-4 propliners disappeared from the fleet. SOUTHERN grew so quickly that by 1976, 70 cities in 14 states were being served with an entirely DC-9 fleet of more than 40 aircraft. As well as these extensive scheduled services SOUTHERN was also active in the holiday charter market, with flights to Canada, the Bahamas, Mexico and the Caribbean. With deregulation of air transport in the USA, the airline became the object of interest from other, and larger, airlines. SOUTHERN AIRWAYS however adroitly aligned itself with NORTH CENTRAL AIRLINES and in 1979

the two airlines were merged to form the new REPUBLIC AIRLINES, itself later to be taken over by NORTHWEST.

Convair 990 Coronado EC-CNG spent twelve years in service with SPANTAX and with its 13 sister aircraft formed the long-term backbone of the company. (Josef Krauthäuser collection)

SPANTAX

Spain

SPANTAX SA TRANSPORTES AEREOS was founded on 6th October 1959 as SPANISH AIR TAXI. It was one of the first private charter companies and enabled a large number of passengers to be carried on their holidays under the Spanish sun during a number of years when other companies came and went. Using a Douglas DC-3, the airline was initially engaged in support of exploration for mineral resources in the Spanish Sahara and the Western Sahara. However in 1960 SPANTAX began flying inclusive tourists from England to Spain.

From 1962 SPANTAX gained a contract to fly a scheduled service to Mauritania. In the same year technical and logistical support was given in the setting up of AIR MAURITANIE. Douglas DC-6s (including one swing-tail freighter) and Douglas DC-7s came into use for flights in Western Europe, with Palma,Tenerife and Malaga as the most popular destinations. During 1967 SPANTAX received

its first Convair 990 Coronado; over the next few years SPANTAX was destined to become the world's largest operator of the type. There seemed to be a good potential for travel to the USA, and flights were first operated there in 1972, first with the Coronados, but then Douglas DC-8-63s, of which two were acquired in 1973. Germany, Switzerland and Scandinavia were all important markets for SPANTAX. As a result of various incidents, however, these became more dubious, and the company was called into question in the German press. In spite of this SPANTAX continued to fly charters and scheduled services especially between the Canary Islands and from here on to the African mainland; these services were carried out in association with IBERIA. A fleet modernisation was called for by the mid 1970s, by which time the company was struggling as a result of the oil crisis. DC-9s replaced the thirsty CV-990s,

though these were retained as back-up aircraft in Majorca for several years. Douglas DC-10-30s came into service from 1977 on the American routes and to Scandinavia. Several bouts of reorganisation failed to bring the desired success and when in 1982 a DC-10 suffered a take-off accident at Malaga, contracts were further reduced. In Spring of 1987 the Luxembourg-based Aviation Finance Group took a shareholding. New management and fresh capital provided a new image and it was possible to undertake a fleet modernisation with Boeing 737-300s and MD-83s replacing the older aircraft. The Spanish government had agreed to a deferment of payment of some 9 billion pesetas. SPANTAX was looking for a partner with which to merge, but this could not be achieved in time to avert collapse with newly accumulated debts of 135 million pesetas. SPANTAX declared bankruptcy on 31st March 1988.

SE 210 Caravelle 10B3 OY-STF c/n 257was delivered to STERLING on 12th February 1962 and it remained in their ownership for 20 years, though at times it was leased out to STERLING PHILIPPINAS and TEA – TRABAJOS AEREOS Y ENLACES. (Josef Krauthäuser collection)

STERLING AIRWAYS   Denmark

In May 1962 STERLING AIRWAYS A/S was set up by independent tour operator Tjaereborg in order to provide necessary capacity for flights to Spain. Tjaereborg was the largest operator of its type in Denmark and had been set up by a priest, Eilif Krogager. Using a DC-6 and operating from Copenhagen, services were begun on 7th July 1962 to Palma de Mallorca.

The fleet quickly grew to ten DC-6s, and Fokker F.27s and Lockheed L-188 Electras were also added, before the first Caravelle was introduced for the 1965 season. This type was to be the backbone of the fleet for many years and STERLING also used these aircraft to fly to the USA. The first Boeing 727 was taken on in November 1973, with Douglas DC-8s arriving from 1984. STERLING AIRWAYS also set up some branch operations, for instance STERLING PHILIPPINES and STERLING AIRWAYS NORWAY, but each of

these was given up. The airline also participated in 1989 in the setting up of AIR COLUMBUS in Portugal and held 34% of its shares.

As a successor to the Boeing 727, Boeing 757s were ordered and the first of these, initially leased, entered service for the 1989 season. With these aircraft, of which the airline's first owned example arrived in 1991, came a new colour scheme. At the beginning of the 1990s came worldwide recession, including in Scandinavia where STERLING was still the major player, and this had its consequences for flying operations. Passenger numbers dropped dramatically and the pressure from competitors continued to increase.

Despite reductions in the numbers of staff and aircraft STERLING was in danger and sought financially strong partners. After a combination of flying operations with the French airline EAS failed to come about,

STERLING AIRWAYS ceased operations on 22nd September 1993 after a life of years and went into bankruptcy.

Based at the Munich-Riem airport, SÜDAVIA used this leased Dornier Do 228 D-CMUC from March 1987 principally on the route from Munich to Saarbrücken. (Christopher Witt)

SÜDAVIA Germany

BN RENT-A-PLANE was founded in Munich in 1980, and used a Beech for charter flights. On 19th June 1984 the name of the company was changed to SÜDAVIA FLUGGESELLSCHAFT. From August 1984 SÜDAVIA took over the Saarbrücken on-request service and converted it into a fixed time schedule. A further service to Verona in Italy was added in 1985. Alongside these weekday operations, still using a Beech 90, regular charter flights were operated at weekends to Elba. SÜDAVIA received its licence as a scheduled operator on 25th July 1986 and began a service to Pisa. For this a Beech 200 was brought into use. At the end of March 1987 SÜDAVIA received its first Dornier Do 228, which was used for a new service to Strasbourg. As the Do 228 did not have a pressurised cabin and was thus not suited to services to Italy which entailed flight at higher altitudes, the first Beech 1900 was leased from November 1987.

A further Beech 1900 was added in February 1988 and SÜDAVIA endeavoured to work closely with DLT, in order to achieve better utilisation and to avoid fruitless competition. Because of the airline's rapid expansion there had already been some financial bottlenecks. In 1989 SÜDAVIA leased Embraer Brasilias from DLT for the Saarbrücken route and a takeover by DLT was in the offing.

However this takeover plan failed and a group of investors who also had shares in AIR EXEL, came into SÜDAVIA in mid 1989, taking 43.9% of the capital and also bringing in two Saab SF340s as new equipment. The leased Embraer Brasilias were returned to DLT.

On 2nd April 1990 the federal transport ministry revoked the company's licence, as its indebtedness had become too great. The two Saab SF340s and the remaining Beech 1900 were returned to their owners.

Thus ended a south German pioneering effort at regional air transport. The lucrative routes passed to companies who had a stronger financial base.

SULTAN AIR's first aircraft was an SE.210 Caravelle leased from TRANSWEDE. TC-JUN is seen here still in the colours of its owners, with SULTAN AIR titling added. (Wolfgang Grond)

SULTAN AIR
Turkey

SULTAN AIR was a joint Swedish and Turkish operation set up in 1988; TRANSWEDE and Turkish business interests held the shares. An SE 210 Caravelle 10B was the first aircraft, and services began in July 1989. In an expansion for the 1990 summer season, two Boeing 737-200s were leased. The development of the company was ill-starred, for the effects of the Gulf War and Turkish domestic problems led many holidaymakers to choose alternative destinations. Many Turks working abroad used the airline to return home, but the management had to look for other possibilities for employing the aircraft. At the beginning of 1991 SULTAN AIR stopped operations on financial grounds and set up a subsidiary company called VIP AIR. This new airline flew domestic schedules with the two remaining Boeing 737s. However, as this did not make money, a return was made to the charter business. VIP AIR was re-integrated into SULTAN AIR, which had made a new start

with Boeing 737-200s for the 1991 summer. In 1992 SULTAN passed entirely into Turkish hands. Two Boeing 737-300s and two Airbus A300B4s were acquired in 1992. Traffic to Turkey goes very quiet in winter. In Spring 1993 SULTAN AIR began what was to be its last

season with two each of Boeing 727s and 737-200s. As a result of safety shortcomings on aircraft, the Turkish authorities withdrew SULTAN AIR's licence. In November 1993 SULTAN AIR ceased operations and was liquidated.

Subsidiary company VIP AIR operated scheduled services only briefly, before it was reintegrated with SULTAN AIR. Boeing 737-200 TC-VAA was flown by SULTAN AIR as the large sticker on the fuselage makes clear. (Josef Krauthäuser collection)

Douglas DC-9-14 N1301T, the first production aircraft of the series built for TEXAS INTERNATIONAL AIRLINES in 1966, in SUNWORLD's old colour scheme. (Josef Krauthäuser collection)

SUNWORLD INTERNATIONAL AIRWAYS USA

Five former members of the BONANZA management team founded JETWEST INTERNATIONAL in 1981. The company began operations on 27th May 1983 using the Douglas DC-9, but under the new name of SUNWORLD.

At first the base was in Las Vegas, but after acute and lengthy disputes with AMERICA WEST AIRLINES, SUNWORLD moved out to Reno and established its hub there. Further expansion initially went to plan and new routes were instituted to Omaha, Portland, Seattle and further destinations in California, such as San Diego and Ontario, for which Boeing 737-300s were ordered, with the first delivery taking place in 1985.

In January 1988 all flights were cancelled for financial reasons; only the route from Las Vegas to Omaha was maintained and some charter work carried out.

It was perhaps no surprise that in April of that year SUNWORLD had to seek Chapter 11 bankruptcy protection. Takeover negotiations with the British PARAMOUNT AIRWAYS were unsuccessful and with debts of over $15 million SUNWORLD took the course of bankruptcy on 7th November 1988.

Douglas DC-9-31 N741L is seen here with the modified and more modern-looking colour scheme. (Josef Krauthäuser collection)

185

Douglas DC-8-32 EC-CCN of TAE at Frankfurt in 1974. This aircraft originally flew with TAI/UTA and AIR AFRIQUE, until passing to TAE in 1973. After the bankruptcy it was stored at Palma and later scrapped there. (Manfred Winter)

TAE   Spain

TRABAJOS AEREOS Y ENLACES SA – TAE was actually set up in 1957 but it was to be ten years until the company operated its first flight in April 1967. The reasons for this long delay were in licencing, finance and the simple organisation of an airline enterprise. The airline's owner was the shipping line CIA Naveira Aznar, which set up a base for TAE in Palma. As early as 1970 TAE ceased all flights as a result of financial difficulties. Three years later the time was apparently right for a fresh start to be made, and the company was reorganised and embarked on the new season's work. The French airline UTA gave start-up help in technical and operational matters, and by way of a leasing arrangement also made available the aircraft, two Douglas DC-8s. Charter and inclusive tour flights were undertaken, with Germany being the most important source of traffic. The oil crisis did not leave TAE unaffected, and efforts were made to secure other potential business. Thus in 1975 and 1976 two SE 210 Caravelles were acquired especially for flights to Germany. When in 1975 AIR SPAIN ceased operations, TAE leased a further Caravelle, in order to fill the gap. Also another DC-8 was ordered, but the anticipated ex DELTA AIR LINES aircraft failed to enter service with TAE. Declining interest in Spain as a holiday destination and increasing business recession at the beginning of the 1980s led to a drop in business for the company, and other newer companies were also providing increased competition in the market. Another factor in the airline's decline was the relatively old fleet of DC-8 and Caravelles which were expensive to operate and to maintain. At the beginning of 1982 TAE filed for bankruptcy and was dissolved.

The most modern and largest aircraft in the TALAIR fleet was the de Havilland Canada DHC-8. Here P2-GVB is ready for its next service. (Christofer Witt collection)

TALAIR   New Guinea

Founded in January 1952 as TERRITORY AIRLINES, activity was confined for the first few years to charter traffic only. In New Guinea, charter means the carrying by air of everything which would otherwise take forever to transport through trackless country. Departure points for these flights were Lae and Madang on the coast. Small Cessna and Beechcraft types were used.

In 1968 TERRITORY AIRLINES was given permission to operate scheduled services from Goroka in the interior. A large route network was quickly built up and extended, soon encompassing service to over 50 locations. By means of the takeover of SEPIK AIR CHARTERS in 1971 and MAC AIR CHARTER in April 1975 the network grew to over 100 destinations. MAC AIR operated mostly in the east, while TERRITORY was mostly active in the highlands. More than twenty aircraft were taken over and integrated into what was a very varied fleet, necessitated by the extreme variety of the contracts on hand and jobs which they were required to do. Britten Norman BN-2 Islanders and de Havilland Twin Otters formed the basis of the fleet over the following years, and were ideally suited to the region. During 1975 the name was changed to TAL-AIR TOURIST AIRLINES OF NIUGINI and the airline was the country's largest regional operator. This position was further strengthened in 1977, when a competitor, PANDA AIR, along with all its routes and aircraft was taken over. This also brought the total number of destinations in the network to over 150. Growing tourism in the region brought with it considerable opportunities for charter flights and a tour operator, Talco Territory, marketed special tours to Guinea.

With the delivery of the first de Havilland DHC-8 in December 1986 along with Embraer 120s, some of the most modern turboprop types with increased capacity were in service. In 1990 TALAIR, with its fleet of over 50 aircraft, dramatically reduced its services, as the operating costs were increasing sharply, as a result of the high inflation rate of the currency. On 25th May 1993 TALAIR suddenly halted all flights in New Guinea on cost grounds and moved most of its aircraft to its sister company in Australia, FLIGHT WEST AIRLINES.

TAT had a very varied fleet, even including the unusual VFW 614. D-BABF, which was leased from the manufacturer, is seen here on a domestic service at Carcassonne. (Manfred Winter)

TAT EUROPEAN AIRLINES France

Founded in 1968 as TOURAINE AIR TRANSPORT, TAT developed from an air taxi concern to become one of France's leading regional airlines. Various other airlines including AIR ALPES, AIR ALSACE, TAXI AVIA FRANCE, AIR PARIS and AIR LANGUEDOC were taken over in the course of the years, along with their varied aircraft and route networks. Thus the airline had Fokker F.27s, Fokker F.28s, Nord 262s, VFW 614s and even biz-jets, as well as smaller feeder aircraft in the fleet. The name was changed to TRANSPORT AERIEN TRANSREGIONAL, so that it would reflect the new aims. A standardisation of the fleet was put in motion at the end of the 1980s and ATR 42s and Fokker 100s were bought. During 1993 BRITISH AIRWAYS acquired a portion of the capital of the company and TAT was entrusted with new tasks. Thus many flights were conducted on behalf of BRITISH AIRWAYS and new european routes opened. Also, TAT aircraft were leased within the BA family, for instance some Fokker 100s went to DEUTSCHE BA. This all led to a further change of name to TAT-EUROPEAN AIRLINES. TAT also sold off its 20%holding in L'AEROPOSTALE, and set the three Boeing 737s thus released, to work on charter flights.

During 1996 BRITISH AIRWAYS exercised its option to acquire further shares in TAT and the airline became a wholly-owned subsidiary of BRITISH AIRWAYS. After BA bought the financially troubled AIR LIBERTÉ in 1996 these two French airlines were merged on 26th October 1997 and the historic TAT name disappeared from the timetables.

Boeing 737-300 G-TEAA was leased to the British TEA-UK and is seen here at Graz in Austria ready for its return flight to Manchester. (Andreas Witek)

TEA   Belgium/Europe

TEA-TRANSEUROPEAN AIRWAYS was founded in October 1970 and began operations with an ex EASTERN AIR LINES Boeing 720 at the beginning of June 1971. At first charter passengers were flown to holiday resorts in the Mediterranean and the Canary Islands. Ad hoc charters to destinations worldwide were also offered, as well as services on behalf of other airlines. Outside the tourist season, TEA aircraft could be seen in service with other companies, since TEA leased its aircraft out long-term in the winter. Year-round tourism as we know it now was not then established.

In 1973 TEA bought three Boeing 707s. A spectacular event in 1985 was the use of a 707 on a top secret air bridge operation from southern Sudan to Israel, for the evacuation of Ethiopian jews. The annual hadj pilgrim flights were flown regularly to Jeddah in Saudi Arabia. In order that the older 707s could be retired, an

initial Airbus A300B1 was taken on, and this was also used on the longer-range routes. For short and medium length services Boeing 737-200s were bought. The idea of a european charter airline was developed during the mid 1980s, and put into practice from 1988. At this time, TEA also adopted a new aircraft livery, which first appeared on the newly-delivered Boeing 737-300s, and was later adopted by the subsidiary companies which were founded over the following years.

These were TEA-FRANCE, TEA-BASEL, TEA-UK and TEA-ITALY. In order that there would be a unity within the fleet, the Boeing 737-300 was chosen as the standard type and shared out according to the needs of the companies in each country. Thus the aircraft were at the disposal of the charter group, to which NORWAY AIRLINES also belonged. The whole framework of this european group began to look unstable in 1991, when

because of Europe-wide recession and developments in the Gulf, there was an excess of charter capacity and a lack of the necessary turnover. Lacking its own financial reserves, the company broke up, with TEA-UK ceasing operations on 27th September 1991.

The bankruptcy of the parent company TEA-TRANSEUROPEAN AIRWAYS took place on 3rd November 1991. Only TEA-BASEL and TEA-ITALY were able to find new support and fresh capital with which to continue as independent airlines, after the bankruptcy of the former owner.

This Nord 262 N106TA was used by TAUSA on its routes to Dortmund and Paderborn and on the demise of the company was passed by the airport authority to the fire brigade for use as a fire and rescue training aid. (Josef Krauthäuser collection)

TEMPELHOF AIRWAYS USA

TEMPELHOF AIRWAYS USA (TAUSA) was set up in 1981 in Fort Lauderdale, Florida. In April 1982 Piper Navajo light twin aircraft were used to inaugurate air taxi services, and a year later ambulance flights, from Berlin-Tempelhof.

From January 1985 scheduled charter flights were begun between Berlin and Paderborn, on behalf of a computer company, and using a Nord 262. A second Nord 262 was used for scheduled services to Dortmund, and sometimes to Luxembourg, Augsburg and Braunschweig.

In 1988, with the advent of Saab 340s, modern regional types came into service on the schedules and Hamburg was given a new service.

Following the reunification of Germany, things became more difficult for TEMPELHOF AIRWAYS, since the aviation authority for Berlin and indeed the whole of the former German Democratic Republic was now located with the Federal Government in Bonn, and showed a preference for other companies to look after Berlin's needs. Additionally there were plans afoot to close the airport at Tempelhof.

At the end of October 1990 all flights on its own account from and to Berlin were ceased. The aircraft, sometimes with crews included, were rented out to RFG and SABENA. Reconstitution of the company and a planned change so that it would be covered by German rather than American law finally came to nothing, on financial grounds.

TEXAS INTERNATIONAL DC-9-30 N3505T with its Lone Star livery approaches to land at Las Vegas. The route network embraced the whole of the southern United States. (Manfred Winter)

TEXAS INTERNATIONAL AIRLINES USA

TRANS-TEXAS AIRWAYS – TTA was originally set up in November 1944 as AVIATION ENTERPRISES. Regional services were carried out and following a name change to TTA in July 1947, Douglas DC-3s were brought into service from San Antonio to Houston and Houston to Dallas. Other routes were served with smaller aircraft. During the following years further expansion took place and with support from the state TTA also built up services to places situated off the main routes. Convair 240s supplemented the DC-3s from 1962 to several destinations. The Convair 240 fleet would later be brought up to Convair 600 standard with Rolls-Royce turboprop engines. The first of the Douglas DC-9s arrived from October 1966, and were used on major routes. Houston to Mexico City was the most popular and profitable route, but many others were making losses. In 1968 the company was bought by Minnesota Enterprises and re-

named as TEXAS INTERNATIONAL. The next couple of years showed no improvement and the major shareholder, Chase Manhattan Bank sent Frank Lorenzo in as an independent expert. With losses of $6 million there was theoretically no alternative to bankruptcy, yet Lorenzo and his Jet Capital Corporation made a takeover bid and purchased 460,000 shares. Lorenzo was up against an offer from HUGHES AIRWEST and on 10th August 1972 took control of the company, as he held 59% of the shares. Lorenzo came in with a new broom and cut out the loss-making routes, in turn setting up new routes with modern aircraft. In 1977 the whole industry was surprised by his introduction of 'Peanuts-Fares'. TEXAS INTER-NATIONAL became the first low-fare airline in the USA and the system brought in passengers, so that the losses were soon transformed into profits. In 1978 it was thanks to these profits that Lorenzo was able to launch an

offer for NATIONAL AIRLINES. This failed however when PAN AM quickly took over NATIONAL. In 1980 TEXAS INTERNATIONAL received 20 DC-9s and wanted to use these to enter into the New York-Washington market, in competition there with EASTERN. In June 1980 the shares passed into the ownership of the new holding company Texas Air Corporation. President and CEO Lorenzo set up NEW YORK AIR a little later, and steadily built up shares in the loss-making CONTINENTAL AIRLINES which was eventually taken over on 25th November 1981. The routes were harmonised and a unified timetable set up. On 13th October 1982 the shareholders decided upon a merger of CONTINENTAL AIRLINES and TEXAS INTERNATIONAL. The new President was Frank Lorenzo and as part of the marketing strategy the CONTINENTAL AIRLINES name was taken on for the combined company.

In front of the hangar at Lethbridge stands Convair 640 C-FPWS waiting for its next service. The Convair came to TIME AIR with the takeover of GATEWAY AVIATION. (Josef Krauthäuser collection)

TIME AIR   Canada

This company was founded in 1963 by Walter R Ross, when with the purchase of a Piper Tri-Pacer he also took over the licence of the small LETHBRIDGE AIR SERVICES. Against the opposition of the large companies, AIR CANADA and PWA – PACIFIC WESTERN AIRLINES, he gained the permission of the state of Alberta for a service from Lethbridge to Calgary. This service began on 18th May 1966 with a Beech 18 and a daily service to Edmonton was also commenced. In 1969 the name was changed to TIME AIR and DHC-6 Twin Otters put into service on this route. Larger aircraft such as the Fairchild F.27 took over these routes in 1974, three Shorts SD-330s were bought in 1976 and the route network continued to be built up. In 1980 TIME AIR took over the Edmonton-based GATEWAY AVIATION with their Convair 640 and small route network. For the first time venturing out of the state

of Alberta, in 1981 a Medicine Hat-Lethbridge-Kelowna-Vancouver service was started, using a DHC-7 fresh from the factory. PWA took over 40% of the shares in TIME AIR in September 1983 and by working together in future ended the effort which TIME AIR had made over the years to come to the market. A further period of great expansion came between 1985 and 1987, when SOUTHERN FRONTIER, INTER CITY AIR SERVICE, NORTH CARIBOU FLYING SERVICE and NORCANAIR were all taken over. In 1987 PWA took over CP-CANADIAN PACIFIC AIR and the two were merged into CANADIAN. This also had consequences for TIME AIR, for a reorganisation after the death of the airline's founder in that year, meant that older aircraft were sold so that the fleet would consist only of DHC-8s and Fokker F.28s. At the end of 1990 CANADIAN bought the balance of the shares in TIME AIR and

integrated it into CANADIAN REGIONAL AIRLINES.

192

Boeing 737-200 SE-DLP was leased and used on TIME AIR SWEDEN services within Europe. (Josef Krauthäuser)

TIME AIR SWEDEN   Sweden

TIME AIR SWEDEN was set up as an air taxi undertaking in Karlstad. In March 1991 a Boeing 737-200 was taken over from TRANSWEDE and it was used for tourist charter flights to the usual resorts in the Mediterranean and the Canary Isles. As a result of the success achieved in the first few months, a second Boeing 737-300 was leased and frequencies increased.

Two Douglas DC-8-71s were also acquired, one however a pure freighter, which was used on behalf of AIR INDIA for freight flights between India and Europe. With the introduction of the passenger-configured DC-8-71 in March 1992 the 'TIME' part of the name was dropped and for marketing reasons the company called itself simply AIR SWEDEN. Further Boeing 737-200s and 300s were leased and an L-1011 TriStar joined the fleet. This was used in the high season from Stockholm to the Canary Isles. Later in 1992, increasing financial difficulties emerged as a result of a poor winter season and the company was obliged to return several aircraft to their leasing companies. The traditionally strong Scandinavian charter market was faltering as a result of mergers amongst the major tour operators, who were then establishing their own in-house airlines or placing business with allied companies. Because AIR SWEDEN could only count on a few passenger contracts for the summer 1993 season, operations were ceased in February 1993. The freight contracts were sold off, the aircraft returned to their owners or lessors and TIME AIR SWEDEN liquidated.

Boeing 707-323C G-WIND flew with TRADEWINDS AIRWAYS from 1978 to 1982 on their regular freight services to Africa, the USA and the Far East. (Josef Krauthäuser collection)

TRADEWINDS AIRWAYS Great Britain

BOBWOOD Ltd was founded in November 1968, in order to take over three Canadair CL-44s from the bankruptcy of TRANSGLOBE AIRWAYS. The latter airline had concluded a lease-purchase agreement for these aircraft with SEABOARD WORLD AIRLINES and SEABOARD had an interest in keeping these aircraft flying.

In the following January BOBWOOD changed its name to TRADEWINDS, but there were problems with the British air transport authorities over the issue of a licence, as TRADEWINDS was financed by United States capital and could not therefore be considered to be a British company. The crews, employed and paid by SEABOARD, helped out at TRANS MEDITERRANEAN AIRWAYS in the meantime. In April 1969 British investors acquired the majority of the share capital of £50,000 and following more bureaucratic delays, the CL-44s were finally able to take to the air

later in the year. At first government-sponsored flights were operated carrying relief goods to Nigeria, where the Biafra conflict was in progress.

After the full licence had been granted at the beginning of 1970, further CL-44s could be taken on in June and at the end of the year. Regular freight flights were operated to Africa, the Middle and Far East. Whilst these were flown from Gatwick, Stansted or Heath-row, TRADEWINDS operated a weekly service to Hong Kong from Maastricht in the Netherlands. The company was also quite actively engaged on work for the Ministry of Defence.

During 1977 TRADEWINDS AIRWAYS was taken over by the Lonrho Group and in the same year the first jet freighter was taken on, a Boeing 707. This was initially set to work on schedules to Chicago and Toronto. These schedules were now being flown from London-Gatwick, where a base was set up to coincide with

the arrival of the jets. Two more Boeing 707s were added to the fleet by 1979 and the company became Britain's largest pure-freight airline.

As well as the schedules, TRADEWINDS was however active worldwide with ad hoc and charter work, covering a very broad spectrum of freight tasks. When the Lonrho Group ran into financial difficulties in the mid 1980s, TRADEWINDS was taken over by HOMAC AVIATION, but business took an increasingly negative turn and one Boeing 707 was sold, with the others being temporarily leased out. On 28th September 1990 TRADEWINDS ceased operations.

TRANSAIR's first Boeing 737-200s came into service from May 1970. The aircraft had a striking yellow colour scheme, but notice that Fokker's version of yellow on the F.28 behind is somewhat different from Boeing's rendition as seen on this 737. (Christofer Witt collection)

TRANSAIR
Canada

Manitoba's best known airline after the Second World War was TRANSAIR, which until 1956 however was known as CENTRAL NORTHERN AIRWAYS – CNA. It was set up as CNA on 8th April 1947 by Milt Ashton and Roy Brown, who had already operated a small flying operation in the 1930s, but which they had sold to CPA in 1941. A scheduled service on the route from Winnipeg to Red Lake was begun in 1951. With a mixed fleet of Curtiss C-46s, Avro Ansons, Avro York, Lockheed L-12/14s, Bristol 170s and smaller Cessnas and Waco aircraft, many bush-flying contracts were under-taken. During 1955 CNA took over ARCTIC WINGS and they merged to form the new TRANSAIR. The company was awarded good long-term contracts in connection with the building of the DEW-line and as well as personnel involved in the building, freight was also carried using Douglas DC-4s. In 1957 routes from Winnipeg were taken over from CPA along with

the DC-3s which operated them. Churchill was an important base, as services running Winnipeg-Churchill-Ottawa-Montreal and Churchill-Resolute Bay were instituted. On 15th April 1963 TRANSAIR took over from TCA the Winnipeg-Calgary route with several intermediate stops. 1966 was an important year for all Canadian regionals, as the government changed their status and allowed them to operate as feeder carriers for the two majors AIR CANADA and CPA. Using the DC-6 and a newly delivered DC-7, TRANSAIR entered the international charter market in 1965. During 1967 TRANSAIR sold its bush-flying operations to HOOKER AIRLINES and NORTHLAND AIRWAYS and took advantage of a strike at AIR CANADA to take over lucrative direct flights for a period. DHC-6 Twin Otters and YS-11s were introduced in 1967 and 1968, the latter used to Yellowknife and from Winnipeg to Toronto. The further development

of the company was shaped by the merger with MIDWEST AIRLINES in November 1969; both continued to fly under their own names. In order that they should not be adversely affected by the reduction in size of the national carrier AIR CANADA, from 1970 regional carriers were allowed to operate routes into other provinces. Jets were deemed necessary for this and Boeing 737s were first used from May 1970. These were also suitable for use on charter flights to Florida, the Caribbean and Mexico. Further jets to join the fleet were Fokker F.28s in 1972 and Boeing 707s in 1973. PACIFIC WESTERN AIRLINES took 72% of the shares in TRANSAIR in 1977, after the airline had been making large losses as a result of the oil crisis and a cutback in charter work. In 1978 TRANSAIR gave up all flights east of Winnipeg and from 1st December 1979 transferred its licences and route rights to PWA.

SE-DDB is a Boeing 727-134 and was delivered to TRANSAIR on 2nd December 1967 directly from Boeing. The logo and 'Sunjet' titling was inherited later from SCANAIR. The aircraft was sold to the Philippines in 1981. (Josef Krauthäuser collection)

TRANSAIR SWEDEN　　　Sweden

NORDISK AEROTRANSPORT AB was founded in 1950 in order to carry newspapers from Stockholm. Curtiss C-46s were used and from 1953 passenger charter work was added to these freight tasks for the first time. The name was changed to TRANSAIR SWEDEN. DC-6s and later also DC-7s came into service for United Nations work in the Congo, with diverse aid and evacuation flights.

In co-operation with FRED OLSEN AIRTRANSPORT nightly freight flights were operated to Malmö, Copenhagen, Hamburg, Amsterdam and Paris on behalf of SAS. The first jet type in the fleet was the Boeing 727, delivered at the end of 1967, but the expenditure of finance was limiting the potential of the company. During 1968 TRANSAIR SWEDEN was taken over by the Svenska Handelsbank, so that the changeover to jet equipment could continue to be financed. Intensive co-operation with the SAS group came into play, with SAS taking a shareholding in TRANSAIR SWEDEN, and then taking it over completely and quickly in 1975.

At first still independent and with unaltered livery, the TRANSAIR 'Sunjets' flew sun-hungry holidaymakers to destinations in the Mediterranean and the Canary Isles. These flights were carried out on behalf of SAS subsidiary company SCANAIR.

The end for TRANSAIR came in 1981. The Boeing 727s were sold, independent operations brought to a close and the employees taken on by the SAS group.

TRANSAMERICA carried out scheduled flights to Europe and Hawaii using DC-10-30s or Boeing 747-200s. Here Boeing 747-200 N742TV is seen on its way to the runway at Amsterdam. (Manfred Winter)

TRANSAMERICA AIRLINES USA

In December 1948 LOS ANGELES AIR SERVICE was founded, operating a single Douglas DC-3 on charter flights. During 1959 and 1960 several Douglas DC-6A/Bs were taken on and these were used overwhelmingly on freight transport duties. In 1960 with the change of fleet, came a change of name and a move of company headquarters. TIA-TRANS INTER-NATIONAL AIRLINES was the new name given by the new owners of the airline, the Studebaker Corpo-ration, and the new base would be Oakland, California. Lockheed L-1049H Super Constellations were acquired, which allowed the airline to conclude long term charter contracts with the USAF's Military Air Transport Service. A Douglas DC-8 leased from the manufacturer was introduced in June 1962 and used for trans-Pacific charters. The next change came about in 1964, when the president of TIA took over the company completely from financially troubled Studebaker.

More DC-8-61s joined TIA, which was now also busy in the charter business, carrying holidaymakers to Hawaii, the southern states of the USA and the Caribbean. The San Francisco based Transamerica Corporation, a conglomerate with many interests, took over the airline in 1968. The first Douglas DC-10 arrived in April 1973. In 1976 a competitor, SATURN AIRWAYS was bought and their fleet of Lockheed L-100 Hercules, Lockheed L-188 Electra and Douglas DC-8s integrated, making TIA at the time, the world's largest charter operator. TIA was given a licence during 1979 for scheduled flights to Europe, but before commencing the first flights from New York to Shannon in Ireland TIA changed its name to TRANS-AMERICA AIRLINES. The prominent 'T' on the tailfin was well known from its use in connection with the films made by United Artists Studios, also a Transamerica Corporation firm. Amsterdam, Frankfurt and Paris

were also served regularly from 1984. Boeing 747s were used for these services, as were DC-10s. In the mid 1980s many airlines were caught out by the deep business recession and in order to try to stay in existence had to reduce capacity and make other sweeping economies. Thus TRANSAMERICA AIRLINES gave up routes to Europe and Hawaii and sold three DC-10s to FEDERAL EXPRESS. Other aircraft were leased out and a non-union company called TIA – TRANS INTERNATIONAL AIRLINES, set up with its base in Louisville, Kentucky. Here the non-union organised staff could be paid low rates and a DC-8 was operated, and thus the old name came to be re-born. Despite all efforts to reduce costs, the two companies continued to show losses and were put up for sale in 1986. The cessation of all services with effect from 30th September 1986 was logical, as no buyer had emerged for the afflicted airline.

SE 210 Caravelle 10R EC-CYI being readied at Frankfurt for another flight to Majorca. This aircraft was with TRANSEUROPA from 1976 and had previously been in service with LTU as D-ABAF. Likewise HISPANIA used it when it started up in1983. (Manfred Winter)

TRANSEUROPA   Spain

TRANSEUROPA-COMPANIA DE AVIACION SA was founded in July 1965. Initially using a single Douglas DC-7B, flight operations began in September 1965. Ad hoc charters, both with passengers and freight, were carried out from and to its base at Palma de Mallorca.

During 1969 TRANSEUROPA converted onto the SE210 Caravelle. Two of these medium-range jets now carried sunseeking passengers on their holidays from the west and north of Europe. Spain was then the leading holiday destination and the demand grew so that more Caravelles could be added to the fleet. Freight only was flown on behalf of IBERIA and aircraft were leased for this purpose. Two Caravelle 11R combi versions were configured for quick conversion. When IBERIA received its own DC-9-33Fs, the Caravelles went back to TRANSEUROPA. The Canary Isles were also served, often with

an intermediate refuelling stop. TRANSEUROPA also had charter rights to Morocco and Tunisia, with several destinations in these countries being served regularly, especially from Germany. From 1976 TRANSEUROPA had more than six Caravelle 10Rs at its disposal, forming a homogeneous fleet which were not too expensive to fuel and maintain. Falling demand as a result of widespread recession in many countries in Europe led to a reduction in the scale of operations during the early part of the 1980s. The Spanish government supported and gave subvention to TRANSEUROPA, though the continuation of the business seemed not to be sensible on cost grounds, as there was not the capital available for the necessary acquisition of more modern aircraft. Thus operations were ceased at the beginning of the 1982 summer season. AVIACO took over most of the assets and some staff.

Canadair CL-44-0 Guppy or 'Skymonster' N447T was leased from the manufacturer and in service with TAC from 1970. Following the merger the aircraft was painted in HEAVYLIFT colours. (Josef Krauthäuser collection)

TRANSMERIDIAN AIR CARGO Great Britain

On 5th October 1962 TRANS MERIDIAN FLYING SERVICES was registered. The founders were a group of pilots, and T D Keegan of KEEGAN AVIATION also had an interest. The latter also provided the Douglas DC-4/ C-54, with which operations were begun on 1st November 1962.

From its base at Liverpool ad hoc freight and passenger charters were undertaken. From July 1963 TRANS MERIDIAN leased another C-54. This was used on regular freight services between Dublin and Paris Le Bourget. The company was prepared to take on all sorts of work, and Ministry of Defence contracts also helped to keep the aircraft busy. At the beginning of 1965 the two C-54s were returned to their lessors and and a Douglas DC-7 was brought into service instead. 1966 brought a move of operations to London-Luton and the delivery of two more Douglas DC-7Cs, which were used predominantly on

services to Africa and the Middle East. TRANS MERIDIAN had taken over a long-term contract for the transport of cattle. TRANS MERIDIAN FLYING SERVICES was taken over at the end of 1967 by TRANS WORLD LEASING. T D Keegan, who owned this company, installed a new board and built up the company to become one of the first European pure freight operators.

The name was changed to TRANS MERIDIAN and the base moved again to Cambridge, with some of the DC-7s going out on long-term lease to other companies. With the introduction of the first Canadair CL-44 in 1968 a new headquarters was established, this time at London-Stansted. TRANSMERIDIAN operated a total of eight of these aircraft with their folding tails. In order to facilitate the carriage of oversize loads, the American company Conroy was contracted to convert a CL-44 with an enlarged fuselage. This modified

aircraft, known as the 'Skymonster' was leased to TRANSMERIDIAN from July 1970. In the same year there was also a further name change to TRANSMERIDIAN AIR CARGO. During 1974 two CL-44s went on lease to the Swiss company TRANSVALAIR, in which T D Keegan also had an interest, and another to LIMBURG AIRLINES in the Netherlands. In order to engage in business in the Far East, TRANSMERIDIAN was set up in Hong Kong in 1975 and operated regular services to Australia. Hong Kong quickly developed as a trade centre for goods of all sorts. In June 1977 the Trafalgar House Group bought 90% of the shares in TRANSMERIDIAN AIR CARGO and merged it with IAS CARGO AIRLINES from 15th August 1979 to form BRITISH CARGO AIRLINES which would later have its name changed into HEAVYLIFT CARGO AIRLINES.

199

TRANS OCEAN Boeing 727-200 N2818W was built for WESTERN AIRLINES and delivered in 1974. GULF AIR TRANSPORT bought it in 1985 and leased it to AIR MALTA until November 1988. (Gerhard Schütz)

TRANS OCEAN USA

At Acadiana Regional Airport, New Iberia in Louisiana in 1979 an airline called GULF AIR TRANSPORT was established. Principal operations were in support of oil exploration and production companies who were drilling in the Gulf of Mexico, but flights were also frequently undertaken on behalf of the state government of Louisiana.

At first a single Convair 440 was used, augmented from 1981 by a Lockheed L-188 Electra and further Convair 580 turboprops. The airline also operated charters into neighbouring Mexico and within the USA, including profitable weekend charter work in connection with sporting events. This was further expanded when the airline's first Boeing 727 was bought in 1984. A further Boeing 727 was also leased, but was in turn leased out to AIR MALTA. During 1986 came the first change of name to GULF AIR Inc, but charter flights to the Caribbean were withdrawn as there was a

problem with international flights. Because of the similarity of name with the Oman-based GULF AIR there were misunderstandings with flights to Europe and GULF AIR changed name again from 1st May 1989 to TRANS OCEAN. The overseas flights were very unprofitable, and then came the general business recession in the

USA at the end of the 1980s which led to fewer contracts and thus to increased losses. At the end of 1989 TRANS OCEAN entered Chapter 11 bankruptcy protection and tried to find new investors. Reduced operations were maintained, but terminated at the end of March 1990, when bankruptcy was declared.

Convair 580 N511GA served with GULF AIR from 1980 to 1988. (Josef Krauthäuser collection)

TRANSTAR MD-82 N9806F at Las Vegas. It was delivered to the airline on 12th December 1986 and flew with them until the suspension of operations, after which it moved on to serve with CONTINENTAL AIRLINES. (Manfred Winter)

TRANSTAR   USA

Lamar Muse, former President of SOUTHWEST AIRLINES set up his own airline in January 1980 called MUSE AIR. With aircraft equipped with comfortable leather seats and a first-class seating section, he entered into competition with SOUTHWEST AIRLINES, compared with whose ticket prices he was 20% cheaper.

In July 1981 the first DC-9 Super 80 began service between Houston and Dallas. The new airline came a cropper right at the outset, as the air traffic controllers strike took place shortly after its start of operations. These resulting start-up losses had not been allowed for and amounted to over $3 million. From 1982 further services to Las Vegas and New Orleans were introduced. A code-share agreement was concluded with AIR CAL thus offering connections to California. Business stabilised after the start-up losses and in only the second year, profits of $11 million were achieved. More expansion was

planned and the fleet of McDonnell Douglas MD-80s and DC-9s grew further. During 1984, founder Lamar Muse withdrew and passed over the company to his son, who set about further expansion and wanted to have up to 24 aircraft in service. The business crisis in the mid 1980s impeded these aims however and the airline again ran into a loss-making situation. It was intended to remedy this by providing a still better service with 2+2 seating and complimentary drinks, thus attracting more business travellers. On 25th June 1985 SOUTHWEST AIRLINES bought the ailing company and created a fresh image for the airline, along with the new name TRANSTAR. With a revised route system and destinations such as San Francisco and Miami, which were not served by SOUTHWEST AIRLINES, operations continued until 9th August 1987, when TRANSTAR ceased all operations as there was no long-term

prospect of emerging from its loss-making position.

SE.210 Caravelle 10B3 SE-DHA had already flown with STERLING AIRWAYS, FINNAIR and MINERVE, before it joined the TRANSWEDE fleet fin 1985. (Josef Krauthäuser collection)

TRANSWEDE   Sweden

This company was founded in 1985 as AEROCENTER TRAFIKFLYG AB. The first aircraft, which was used for charter work throughout Europe was the Fokker F.27. With the delivery of three SE 210 Caravelles in 1986 the company changed its name to TRANSWEDE and the aircraft were given a striking light blue and yellow colour scheme. In the following years the fleet was built up and MD-83s, MD-87s as well as Boeing 737-200s were acquired. The SE 210 Caravelles were either sold, or passed on to equip Turkish subsidiary SULTAN AIR. For regional scheduled services the Boeing 737s proved to be too large and uneconomic and so TRANSWEDE disposed of the Boeing 737s and instead ordered five Fokker 100s from the Dutch manufacturer. These were used on internal services and on some European routes.

The Norwegian airline BRAATHENS SAFE took a 50% share in TRANSWEDE's scheduled services in June 1996, whilst holiday traffic continued independently under the TRANSWEDE LEISURE banner, this part of the operation being renamed in 1997 as BLUE SCANDINAVIA, before being sold on again in 1998 to the UK charter airline BRITANNIA AIRWAYS as the nucleus for their Swedish operation. Early in 1998 BRAATHENS SAFE took over the company completely and retitled it as BRAATHENS SVERIGE.

Boeing 757 SE-DUL of TRANSWEDE LEISURE, which flew as BLUE SCANDINAVIA. This name was chosen for marketing reasons in order to set the airline apart after BRAATHENS SAFE had begun scheduled services. In 1998 BLUE SCANDINAVIA was acquired by BRITANNIA and transformed into BRITANNIA SWEDEN. (USP)

Boeing 747SP ZS-SPB leased from LUXAIR, ready to depart from Munich on its weekly service to Johannesburg. The flights were marketed by LUXAVIA as indicated by the titling on the forward fuselage. (Uwe Gleisberg)

TREK AIRWAYS
South Africa

Alongside SAA, the best known of South Africa's international airlines was TREK AIRWAYS, founded in August 1953. Even then it was an attractive idea to fly passengers from South Africa to Europe and back at especially favourable prices. This was achieved by means of the so-called Flycruises. Passengers made an overnight stop en route and flew on to their final destinations on the following day. As the aircraft in use at that time, Vickers Vikings, did not have the range for non-stop flights, a virtue was made of necessity. The Vikings were however quickly replaced with Douglas DC-4s and Lockheed L-749A Constellations and later by Lockheed L-1649 Super Constellations. These made the long-distance flights less exhausting for passengers.

During 1958, a subsidiary company PROTEA AIRWAYS was founded to operate charter flights in South Africa. TREK inaugurated the Johannesburg-Luxembourg route in 1964, and operating this route in co-operation with LUXAIR, attractive non-IATA tariffs were offered, quickly achieving a great popularity. Having arrived in Luxembourg from South Africa, connecting flights to destinations such as London and other european cities were provided for passengers by Luxair. During 1979 this service was turned over to operation by Boeing 707s, but the service had to be given up because of overflight embargos by some African countries against South African-registered aircraft.

After a long period of inactivity TREK re-appeared in the market after the ending of apartheid. Many internal services within South Africa were opened in 1991 by TREK subsidiary company FLITESTAR in competition with SAA-SOUTH AFRICAN AIRWAYS.

Working in co-operation with LUXAVIA, the international route to Europe was re-established in 1993, using LUXAIR/LUXAVIA's Boeing 747SP painted in the old TREK colours. FLITESTAR's operations in South Africa met with large losses, whilst the European route developed positively. No solution to this dilemma seemed immediately apparent, and thus on 11th April 1994, TREK AIRWAYS surprisingly ceased all operations and the airline was liquidated.

This Boeing 727-25 was originally delivered to EASTERN AIRLINES on 12th November 1964 as N8121N and was acquired by TRUMP SHUTTLE as N903TS in June 1989. It passed to US-AIR for continued shuttle operations when TRUMP was sold in 1992. (Josef Krauthäuser collection)

TRUMP SHUTTLE USA

On 30th April 1961 EASTERN AIR LINES used several Lockheed Constellations to set up a shuttle service between Boston, New York and Washington. Cheap, comfortable, and without the need to buy a ticket beforehand, the Air Shuttle met with great success. The Lockheed L-188 Electra succeeded the Constellation on this service and from the mid 1970s these too were replaced by Douglas DC-9s or Boeing 727s. The successful shuttle services attracted finance managers in 1988 when the ailing EASTERN AIR LINES was obliged to dispose of various of its activities in order to try to maintain liquidity. Thus in 1988 Donald Trump took over the shuttle with all its route licences and aircraft, after a bidding war with AMERICA WEST AIRLINES. Trump was well known, even notorious, in financial circles, having made his money in property dealing and obviously could afford the purchase. After

the takeover, 22 Boeing 727s were painted in a smart new livery and plied the routes to the accompaniment of the excessive publicity with which Trump was associated. He described the first flight as 'the small beginning of great plans for the world's best transport system'!

The Shuttle provided hourly connections in each direction from 7 am to 9 pm and was aimed at business people in a hurry. At weekends a two-hourly schedule was flown, and in order to provide other work for aircraft at weekends TRUMP AIRLINES was used as a charter carrier. Principally they were used to destinations such as Miami, Orlando or Tampa, which formed an ideal rotation. The system all worked while the economy was booming. By the end of the 1980s in the USA this was however no longer the case and passenger totals fell back dramatically. Trump's other business activities were also not producing enough

income to maintain his empire which had been built on credit. By 1990 he was therefore selling property and interests in various businesses in order to raise cash.

During 1992 a banking consortium took over the TRUMP SHUTTLE as a realisation of their security, formed a new operating company called SHUTTLE Inc and contracted US-AIR to take over the operation of the shuttles.

US-AIR took over the company on 1st April 1992 with a purchase option which could be exercised after five years and Donald Trump devoted his attention to other businesses.

Boeing 727-200 with the appropriate registration TC-TUR taxies for take-off from Düsseldorf in August 1988 with sun-seeking holidaymakers bound for Antalya. (Josef Krauthäuser collection)

TUR EUROPEAN AIRWAYS Turkey

The owner of TUR EUROPEAN AIRWAYS, set up in 1988, was the Kavalla group, one of the largest businesses in Turkey with various sales and service companies.

Using two Boeing 727-200s, both former LUFTHANSA Aircraft, charter operations were begun in April 1988. In the first year traffic consisted overwhelmingly of German tourists to Turkey and expatriate Turkish workers from and to their homeland.

The mounting tourist boom in Turkey made for a good start to business and in 1991 the fleet was for a short time augmented by a McDonnell Douglas MD-83, with another following in 1992. The routes were intensified to include Belgium, Great Britain, France, the Netherlands and other countries in northern Europe. In order to meet demand, further Boeing 727-200s were added to the fleet, one each in 1991 and 1992, as no more MD-83s were available in the marketplace. From its maintenance base and home airport at Istanbul, scheduled flights were also operated to Ankara, Izmir and several other Turkish domestic destinations; all of these routes were implemented quickly after licences had been granted.

The Gulf War and conflicts with the Kurds in Turkey had negative consequences for the tourist industry and led to a dramatic reduction in tourists from Western Europe. This brought major problems for TUR EUROPEAN AIRWAYS, and led to the sale of two Boeing 727s and the reduction of scheduled services. Finally in 1993 these were given up altogether and the airline concentrated on charter business. However many planned charter flights were unable to be carried out.

TUR EUROPEAN AIRWAYS suddenly ceased operations on financial grounds in 1994 and the airline was liquidated.

Boeing 727 N12305 was with TWA for many years, before it was leased to ULTRAIR for a year and a half. As if to emphasise the stylish first-class service, the aircraft wore an appropriately impressive colour scheme. (Björn Kannengiesser)

ULTRAIR   USA

Established in Houston, Texas ULTRAIR began life at the end of 1992 and began operations in January 1993 with five leased Boeing 727s. As so often, the model for the airline was the successful SOUTHWEST AIRLINES, though it was intended that the new airline would offer something fundamentally different in terms of quality and price. A route network to business centres in the east and west of the USA was quickly built up, as a 'business class service' was offered, with advertising targeting business travellers. The way that the aircraft were fitted out did not however correspond to their wishes and expectations, and so after only a few months the route network and number of flights had to be cut back.

After a brief and initially only transitory suspension of operations, accompanied by a change in management, the second episode of the ULTRAIR story began in November 1993.

With a more modest offering and now more attractive prices, a new start was made and new routes built up again. The airline concentrated especially on apparently strong routes in the east of the USA. Competition from established companies, particularly on the routes between New York and Florida, turned out to be exceedingly strong and funding from further investors which would be necessary to hold out against the pressure of competitors was not forthcoming. On 13th July 1994 ULTRAIR pulled out of the business and was liquidated.

MD-83 EI-BTY after take-off from Frankfurt for another flight to Rome shows off the attractive colour scheme of UNIFLY EXPRESS to particularly good advantage against the blue of the sky. (Josef Krauthäuser)

UNIFLY EXPRESS   Italy

This private charter company was founded in 1980 as UNIFLY and at first occupied itself with business flights. Overnight packages were also carried for an express parcel concern. In 1984 the company entered the passenger business with group charters, for which larger aircraft were needed; thus the first Fokker F.28 was acquired. A further F.28 followed in 1985 and co-operation was established with ALITALIA, whereby some routes were taken over from them, and others operated on their behalf. From 1988 there were also freight charters with post and newspapers, flown by DC-9s. UNIFLY EXPRESS emerged from UNIFLY in 1989. Three leased McDonnell Douglas MD-83s came into passenger service a year later and these colourfully painted aircraft were to be seen at many european airports. Early in 1990 UNIFLY took over the regional airline ALINORD with its route network and Fokker F.28 fleet. Thus routes

from airports in northern Italy were added. However during 1990 UNIFLY ran into financial problems. As a result of pressure from the lessors the company's MD-80s were temporarily grounded and then had to be returned to the leasing companies on account of outstanding payments. All passenger flights were suspended and only the freight contracts fulfilled. An attempt at re-organisation and the provision of fresh capital failed, so the company had no alternative to bankruptcy in May 1990.

Fokker F-28-100 I-TIAP flew with BRAATHENS SAFE and was taken over by UNIFLY EXPRESS in October 1986. ALINORD leased the aircraft from 1988 and with the purchase of this company it came back into the UNIFLY EXPRESS fleet. (Josef Krauthäuser)

Leased Douglas DC-10-30 N54629 served with UTA from 1973 and crashed on 19th September 1989, after a bomb exploded on board, over the Sahara. (Josef Krauthäuser collection)

UTA   France

By a merger on 1st October 1963 the two French scheduled service airlines TAI-TRANSPORTS AERIENS INTERCONTINENTAUX and UAT-UNION AEROMARITIME DE TRANSPORT became the new UTA-UNION DE TRANSPORTS AERIENS. The two precursor airlines were independent and operated a strong set of routes principally to the French overseas provinces and to France's former colonies. Douglas DC-6s, DC-7s and from 1960 DC-8s were the main equipment used. In 1965 UTA received its first jet for short and medium range routes in the form of an SE.210 Caravelle. The services to Africa from France and from New Caledonia to other points in the Pacific Ocean were served by this type, until more efficient DC-8-62s took over more and more routes. For many years the UTA fleet consisted only of DC-8s until in 1973 the first widebody, a Douglas DC-10 was delivered. The last DC-8s were taken out of service in 1984 and

replaced by larger Boeing 747s. UTA was also making a name for itself in other business activities, including the construction for Airbus Industries of several Super Guppy freighters for the transport by air of Airbus aircraft structures. It was also a leader in the conversion of DC-8s to use the far more efficient CFM56 engines. UTA also gave considerable support to other airlines, particularly in Africa, and had shareholdings in other companies including 99% in AEROMARITIME, its own charter company, over 70% in AIR AFRIQUE, 62% in AIR POLYNESIE, 14% in AIR INTER and modest holdings in AIR CALEDONIE, AIR MAURITANIE and AIR TCHAD.

The newest version of the Boeing 747, the 747-400 was introduced at the end of 1990, at a time when the company was battling against worldwide business difficulties. The relatively long routes to only a small number of destinations were

expensive to maintain and used by about a million passengers a year. Co-operation agreements were forged with AIR FRANCE, leading to AIR FRANCE taking over 70% of UTA's shares at the end of 1990. As a result UTA became a member of the newly created Groupe AIR FRANCE and there was a redistribution of routes, whereby the subsidiary charter company AEROMARITIME was also affected.

The takeover of the balance of the shares by AIR FRANCE late in 1991 heralded the end for the once profitable UTA. The airline was merged with the government-owned AIR FRANCE in 1992 and its fleet integrated, thus bringing to a conclusion the history of what had been a major private airline.

DC-9-32 N 909VJ on approach to land at Tampa. Until the temporary suspension of operations, the DC-9-32 formed the majority of the VALUJET fleet. (Josef Krauthäuser)

VALUJET

USA

VALUJET was set up in June 1993 with the aim of following the example of the hugely successful SOUTHWEST AIRLINES, and began operations only a few months later, on 26th October 1993 with service from Atlanta to Tampa. The concept of the 'no-frills' airline was popular with customers as it made the ticket prices very attractive.

With a fleet of DC-9-32s, the airline was flying to 20 destinations in the eastern USA after a year. As the market in used DC-9-32s was practically exhausted, MD-80s and DC-9-20s were also brought into use and the fleet grew to over 50 aircraft. 50 of the new MD-95s were ordered from McDonnell Douglas as launch customer, which is now in production and being marketed as the Boeing 717 following the Seattle giant's takeover of McDonnell Douglas. VALUJET's rapid expansion however also attracted the attention of the FAA, as there were obviously some

irregularities taking place. VALUJET was thus obliged to restrain its expansion in the following years.

Following the crash of a DC-9 on 11th May 1996, the company's licence was withdrawn, even though the reason for the regrettable accident had not at that time been established. Stimulated by sensational media reporting, the BIRGENAIR effect set in in the formerly aviation-friendly US media, and back-bench politicians in the House of Representatives, leading the FAA into a hectic bout of action. After a suspension of several months, VALUJET was allowed to re-start operations in September 1996, but with a smaller fleet and a restricted route network. VALUJET battled against its loss of image with the travelling public and found it difficult to combat these prejudices. Even though in the meantime the cause of the accident had been established and VALJUJET at last shown not

to have been at fault, the name was no longer marketable.

As a result it was decided to merge with AIR TRAN and to adopt the latter name for future operations. the merger took place from September 1997 and by the second quarter of 1998 the new (old) company was operating in the black.

As well as their McDonnell Douglas MD-83s and Boeing 727s VENUS AIRLINES used leased Boeing 757-200s. SX-BBY is seen here bringing holidaymakers back to Zurich from the Greek islands. (B I Hengi)

VENUS AIRLINES

Greece

At the end of 1992 the Greek Karabatis group set up an airline. Using leased McDonnell Douglas MD-83s, charter flights were begun in April 1993 to Scandinavia and West Germany. VENUS AIRLINES took on more MD-83s before the end of the season and used them to fly for tour operators in Austria and Switzerland. The aircraft were apparently leased only on a seasonal basis, and for 1994 the airline received MD-87s and Boeing 757s. These had longer range and were thus better suited for the Scandinavian flights. In the early years the company obviously suffered from organisational problems and were at the bottom of the league when it came to punctuality for holiday flights. However VENUS AIRLINES did serve many points on the smaller Greek islands which were not otherwise available by direct flights. Brussels and Luxembourg were added as new departure points and the airline also participated in the setting up of a new airline in Switzerland, EDELWEISS AIR. During the winter months of 1995/96 a much reduced service was operated and for the following summer season 1996 Boeing 727s were used alongside MD-80s.

However this was to be the last season, as more and more tour operators baled out and left VENUS AIRLINES with no basis on which to work. Operations were ceased at the end of 1996 and the aircraft returned to their lessors.

One of VIASA's Douglas DC-10-30s landing at Miami. The daily service between Caracas and Miami was one of the airline's most important routes. (Josef Krauthäuser)

VIASA   Venezuela

At the instigation of the Venezuelan government, on 21st November 1960 a new international airline VIASA – VENEZOLANA INTERNACIONAL DE AVIACION SA was founded. It was to take over the existing international routes of AVENSA and LAV-AEROPOSTAL. Both of these companies had shareholdings in VIASA; 55% and 45% respectively. From the outset a close co-operation was established with the Dutch airline KLM, who brought the new airline up to international standards and were responsible for the provision of the aircraft. Services to Europe were begun on 2nd April 1961 using Douglas DC-8 jets. The official start with the airline's own Convair 880s, which had been ordered by AVENSA, took place on 8th August 1961 with a service to New York. Combined services to Europe were operated with KLM, IBERIA and ALITALIA. When VIASA took delivery of its own DC-8s, it was able to take a greater share of the traffic on these routes. In 1971 the shares on these routes were re-assessed and all the partners re-equipped with Boeing 747s. However, VIASA was more flexible with the DC-10 and was able to ride out the first recession in 1984, though older DC-8s, CV 880s and the Boeing 747 were sold, leaving only the DC-10s for longer range routes. There was a reduction in the number of employees and a thinning out of the routes so that the airline was shrunk to a point where it operated only its most important routes. MD-80s were acquired for use on regional international services, such as those to the Caribbean and to the USA.

VIASA was once again having to fight against a mounting business crisis and there was a lack of black figures in the accounts. Thus everyone was happy when in the mid 1990s IBERIA took over 45% of the shares in the company as part of a change of strategy in relation to its commitments in South America; it was also similarly engaged in Argentina. A re-organisation meant that the only aircraft types remaining in the fleet were the Boeing 727-200 and DC-10-30 and these were decorated with the IBERIA livery. Despite all economy measures and large payments to compensate for the company's debts, in January 1997 bankruptcy came to VIASA with a complete cessation of operations, when IBERIA declined to make further payments.

Boeing 737-300 EC-FLG, just landed in Zurich, with the wonderfully abstract tailfin motif symbolising sun, sand, sea and green hills. (B I Hengi)

VIVA AIR
Spain

On 24th February 1988 VUELOS INTERNACIONALES DE VACACIONES – VIVA AIR was set up by two national airlines, IBERIA from Spain and LUFTHANSA from Germany.

Operations began on 15th April 1988 with a Boeing 737-300 making the inaugural flight from Nuremberg to Palma de Mallorca. Three Boeing 737s formed the equipment for the first season, with two more added for 1989. The two partners separated quite quickly and IBERIA took over all the shares in the company in 1992.

VIVA began scheduled services using Douglas DC-9s, which had been taken over from IBERIA, for whom these services were operated. Flights to Tel Aviv and London appeared in the timetable. During 1993 the DC-9s were withdrawn from service and replaced by more Boeing 737s. It became more difficult to find a marketplace for the airline, in that parent IBERIA had no key

concept for its subsidiary. VIVA AIR's scheduled operations produced only losses and after several bouts of reorganisation IBERIA once again took these services under its own wing in 1995.

For VIVA AIR the future was to lie in charter work within Europe. The fleet of 10 Boeing 737-300s had reached a flexible size and could be specifically marketed. However, there was increasing competition in this area; again operations led to losses and in only the last two years of operation, 1997 and 1998 these losses amounted to the equivalent of some £20m/$30m.

This experience was no basis for successful operations in future and IBERIA decided to give up this subsidiary. In November 1998 VIVA AIR ceased operations and was liquidated. The staff, aircraft and route licences were taken over by IBERIA.

In December 1974 WARDAIR CANADA took on this Boeing 747-100 C-FFUN from former operator CONTINENTAL AIRLINES. The aircraft carries the name of the Canadian aviation pioneer 'Romeo Vachon' and is seen here landing at Frankfurt. (Josef Krauthäuser)

WARDAIR CANADA   Canada

Maxwell Ward first began his company in 1946 in Edmonton as POLARIS CHARTER CO and using a de Havilland DH.83C Fox Moth, which is now exhibited at the National Aviation Museum in Ottawa, flew support flights for mining workers from Yellowknife to the far north of the country. Then in 1952 Maxwell Ward set up the airline taking his own name, WARDAIR Ltd. Using the de Havilland DHC-3 Otter, Ward stuck with bush flying until 1961, when the company name was changed to WARDAIR CANADA.

The ambitions of the company had also changed, for in Spring 1962 it entered the charter business using the Douglas DC-6. Europe was the leading destination, but Florida was also served seasonally. However WARDAIR still remained active in Canada; using Bristol 170s, three DHC-3 Otters and DHC-2 Beavers, routes from Yellowknife were flown. A Boeing 727 delivered in April 1966 was the first jet, and this operated

across the Atlantic; additional tankage was fitted to the aircraft to allow this. In order to provide increased capacity, two Boeing 707s entered service on European routes from 1968. To finance this quick expansion, in 1967 WARDAIR became a joint stock company.

Over the years good service made WARDAIR into Canada's most durable and popular charter airline, setting the standards in many aspects of its business. Boeing 747s were used on charters from May 1973, at a time when other companies were still using propeller-driven equipment. From many Canadian airports such as Calgary, Edmonton, Montreal, Ottawa, Saskatoon, Toronto, Vancouver and Winnipeg, WARDAIR operated charters to Mexico, the Caribbean, and the southern USA as well as to many points in Europe. During 1976 the company underwent a reorganisation and WARDAIR CANADA became a division of WARDAIR International, a holding company

which also had interests in hotels and tour companies. DC-10s supplemented the 747s from November 1978.

During the 1980s WARDAIR suffered mounting problems, which made a reconstruction necessary and it was decided to change the whole fleet over to the Airbus A310-300 from 1987. The first was introduced in November 1987 and operated schedules from Toronto to London-Gatwick. By late 1988 twelve A310-300s had been delivered and the DC-10s and two 747s sold. Within Canada WARDAIR had increased its scheduled services to become a third force after the two leading national airlines. MD-80s were ordered, for use on Canadian domestic services. However these were not delivered as at the end of 1989 WARDAIR was bought in a surprise move by CANADIAN AIRLINES. From 15th January 1990 the two companies merged, and the impressive history of WARDAIR came to an end.

213

WESTERN AIRLINES Boeing 727-200 N295WA which was delivered in May 1981 and went on to join the DELTA AIRLINES fleet after the two airlines were merged from 1st April 1987. (Josef Krauthäuser collection)

WESTERN AIRLINES   USA

A small company began airmail services between Los Angeles and Salt Lake City on 17th April 1926. By 23rd May this company known as WESTERN AIR EXPRESS also had permission to carry passengers on this route. In 1928 a service between Los Angeles and San Francisco followed, and in 1929 this was extended to Seattle. Likewise in the same year Kansas City became the most easterly point to be served, via several intermediate stops. During the course of 1930 WAE bought up four other airlines and thus increased its own route network, only to merge however in the same year with TAT to form the new TWA-TRANSCONTINENTAL & WESTERN AIRLINES. In 1934 William A Coulter bought back the WAE share from TWA and this became GENERAL AIRLINES, in which guise it operated between Salt Lake City and Los Angeles until it was again renamed as WESTERN AIRLINES on 17th

April 1941. During 1942 WESTERN AIRLINES equipped itself with DC-3s and Boeing 247s and in 1943 was able to acquire 87% of the shares of INLAND AIR LINES. WA took over the important route between Los Angeles and San Francisco in 1944 and when the DC-4s came into service in 1946, this was extended to Portland and Seattle. In 1948 Convair 240s arrived and in 1949 WESTERN AIRLINES was the leader in introducing 'coach class' in the western USA, thus bringing the notion of air travel to a much wider audience.

The first service from Los Angeles to Mexico City came in 1957, and this coincided with the introduction of the modern Lockheed Electra turboprops. WESTERN also began jet service using two leased Boeing 707s and this process continued with more 707s, 727s and 737s all being acquired by 1969. After the airline took over PACIFIC NORTHERN AIRLINES in 1967,

the route network reached from Alaska to Mexico and from Hawaii to Minneapolis. WESTERN received its first Douglas DC-10 in April 1973, and these widebodies were used principally on the international routes. The Bahamas and London were served from 1980, if only briefly. Salt Lake City was the company's most important hub, followed by Los Angeles, where WA operated several hundred flights daily. During 1981 WESTERN AIRLINES showed interest in a merger with CONTINENTAL AIRLINES, but TEXAS AIR beat them to it. Likewise merger negotiations with WIEN AIR ALASKA failed two years later.

However from 1st April 1987 WESTERN AIRLINES quickly merged with DELTA AIR LINES and with the integration ended the story of one of the oldest of the US airlines.

WESTERN PACIFIC's colourful and inventive 'flying billboard' Boeing 737s, such as this N962WP, ensured a high level of public recognition. (Josef Krauthäuser)

WESTERN PACIFIC AIRLINES USA

In airline circles Edward R Beauvais is well known for his inspiration in founding AMERICA WEST AIRLINES in 1981 and leading it to success. However in 1992 he left the airline, to reappear on the scene in September 1994 at the start up of COMMERCIAL AIR. He chose Colorado Springs, to the south of Denver in Colorado, as the base of the company. The airport at Colorado Springs which had until that time seen only use by the military, was released for civil use in 1992 and had the longest runway in the whole state of Colorado. The rents and user costs at this location were very attractive to the new airline.

For marketing reasons, before the start of scheduled services with Boeing 737s on 28th April 1995, the name was changed to the much better sounding WESTERN PACIFIC AIRLINES. Initial destinations were Los Angeles, Phoenix, Las Vegas and Oklahoma City. WEST PAC, as

the company was also known for short, was at first only one of several new companies, to which no one paid much attention, but this was quickly altered with the introduction of the first of the so-called 'logo jets'. In doing this WEST PAC stood out from the former humdrum world of aircraft liveries, as the Boeing 737s were rented out as complete advertising hoardings. The airline quickly gained recognition for this flying advertising, as several aircraft were painted in diverse schemes for hotel, car rental, rodeo show, and casino interests, and even for the State of Colorado itself.

An alliance was negotiated by WESTERN PACIFIC AIRLINES with Denver-based MOUNTAIN EXPRESS and WEST PAC took a shareholding in this regional and feeder airline. Quick expansion brought new aircraft and new routes on line, with service extending from San Francisco to Washington, DC. During the

course of 1997 financial difficulties emerged and there was a change of management. There were negotiations for a possible merger with or takeover by Denver-based competitor FRONTIER AIRLINES, but these failed.

On 6th October 1997 bankruptcy protection under Chapter 11 was granted and a re-organisation attempted, but this too was unsuccessful. To the sadness of all those who appreciated seeing the out-of-the-ordinary aircraft markings, WESTERN PACIFIC ceased operations at the beginning of February 1998 and was liquidated.

Boeing 737-210C N4952W in the colours of WIEN AIRLINES as the company was known from mid 1983. It was delivered new to WIEN AIR ALASKA in May 1975 and served for ten years before passing on to AIR CAL. (Josef Krauthäuser collection)

WIEN AIRLINES   USA

WIEN CONSOLIDATED AIRLINES came into being as the result of the merger between WIEN ALASKA AIRLINES and NORTHERN CONSOLIDATED AIRLINES in 1968. The company adopted the name WIEN AIR ALASKA in 1973, after a hoped-for merger with ALASKA AIRLINES failed to go ahead; it thus continued the name of its famous founder and aviation pioneer Noel Wien. He had been in the airline business in Alaska since 1924 and set up his own airline in Fairbanks. WIEN AIR ALASKA built up a strong network serving over 100 destinations in Alaska, supported by feeder services from many smaller companies.

Following the implementation of deregulation in the US airline market in 1968, WIEN AIR ALASKA built up its routes and expanded strongly. As there was not much further opportunity for expansion in Alaska, the extra services were added in the 'lower 48', as the rest of the continental USA is known to Alaskans.

Seattle, Boise, Reno, Portland, Salt Lake City and Albuquerque were all added as destinations, whilst in Alaska a price war broke out in the regional market with the persistent competitor ALASKA AIRLINES. Only three years after it had been taken over in 1980 by Household International, during 1983, WIEN AIR ALASKA was sold again. The new owner this time was JJF Investments, led by James J Flood, who was at that same time the Manager at WIEN AIR ALASKA. The new owner cut back the expansion drive and sold the Alaskan route licences to competitor MARKAIR. In order to oblige the new owner, the company took on the new name of WIEN AIRLINES, thus showing that it was no longer closely associated with Alaska. 1984 was to be the company's last year and was marked by widespread reductions in routes, as mounting losses were being suffered.

Likewise the staff numbers were reduced and the airline cut back to a point where service was provided to only ten destinations. In November 1984 WIEN AIRLINES placed itself under Chapter 11 bankruptcy protection.

In order for a re-organisation to be undertaken, an application was made to cease all flying operations for 25 days, but the law did not permit this. On 28th November 1984 WIEN AIRLINES finally did cease operations. The losses for the year 1984 alone had run up to $11 million. Since that time, the company has acted only as a broker and leasing agent.

Built as an L-1011-1 for PSA in 1974, this TriStar was converted to -100 series by Lockheed and passed to AERO PERU in 1979. It came to WORLDWAYS CANADA as C-GIFE in 1985 and after the bankruptcy was parked in the Arizona desert. (Josef Krauthäuser)

WORLDWAYS CANADA   Canada

The company WORLDWAYS AIRLINES was founded in 1974 by Roy Moore in Toronto with the intention of operating as a charter concern for both passengers and freight. Using two Learjets and a Douglas DC-4, freight and courier flights were initially operated from 1975. During 1976 two Convair 640s were acquired for use especially by sports teams, for instance baseball clubs, so that the teams and fans could fly together to away games. The DC-4 was also used during the winter for group charters to Florida.

The first transatlantic flights began with a service on 21st June 1981 from Toronto to Terceira in the Azores. A Boeing 707-320C was bought from BRITISH CALEDONIAN for these services which were then extended to London, Paris and Frankfurt. The company which had now changed its name to WORLDWAYS CANADA LTD. used a total of three Boeing 707s, before these were replaced in

1983 by Douglas DC-8-63s.

From 1986 a DC-8-63 was on long term charter to the Canadian Department of Defence for troop transport work, flying regularly on the route Trenton-Gatwick-Lahr. Further long term contracts with Echo Bay Mines saw the use of a Lockheed Hercules and a Convair 640 was in permanent use for Petrocanada in Newfoundland. In order that they would be allowed to continue to fly into the United States, the DC-8s were fitted with hushkits from 1986.

The first widebody was introduced in June 1985 in the form of a Lockheed L-1011 TriStar. WORLDWAYS CANADA was to use a total of four of this type and used them on the routes to Europe, the Caribbean and to Central America. the worldwide recession of the late 1980s had its inevitable effect at WORLDWAYS CANADA. Routes were dropped and employees laid off, as the whole business situation of the company began

to lurch. The continuing financial problems led first to a suspension of services at the end of October 1990 and to bankruptcy at the beginning of 1991.

ZAMBIA AIRWAYS used this 1969-build Douglas DC-8-61 9J-AFL from 1989 until the dissolution of the company. Here considerable maintenance and the installation of new jet engines is being undertaken at Santa Barbara. (Josef Krauthäuser)

ZAMBIA AIRWAYS   Zambia

ZAMBIA AIRWAYS was founded as a subsidiary company of CENTRAL AFRICAN AIRWAYS in 1964. Operations were begun on 1st July 1964, with a fleet consisting of two Douglas DC-3s and several de Havilland DHC-2 Beavers. During 1967 ZAMBIA AIRWAYS became independent. Two British Aerospace BAC 1-11s and two HS.748s were bought, and a DC-8 leased from ALITALIA was used from 1st November 1967 to start a scheduled service to London. The Italian national operator also supported ZAMBIA AIRWAYS and gave assistance in the development of the airline by way of a management contract. Initially the London route was flown twice a week with intermediate stops in Nairobi and Rome. During 1975 the fleet was renewed, with the Boeing 707 coming in place of the DC-8 and the One-Elevens being replaced by Boeing 737s. ZAMBIA AIRWAYS ordered a DC-10-30 as its first and only widebody, and

this was introduced from August 1984. In the meantime the route network had reached New York and had become well established in southern Africa. ATR 42s replaced the older HS.748s in 1989 and a Boeing 757F came as a pure freighter substitute for one of the older 707s. An order for a McDonnell Douglas MD-11 was intended to continue the fleet renewal process, with a further DC-8-61 being leased in until delivery. However, trading difficulties coupled with political restructuring in southern Africa, led the airline to bankruptcy in December 1994.

Lockheed Electras from the ZANTOP fleet seen in storage at Detroit's Willow Run Airport, after the operation had been sold to KALITTA. (Josef Krauthäuser)

ZANTOP INTERNATIONAL AIRLINES USA

The history of this company goes back to 1946, when the Zantop family set up the Flying Service bearing their name. In 1952 this small company was granted its licence for commercial flying and ZANTOP AIR TRANSPORT became active in the freight business, principally for the automobile industry, in view of their location at Detroit. With the takeover in 1962 of COASTAL AIRLINES, came a scheduled service licence, for freight and passengers. During 1967 the Zantop family sold the company, and it flew under the new name of UNIVERSAL AIRLINES, but it went into bankruptcy early in 1972.

It was again the Zantop family who took over the legacy of the bankruptcy. On 24th May 1972 ZANTOP INTERNATIONAL AIRLINES was founded, with its headquarters at Willow Run near Detroit. Until this time the fleet had consisted of DC-6, Lockheed Electra, Convair 640 and several DC-8 freighters. From April 1978

the DC-8s were not only used for charters, but also for schedules. With the purchase of the freight division of HAWAIIAN AIRLINES, more Electras came into the fleet and ZANTOP INTERNATIONAL was one of the largest in the freight business. With deregulation, there was also a move towards consolidation in the freight business, as firms such as FED EX and DHL were making their presence felt. In May 1993 ZANTOP sold its whole operation to AMERICAN INTERNATIONAL (a KALITTA company), which operated from next door to them at Willow Run.

A shot from the time when ZANTOP INTERNATIONAL AIRLINES was active shows a DC-8 on approach to Amsterdam. (Patrick Lutz)

Up to seven Boeing 707s served with ZAS AIRLINE OF EGYPT over the years. SU-DAA was used only as a freighter. (Gerhard Schütz)

ZAS AIRLINE OF EGYPT Egypt

Emir Zarkani founded his airline in 1981, and it was initially licenced as a freight carrier.

The beginning of flight operations came about on 23rd November 1982 with a flight from London, via Amsterdam to Cairo. In Autumn 1987 ZAS was also licenced for passenger charters. At first this was for the carriage of pilgrims to Jeddah, but then in 1987 the licence terms were broadened and ZAS began flights to Western Europe. Here Boeing 707s were first used on the service from Luxor to Bordeaux. Scheduled flights within Egypt were also operated from 1988. More modern aircraft, McDonnell Douglas MD-83s and MD-87s came into service, and at peak times Airbus A300s and A310s were also leased. After the collapse of tourism to Egypt brought about by the Gulf conflict, ZAS experienced mounting business difficulties, which led in April 1995 to the cessation of all services.

This Airbus A300B2 which had previously flown with CONAIR, SCANAIR and SAS came to the ZAS fleet in 1991 and was used on a seasonal basis. (Josef Krauthäuser collection)

220

Commonly used abbreviations

ABC   Advanced Booked Charter
CAA   Civil Aviation Authority (UK)
CAB   Civil Aviation Board (US), predecessor of the FAA
CRS   Computer Reservation System
DEW   Line Defence Electronic Warning Line
DOT   Department of Transport (USA)
FAA   Federal Aviation Administration (USA)
IATA   International Air Transport Association
IT-Flight/Charter Inclusive tour flight (both flights and accommodation)
MAC   Military Airlift Command
MATS   Military Air Transport Service
UN/UNO   United Nations
RAF   Royal Air Force
USAF   United States Air Force

Cross reference index

We hope you enjoyed this book . . .

Midland Publishing titles are edited and designed by an experienced and enthusiastic trans-Atlantic team of specialists.

Further titles are in preparation but we welcome ideas from authors or readers for books they would like to see published.

In addition, our associate company, Midland Counties Publications, offers an exceptionally wide range of aviation, spaceflight, astronomy, military, naval and transport books and videos for sale by mail-order around the world.

For a copy of the appropriate catalogue, or to order further copies of this book, please write, telephone, fax or e-mail:

Midland Counties Publications
Unit 3 Maizefield,
Hinckley, Leics, LE10 1YF, England

Tel: (+44) 01455 233 747
Fax: (+44) 01455 233 737
E-mail: midlandbooks@compuserve.com

US distribution by
Specialty Press – details on page 2

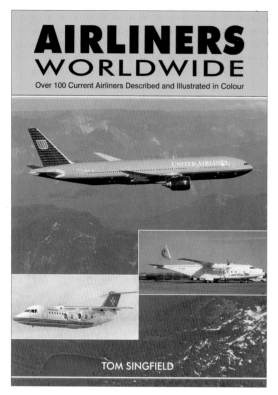
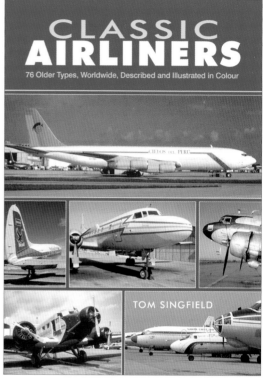